Mississippian Towns and Sacred Spaces

Searching for an Architectural Grammar

Mississippian Towns and Sacred Spaces

Searching for an

Architectural Grammar

Edited by
R. Barry Lewis and Charles Stout

The University of Alabama Press
Tuscaloosa and London

Library of Congress Cataloging-in-Publication Data

Mississippian towns and sacred spaces : searching for an
architectural grammar / edited by R. Barry Lewis and Charles Stout.
p. cm.
Includes bibliographical references and index.
ISBN 0–8173–0947–0
1. Mississippian culture.   2. Mississippian architecture.   3. Indians of
North America—Urban residence—Southern States.   4. Indians of
North America—Urban residence—Mississippi River Valley.   5. Sacred
space—Southern States.   6. Sacred space—Mississippi River Valley.
7. Southern States—Antiquities.   8. Mississippi River
Valley—Antiquities.   I. Lewis, R. Barry.   II. Stout, Charles B.
E99.M6815 M575 1998
306′.09762—ddc21
98–19772

British Library Cataloguing-in-Publication Data available

EN

Contents

Contents

Figures and Tables

Figures

Tables

Preface

Between A.D. 900 and 1700, many prehistoric groups in the southeastern United States shared an agricultural economy based on maize, beans, squash, and other crops. Although they spoke many languages, these groups also shared symbols, decorative motifs, and styles that linked them archaeologically in the Mississippian cultural tradition. The centuries during which these societies thrived is called the Mississippi period.

Mississippian societies differed considerably from those of earlier periods. In formal anthropological terms, they were ranked societies or chiefdoms. Only a few individuals could fill some leadership roles and achieve other special privilege statuses in Mississippian society. Only a few could be chiefs, war leaders, or shamans. Some of these statuses and social roles were inherited, and they were passed down within one family or clan for generations.

The settlements of the Mississippian chiefdoms formed a hierarchy of different kinds of sites, the most archaeologically visible of which were planned towns and mound centers. The dominant architectural feature shared by these sites was one or more large plazas, each of which was often flanked by buildings set on platform mounds. These social, political, and religious centers of Mississippian society are among the largest and most complex archaeological sites in the eastern United States.

The towns and mound centers dominate the popular and scientific images of prehistoric Mississippian societies. Much has been written about the regional spatial patterning of these sites and the larger social context in which they existed. What is missing from the eastern North American archaeological literature is a detailed consideration of the common design themes, construction patterns, and developmental trends shared by these settlements. This book fills that need. It describes the essential characteristics of Mississippian towns and central places and interprets a basic architectural grammar of these places. Most of these generalizations are familiar to researchers who have worked on many town sites, but, with few exceptions, they have not yet been communicated to a larger audience.

The ten chapters cover the Southeast and southern Midwest—specifically, Georgia, northwestern Florida, central Alabama, the Yazoo Basin in Mississippi, eastern Tennessee, western Kentucky, the Cahokia site in Illinois, and the Lower Ohio Valley.

R. Barry Lewis
Charles Stout

Acknowledgments

Portions of the chapters in this book were presented in 1993 in the Mississippian Towns and Central Places Symposium at the Fifty-Eighth Annual Meeting of the Society for American Archaeology, St. Louis, Missouri. We thank Christopher Peebles for the many insights he offered as the discussant for this symposium.

As part of the research for this book, Lewis went to India in 1993 to study the traditional Asian city. In his case, the search for comparative perspective, a traditional anthropological tool, led not only to a deeper understanding of the nature of Mississippian towns, but also to an acquaintance with several extraordinary researchers whose ideas influenced this book. Drs. John Fritz and George Michell have been invaluable mentors and generous hosts at Agra and many times at Vijayanagara. Through the kind hospitality of the Directorate of Archaeology and Museums and the cooperation of its Deputy Director, Dr. C. S. Patil, Lewis recently began a collaborative study of medieval and early modern forts in Karnataka, which will eventually come full circle back to a comparative study of Mississippian towns and South Indian fortified towns.

Part of Lewis's research for this book was supported by grants from the University of Illinois Research Board and by a Senior Scholarly Development Fellowship from the American Institute of Indian Studies (AIIS). He wishes to thank Drs. Pradeep Mehendiratta, Kaye Hill, L. S. Suri, and Philip Lutgendorf for the many contributions the AIIS fellowship experience made to this book. It would not have been possible without the AIIS.

In Chitradurga, Jagadeesh C. and his extended family, the S. V. Reddy family, and Shankar S. Athani went out of their way repeatedly to ensure that this project and Lewis's fort research, which has yet to be written up, went as smoothly and productively as possible.

Robert Connolly, Sue Lewis, Ian Brown, and an anonymous reviewer read and commented on several drafts of the manuscript. Jarrod Burks served as sounding board and research assistant for Stout on many aspects of this project. Kathy Cummins did an outstanding job with the copyediting and index.

Finally, we extend our sincere thanks to the authors who contributed chapters to this book and to Judith Knight at the University of Alabama Press. They put up good-naturedly with Barry's tendency to wander off to India every time a deadline approached and Chuck's apparently compulsive household moves.

Mississippian Towns and Sacred Spaces

Searching for an Architectural Grammar

1

The Design of Mississippian Towns

R. Barry Lewis, Charles Stout, and Cameron B. Wesson

Architecture is the most visible physical manifestation of human culture. As such, it encodes much information about a society—political organization, economy, subsistence, aesthetics, cosmology, and gender relations, to list only a few topics—and the limits of this information expand as we learn more about the dynamic relationships between people and their environments. Archaeological investigations seek to decode this information and reconstruct the cultural meanings assigned to architecture by the men and women who created it.

Stella Kramisch (1976), in the preface to her book *The Hindu Temple,* writes, "The Hindu temple is the sum total of architectural rites performed on the basis of its myth. The myth covers the ground and is the plan on which the structure is raised." This statement captures the essence and spirit of one new direction in which studies of prehistoric American architecture are moving. This book also steps in that direction. Some of the chapters move boldly; others may appear tentative, but together they advance a view of the larger late prehistoric communities of the midwestern and southeastern United States that is more centered on a search for meanings than on settlement patterns and site function. Like Kramisch, we (Lewis, Stout, and Wesson) believe that the architecture we study reflects design decisions that were based on widely shared meanings. This assertion is, in itself, unremarkable, but having to reconcile it with the fact that the architectural similarities of town planning in the Mississippian world transcended linguistic and cultural boundaries as substantial as the differences between medieval Poland and Spain makes it of considerable research interest.

This book is motivated primarily by the hypothesis that the design of Mississippian towns was ritually prescribed. Following (and rephrasing) Kramisch, we believe that each Mississippian town site owes its general design to the sum total of architectural rites performed on the basis of its myth. The myth covered the ground and was the plan on which the town was raised. Our goal is to understand the congruencies of design in time and space, the main elements of the designs, how and why these congruencies existed, and the regional variants and, generally, to begin to answer questions about these towns that consider them more as *communities* than as archaeological sites, settlement patterns, site plans, or excavations.

As one might expect, we are only partly successful in reaching our goal. To anticipate our conclusions, this book describes and examines the elements of a Mississippian *architectural grammar*. We find it easier to trace the major dimensions of this grammar across space than through archaeological time. It is unlikely that a coherent town plan "myth," formalized in the same sense as the *shastras* that guide the construction of Kramisch's Hindu temples, existed consciously in the Mississippian world except perhaps at the most superficial level. Nevertheless, a shared architectural grammar is both sufficient and necessary to account for the observed patterning.

So what is an architectural grammar and why should we concern ourselves with it? A fundamental distinction to be made here is between an architectural grammar and an architectural style. Both address the same phenomena, but an architectural grammar focuses on the rules by which elements were combined in architectural expression, while an architectural style emphasizes the classification of compositions by their shared expressions. Classification is an important component of the research described here, but only as a means to an end. Our definition of architectural grammar is similar to that of Mitchell (1990). Like him, we assume that "design worlds may be specified by formal grammars" (Mitchell 1990:x). Even in cases such as the Mississippian town, about which very little is known, there is much to be learned by delineating fundamental design relationships.

To further explain what is meant by an architectural grammar requires that we reaffirm the obvious—but not the obviously trivial. Although interesting in their own right, architecture and settlement patterns cannot be divorced from the unique cultural contexts in which they were formed. And, while it is usually impossible to learn language, economics, cosmology, or other complex cultural phenomena from *direct* analyses of a society's architecture, these other systems are often revealed *indirectly* by their articulation with constructed forms. This, therefore, is the argument of architectural relevance: architecture is one instrument, of widely accepted face and criterion validity, by which we may compare the differences and similarities of societies through time and across space.

To build on this argument, but still stay close to the obvious, it is also uncontroversial to assert that all societies assign meaning to spaces that denote, connote, or secure privacy; that segment activities; that expose or elaborate openness; and that convey water, people, or machines. They appropriate hills, trees, bushes, bluffs, and rockshelters to serve as walls, fences, hedgerows, screens, and homes. They create landscapes filled with terraces, pits, roads, bridges, canals, aqueducts, and other socially defined spaces in places where nature did not provide them.

One important dimension of the latter behavior is the anticipation of future use. The elements of cultural landscapes are of differential duration. Some spaces, such as campsites, may be both architecturally simple and of short duration. Spaces that are designed to be used for long intervals tend to be more architecturally complex and show a greater investment of time and effort in their construction. This is the argument of design intent: the architectural complexity of cultural spaces tends to vary directly with the cultural "memory" of these spaces. This argument, or more accurately this relationship, was one of the more fruitful ideas underlying the settlement pattern studies of the 1960s and 1970s. It is yet another instrument by which we may reconstruct and compare cultural landscapes.

Finally, if we glance again at design intent, we also can see that architectural complexity cannot be divorced entirely from considerations of function. Societies generally prescribe the design of long-term structures and sites so that they can serve multiple complementary ends. Witness the Khyber railway line booking office blueprint that identified one of the rooms as a "Combined Booking Office Window and Machine Gun Loophole" (Aitken 1995:25). The general idea, which seems to be true cross-culturally, is the more features that are included in a design, the more functional the space becomes, but only if the features are well integrated and only if there are no more than a few main features. The inherent limits of spatial functionality are quickly reached. A few minutes spent with any of the world's baroque styles—or in trying to adapt a church's "multipurpose room" to do what you really need (perhaps we could call this a *faroque* space, one with an over-

elaboration of assigned functions)—is sufficient to demonstrate that the relationship between architectural complexity and designed functions is every-
where nonlinear. This aspect of design intent we call the argument of functional limits: the number of designed functions increases in a nonlinear, but
asymptotic relationship with architectural complexity.

If we step beyond a consideration of limitations on the *objects* of architectural design to the *contexts* of designs, we must come to terms with the
cultural meanings of exterior space or setting, that which lies outside of the
domain of a given design, but which stands in the same relationship to it
as does a vase to a rose bud (or, depending on your mood, an alley to a
garbage can). A problem here is to capture accurate cultural meanings but
also to avoid infinite regress. Were the design limits of a Mississippian town
the mound-and-plaza complex, the palisade, the outermost cluster of houses,
the outlying fields, or the homes of everyone who viewed himself or herself
as a member of that town, and so on? To push the question into our world,
where does Chicago really end? At the Loop? The Cook County line? Joliet?
The answers to these questions require that we understand both the objects
of design and their contexts. This is the argument of architectural context:
a given design cannot be understood in cultural terms if you divorce it from
its context; the setting of a design is as much a cultural artifact as is the
building, space, or landscape itself.

With these ideas in hand, we can now develop the notion of an architectural grammar. Just as language is imposed order on selected sounds, the
grammar of human constructions and appropriations is ordered by design
intents, functional limits, and contexts. Like language, which takes as elements those vocalizations that can be readily recognized and generated by
humans, architecture arranges such elements as visual images, colors, shapes,
materials, textures, and motives in terms that are culturally meaningful and
interactive with the environment. Architecture often even arranges odors
and sounds, making the desirable more noticeable and the unwanted as invisible as possible. As a society builds upon its architecture, its own accidental
and historical additions and nuances become part of a distinctive, but changing lexicon. It is this architectural grammar, the instances of which recall
Rouse's (1939) *procedural modes,* that we seek to capture in our investigation
of Mississippian towns. We use the architectural grammar notion as a heu-
ristic, not, as Mitchell (1990) has done, to construct a critical language about

designs. Although we are interested in pursuing the latter, it is a goal feasible only in the long term.

The remainder of this chapter introduces the reader to the history of research on Mississippian architecture and the major elements of Mississippian town design. We conclude with a brief guide map to the book's organization.

Architecture of Mississippian Towns and Mound Centers

The fundamental architecture of built communities in the southeastern United States between the tenth and seventeenth centuries A.D. is clearly distinguishable from that of societies in other places and times. This unifying system arose from the collective cultural histories and natural environments of the many distinct peoples who are now lumped together by archaeologists under the rubric of "Mississippian culture" (Figure 1.1). The main architectural elements include plazas, platform mounds and other earthworks, entryways, various means of segregating space and activities, defensive works, and natural terrain features (Figure 1.2).

Out of this context, archaeologists have, thus far, extracted only the major spatial and temporal patterns by which these elements were melded together to create spaces that were socially meaningful in the Mississippian world. Among these patterns are towns and mound centers. We define a Mississippian *town* as a habitation center with a public area, such as a plaza or courtyard, that may be flanked by one or more mounds. Many archaeologists who study the Mississippi period also recognize *mound centers,* which are planned sites with earthworks but little or no archaeological evidence of habitation. The term *ceremonial center* has also been applied to most Mississippian towns and mound centers. We believe that the latter label, and those like it, are misleading in that they emphasize only one functional aspect of these complex sites. It is unlikely that any town or mound center existed only for ceremonial uses, just as it is quite likely that Mississippian rituals and ceremonies were carried out at sites that lacked mounds and plazas. In our view, at least, Mississippian earthworks and plazas were a sufficient but not a necessary condition of rituals in the Mississippian world. The label "ceremonial center," therefore, is as meaningless when applied to Mississippian towns and mound centers as would be such labels as "trade center,"

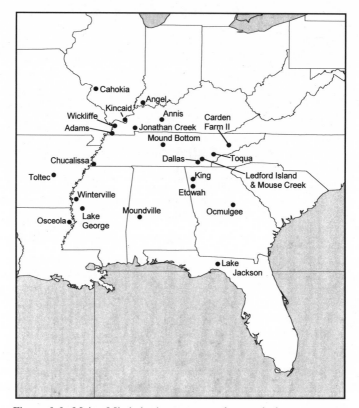

Figure 1.1. Major Mississippian towns and central places.

"habitation center," "administrative center," "defensive center," and "storage center."

The two major information sources for Mississippian town planning are, first, the narratives of early European and American explorers (e.g., Adair 1986; Bartram 1996; Clayton, Knight, and Moore 1993; d'Iberville 1981; Le Page du Pratz 1972; Pénicaut 1988) and, second, archaeological investigations. The ethnohistorical accounts provide rich contextual information about these towns and how they were used. Nevertheless, it is corroboration by the physical evidence, which only archaeology can provide, that gives these accounts true interpretive value.

Mississippian town planning has been studied by archaeologists for more than a century and a half. Early surveys of earthworks, such as those by Squier and Davis (1848), Thomas (1894), and Potter (1880), helped

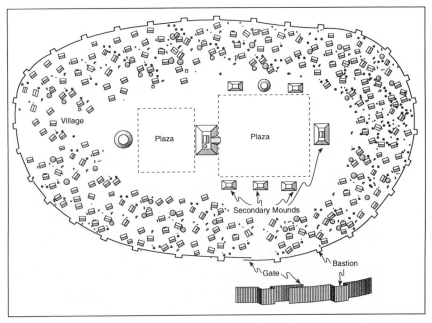

Figure 1.2. Mississippian architectural design elements.

to identify the main features of Mississippian towns and mound centers throughout the Southeast. The first systematic examination of Mississippian site design patterns did not come, however, until shortly after World War II when Phillips, Ford, and Griffin (1951:309–44) described and analyzed a taxonomy of sites in the first major report of the Harvard Peabody Museum's Lower Mississippi Survey. Their taxonomy recognized villages without mounds, sites with one or more conical burial mounds, small ceremonial centers with rectangular mounds, large ceremonial centers with rectangular mounds, large rectangular villages with temple mounds (St. Francis type), large irregular villages with rectangular mounds, and sites too damaged to classify (Phillips, Ford, and Griffin 1951:310–35).

In general, Phillips, Ford, and Griffin (1951) described a Mississippian town design pattern that was already well known to other southeastern archaeologists. The big difference between what Phillips, Ford, and Griffin did and what researchers like Thomas and Potter were able to accomplish was that Phillips and his coworkers had a much better command of the temporal dimension of their data. Their main contribution was to pull together the first systematic look at the dynamics of site planning in one region of the prehistoric Southeast. They described a pattern in which mounds, when present at a Mississippian site, are found along the edges of a central plaza. When there is more than one mound, the axes of the mounds usually are parallel with the plaza's axis. Commonly, one of the mounds that flank the plaza is larger than the others. Often, the plaza lies to the east or southeast of this "primary" mound.

Study of the design patterns described by Phillips, Ford, and Griffin and their predecessors has dominated subsequent examinations of Mississippian architecture and settlement patterning. For example, Reed (1977), Wahls (1986), and most recently Payne (1994) have explored the alignments of Mississippian mounds with respect to plazas and nearby rivers and found a close relationship between plaza alignments and the courses of adjacent rivers. Morgan (1980), an architect, also examined these and many other aspects of Mississippian settlement patterns and design elements in an ambitious but visually outstanding study of prehistoric earth architecture in the eastern United States.

Other studies, such as Sullivan's (1987, 1995) investigation of the Mouse Creek site in eastern Tennessee and Mehrer's (1988, 1995; Mehrer and Collins 1995) research on American Bottom hinterland communities in western Illinois, trace the relationships between the evolution of villages into towns and the interrelated effects of this transition on households and site plans. Williams's (1995) look at "chiefly compounds" in Georgia addresses questions about population estimates and community composition and concludes that most Mississippian societies in the Southeast basically had a two-tiered settlement system of compounds or sites with various numbers of farmsteads, with rare exceptions like Cahokia and Etowah, which were larger and more complex.

Sherrod and Rolingson's (1987) investigations at Toltec Mounds led them to conclude that the distance between principal architectural features was measured in multiples of 47.5 meters and that these features were aligned with significant celestial landmarks. They assert that these practices may represent an elaborate engineering scheme, the focal point of which may have been a post that marked the position of a future mound until it was built. Sherrod and Rolingson's work recalls Fowler's (1977) earlier observations about the possible use of post markers and small "secondary" mounds at Cahokia and other Mississippian sites. Fowler suggested that there might be a pattern to the location of these mounds. Benchley (1974) investigated these mounds at several southeastern sites where they have been recorded or were said to have once existed. The results of her study indicate that these mounds were substructures, their location on a primary mound was predictable, and they may have served as physical markers of some kind or they were constructed for some reason especially where a wooden post marker had once stood.

Mehrer (1988, 1995; Mehrer and Collins 1995) found that as hinterland groups gradually developed a degree of autonomy from Cahokia, villages grew larger and hamlets smaller. Dispersed hinterland communities possessed the same functional elements, but had no apparent formal plan. In a somewhat similar examination of Mississippian site patterning, Healan (1972) conducted a controlled surface reconnaissance and spatial analysis of Beckwith's Fort, a Mississippian town in southeastern Missouri. Healan's research identified some gross differences between Late Woodland and Mississippian material culture distributions that might reflect changes in community patterning as the site developed. O'Brien (1977) also used controlled surface collections to investigate the North Mound Group at the Mound Bottom site in central Tennessee. The primary goals of this study were the location of habitations and the development of a model of community residential layout. Both gross functional areas and activity areas were identified.

Hatch's (1995) examination of Lamar period upland farmsteads of the Oconee Valley in Georgia highlights the life and duration of a Mississippian community, with its internal constructions and external relationships, including the basic relationship with the natural environment. The built communities of the Oconee Valley were composed of circular winter houses and rectangular summer houses. These sites were occupied for only ten to thirty years, probably depending on soil fertility. Likewise, Scarry (1995) identified several important architectural elements in his study of the homesteads of Apalachee Mississippian chiefdoms. The patterning of homestead locations demonstrates the importance of natural resources, such as water and firewood, and the ease of social interaction with other homesteads as factors in settlement decisions.

Daniel (1980; Daniel-Hartung 1981), in an attempt to test for cultural connections between Mesoamerican and Mississippian peoples using astro-archaeological data, demonstrated a Mississippian "interest in solar movement and knowledge of the cardinal points" (1980:iii). It is noted that in the absence of a compass, north or south can be found accurately as the bisector of the angle of any nonequinox sunrise and sunset or by tracing a noon shadow.

Rolingson (1982, 1983, 1984) and Sherrod and Rolingson (1987) have identified primarily solstice alignment patterns at Toltec Mounds, a proto-Mississippian center in Lonoke County, Arkansas, and at several Mississippian sites in the Mississippi Valley. Nassaney (1992) interprets the spatial arrangement of mounds and other features at Toltec as a struggle between elite and nonelite members of the community at a low-ranking site, which left the site design to enduring community prescriptions.

Wittry (1977) has interpreted circular arrangements of postmolds at Cahokia as observatories, called woodhenges, for tracking solstices and equinoxes, an interpretation not without skeptics (e.g., Daniel 1980; Daniel-Hartung 1981), who cite ethnohistoric examples of alternative uses of circular arrangements of posts in the Southeast. Likewise, Smith (1992) questions the postulated use by Mississippian elites of solar observatories, such as Cahokia's woodhenges, as a means of maintaining control over the masses. Demel and Hall explore some of these same questions in Chapter 9.

Stout's studies of Mississippian towns in western Kentucky have focused on how observed spatial relationships at these sites reflect relationships among the people who lived at or visited these sites and relationships between these people and their universe (e.g., Burks and Stout [1999]; Stout 1984, 1989, 1991; Stout and Lewis 1995; Stout, Walz, and Burks 1996). Using primarily topographic and extensive surface collection data, he and his colleagues have explored how community segments related to each other and to their constructed world, how their constructed world indicated or reinforced social meanings and prescription, and how these might have changed among indigenous Late Woodland peoples as they developed what archaeologists would later call Mississippian ways of life. Although mounds dominate the landscape, he notes, the plaza and houses dominated site area. At the Adams site, as at Snodgrass in southeastern Missouri, Stout observes that houses appear to be located at nearly regular intervals from each other and that the mound-plaza layout is similar to that of at least two other sites in the immediate vicinity (Turk and Beckwith's Fort), perhaps reflecting common design concepts; these ideas are explored by each of the authors in this volume.

Knight's (1981, 1985) interest in Mississippian architecture emanates from his tracing of the lineage of Mississippian ritual. He brings to his study ethnographic and archaeological data, apparent analogies, and linguistic equivalents to piece together meanings and possible origins of Mississippian ritual. In the process, Knight interprets heretofore incomprehensible elements of Mississippian cosmology, politics, religion, engineering, and technological understanding of the physical world, all of which are essential for any thorough study of Mississippian communities.

Basic Mississippian Design Elements

Although the research questions have changed since Phillips, Ford, and Griffin (1951) published their important study of Lower Mississippi Valley site distributions, one thing that has remained constant is our understanding of the essential design elements of Mississippian towns and mound centers. The key elements are plazas, mounds, boundaries, and gates. This section considers each element in turn.

Plazas

Architecture is composed of two basic elements, mass and space (Bacon 1976:15). Most Mississippian architectural analyses emphasize mounds (mass), while plazas (space) are viewed as liminal and unimportant. We believe this emphasis to be misplaced. Although plazas may not present archaeologists with the same type of information as mounds, they were an integral part of the Mississippian world.

It is unproductive to view plazas merely as residual spaces around which structures are raised. In the Mississippian architectural grammar, for example, mounds and plazas were intimately linked through the very nature of the building enterprise. While the structures (mounds, courthouses, temples, etc.) that flank such spaces were often circumscribed by use or status (e.g., the mounds that flank Mississippian town plazas have long been considered as elite structures), the plazas themselves are, the world over, places of the people. Plazas are communal spaces that allow all members of society to share in the ceremonies, rituals, and daily life experiences that unite and define a community.

Consider, for example, the typical developmental pattern of European cities. These cities have traditionally been organized around a network of interconnecting streets and squares, with the city's open spaces considered as important as the buildings that surround them (Trancik 1986:67). Most of these cities have several open squares or plazas, with the number of such spaces directly tied to the size and prestige of the city itself. As cities developed across Europe, plazas were the first spaces to be dedicated to the interests of the community at large and the social needs of the populace.

The traditional spatial pattern of these European plazas began with the construction of a church and a seat of municipal government, sometimes placed directly opposite each other at the ends of the plaza. The division between ecclesiastical and secular authority within society was given physical expression within these plazas (Sitte 1965:3–12). As the town grew, domestic and commercial structures were built near these structures and completed the spatial definition and form of the communal areas. The result, in many European cities, is densely packed clusters of buildings, with only the streets and public squares serving as places for public activity. As Trancik (1986:67) contends, "the square was probably the first organizing form of urban space and the street was an extension of the square once the periphery had been filled with houses."

The Piazza San Marco (Figure 1.3, *A*) in Venice, Italy, for example, serves as the largest open area in a city surrounded by water. Part of the city's original design, the Piazza San Marco is the heart of the city. It is formed by the intersection of two rectangles, joined to create an L-shaped open space. The dense mass of structures that surrounds the Piazza San Marco screens it from the canals and other areas of the city. A colonnade links the spaces and provides a unifying element around the plaza (Fletcher 1963:611). Named for the Cathedral of Saint Mark, located on its eastern boundary, the piazza follows the European tradition by serving as the center of religious, political, and commercial life for the city (Sitte 1965:58–59). A parade of social classes and nationalities marches through the plaza every day, and individuals pause to rest at a table in the shade, take pictures, or stop to talk. Like plazas throughout the world, this is a public place. The activities taking place within this forum change as needed. It can be a church, polling place, board room, concert hall, or any other socially defined forum. Although the structures surrounding the plaza define the space and command attention simply by their obtrusiveness, the majority of social life is acted out on the flagstones of the plaza, not in the structures.

Although geographically a non-European plaza, the Zocalo (Figure 1.3, *B*) in Mexico City, like plazas in many Spanish colonial cities, contains strong

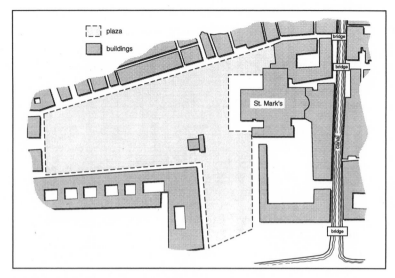

Figure 1.3. *A*, Piazza San Marco

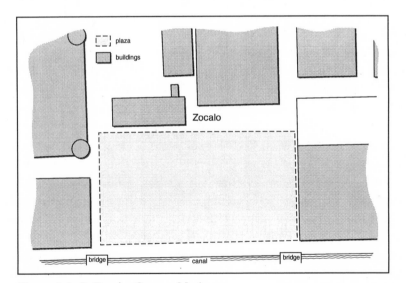

Figure 1.3. *B*, Zocalo, Oaxaca, Mexico

Figure 1.3. Public spaces: *A*, Piazza San Marco, Venice, Italy; *B*, Zocalo, Oaxaca, Mexico; *C*, Hampi bazaar and Virupaksha temple, Karnataka, India (*A* adapted from Fletcher 1963:611, D; *B* adapted from Kubler 1948:plate 63; *C* adapted from Aspiration Stores 1995).

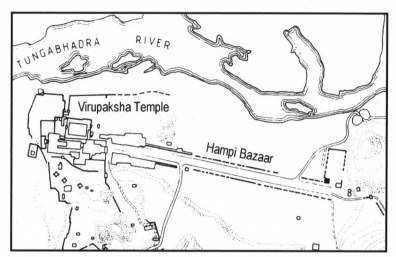

Figure 1.3. *C,* Hampi bazaar and Virupaksha temple, Karnataka, India

European influences. This is no accident as royal ordinances governing the planning of colonial towns and cities were in force in Spanish America as early as the late sixteenth century (Morris 1994:305). Much like its European counterparts, the Zocalo is surrounded by important government buildings, a cathedral, and the central business district of the city. Although the government, the Church, and the economy dominate the life of the average Mexican, the Zocalo remains fundamentally the people's place. Its complexion changes with the daily and seasonal cycle of life in the city. What may be a parade ground for soldiers in the morning can become a market by midday and a promenade for tourists and lovers by nightfall.

Lest our emphasis on European cases be misunderstood, we take as our final example one of the similar spatial expressions found in many non-Western architectural traditions. Hampi (Figure 1.3, *C*), located in central Karnataka, India, is an ancient Hindu pilgrimage town of about 5,000 inhabitants. The key architectural foci of the town are the Virupaksha temple complex and its associated bazaar street. Like the Piazza San Marco and the Zocalo, Hampi bazaar is the structural analogue of the plaza and it figures prominently in the life of the community. Ritual prescriptions, described in architectural *shastras* (e.g., Dagens 1984), and the worship of Virupaksha, a form of Siva, dictated the bazaar street's shape, length, and orientation and created the architectural elements that anchor each end of the street (an outer gateway or *gopura* at the west end and a massive image of Nandi, Siva's mount, at the east end). At set times during the year, such as during the betrothal ceremony of Virupaksha and the local goddess Pampa, the bazaar street becomes the central focus of ritual. At all other times, however, the colonnaded halls that line the street and the space of the street itself are the lifeblood of both Hampi and Virupaksha temple as devotees make small purchases for offerings to the god; as shops, street vendors, sadhus, beggars, and sacred cows vie with each other for the attention of pilgrims and European tourists; and as the latest rumors ripple from one end of the bazaar to the other.

As these examples show, plazas and their structural counterparts are flexible, dynamic settings for human activities. From the Piazza San Marco to Hampi bazaar to "downtown" Cahokia, plazas have found architectural forms that express individual cultural needs, while simultaneously expressing universal desires for communal spaces in human settlements. They are capable of expressing religious, political, communal, and social sentiments, often at the same time. They provide a public space that is an intermediary between the sacred and profane, but they are also areas from which protests against the authority of both powers can be waged. Above all, plazas are public areas, where individuals interact and community consensus is built. They are not independent worlds within a community; they are a means of orientation and a representation of shared community spatial concepts (Norberg-Shulz 1980:175).

So what can be learned about Mississippian peoples from the archaeological examination of their plazas? Probably more than we suspect. We certainly disagree with artistic reconstructions of Mississippian plazas that show them as desolate "no man's lands" where activities and access were extremely limited. This, we believe, is an image of Mississippian towns that is probably wrong. Although plazas, when viewed archaeologically, are neither visually obvious nor especially interesting, they are architecturally, historically, and symbolically dominant elements of Mississippian towns and central places. As such, they are crucial to the understanding of Mississippian town designs.

Mississippian plazas come in a variety of sizes and shapes. Some plazas were square, others rectangular, and still others rounded, and virtually all of them are delimited archaeologically according to the edges of surrounding mounds. Since most of these mounds were necessarily constructed after the creation of the plaza, the size and shape of a plaza may indicate something of early site planning, intended use, and perhaps the size and centralization of the population that made and used it. At towns constructed on locations where the layout was fixed by the terrain, increased plaza size or construction of a second plaza was not an option. New plazas, of course, were established at towns with physiographically circumscribed settings, as sites expanded in population and, presumably, in services to the community or surrounding support region.

The origins and development of the Mississippian mound-and-plaza complex are anything but clear. Such a seemingly simple question as "What came first, the plaza or the platform mound?" is impossible to answer in large regions or the Mississippian world as a whole, if for no reason other than the differential visibility and obtrusiveness of these elements. Mounds stand out, sometimes even on topographical maps. A plaza, which is nothing more than cultural meaning assigned to a defined space within a site, is effectively invisible unless it is framed by a mound group or some other obtrusive feature.

Mounds

Although the origins of the relationship between mounds and plazas in the Mississippian world are hard to trace, it is undeniable that this relationship was both primary and reciprocal. Stand in the plaza of any well-preserved Mississippian town site and your attention is drawn by the mass of the main mound that flanks it. Stand on the main mound and your attention is dominated by the space of the plaza, framed by smaller mounds, that lies before you. Just as one cannot separate the design of the nave of a church from its chancel, the design of the Mississippian town plaza cannot be divorced from the mounds that flank it. They are contextually interrelated in the Mississippian architectural grammar.

The manipulation of earth for the construction of mounds and earthworks is of considerable antiquity. Such constructions have been part of the architectural traditions of many societies and have been identified on every inhabited continent. Although the form and function of these structures vary greatly, they share many elements of construction and assigned cultural meaning. The human desire to rise above the earth's surface on a supportive structure is an old one. This desire can be psychologically met by raising a structure just a few centimeters above the ground. In the children's game called King of the Hill, the important question is not the height of the hill, but how many kids can be King of the Hill at the same time. The answer would not be lost on the builders of the ziggurats in Mesopotamia, the pyramids at Giza, the Acropolis at Tikal, Monks Mound at Cahokia, or the mounds of any other Mississippian town.

A mound's height, therefore, is of little interpretive value. What is important is that it placed one or more architectural features (and the individuals who controlled them) at odds with the rest of the community by creating a visible differential between it and the surrounding elements of the total community design. This differential may have served to elevate the status of an individual, a family, a lineage, a god, or some combination of these.

Mounds, large and small, were commonly built around the public center or centers of Mississippian communities. From ethnohistorical evidence, we know that the structures on top of platform mounds included the dwellings of high-ranked individuals, religious structures, charnel houses, and buildings for public meetings. Although many Mississippian mounds were designed as substructures upon which buildings were constructed, others were clearly intended for mortuary use and others still—ridge-topped mounds, conical mounds, and even some truncated pyramidal mounds—apparently served additional needs of the community. Platform mounds were usually rectangular, but circular ones (distinguished from conical) are also known. Mississippian towns were frequently dominated by a large mound with more than one level.

The largest mounds at important town sites were sometimes divided into multiple levels, one or more of which could be crowned with submounds (e.g., Monk's Mound at Cahokia, the Angel site in southern Indiana). Besides buildings, second platform levels and additional mounds were sometimes built on top of the largest mounds at important town sites. Structures situated on tall mounds could be reached by way of ramps, although it was certainly possible for any slope to have been climbed.

Knight (1981, 1985, 1989) has explored extensively the symbolism of Mississippian mounds and we cannot pretend to improve on his delightful exposition. He suggests that platform mounds and their relationship to the plaza had an indigenous but independent origin, arising from ritual sweeping of the plaza resulting first in ridges along the plaza edge and evolving into constructed mounds in these arrangements. Pauketat (1992) suggests for Cahokia and the nearby Lohmann site that mound construction was a periodic event repeated on an annual cycle and that the additional size and height were in part intended to increase the distance between stratified social classes, thus permanently defining these social relationships in the community's physical structure. Kidder (1992a, see also Chapter 6) notes that hundreds of years before maize agriculture became dominant in Coles Creek culture (ca. A.D. 1400), multistage platform mounds reaffirmed generations of elite dominance.

Boundaries and Gates

Mississippian towns were constructed with barriers between public, private, and ceremonial spaces (Stout 1989). In urban settings, these barriers are called "locks" (Rapoport 1977) because they restrict public access to private space much as a locked front door facing a city street does. At many Mississippian sites, the locks between plazas and the rest of the site were arguably both physical and symbolic, but the physical boundaries between major functional areas appear to have provided mainly a reminder of the symbolic ones (cf. Knight 1981, 1985). Although all locks control access, one useful distinction is between *boundaries,* locks that cover large units of space, and *gates* (where the term is used loosely), locks that control points.

The boundaries of Mississippian towns are largely unexplored by archaeologists. As noted earlier, the tendency is to define the limits of Mississippian towns by physical boundaries such as ditches (e.g., Lake George in Mississippi [Williams and Brain 1983]), palisades (e.g., Snodgrass in Missouri [Price and Griffin 1979]), or natural limits of terrain (e.g., Adams in Kentucky [Lewis 1986; Stout 1989]). The main interpretive problem with using these physical features to bound a town is that it implicitly maps our own cultural associations onto the Mississippian landscape. While doing so may often yield an accurate understanding of the boundaries of Mississippian towns, we will be unable to tell when it fails unless our research is designed to leave open alternative explanations. What is needed, therefore, is research that seeks to define site limits in Mississippian terms. Since these terms are hidden from us, except where ethnohistorical accounts exist to inform us of details, the task is not necessarily an easy one. In the absence of these details, one productive course of action is to examine town boundaries at several spatial levels: at the boundaries that existed between the mound-and-plaza core and the rest of the town, between neighborhoods within a town, between the parts of the town enclosed by defensive works and those that were not, between a town and its hinterland, and so on.

When we turn to gates, we face essentially the same interpretive problems as with boundaries. Few archaeological excavations reveal such clear evidence of Mississippian town planning with respect to gates as that revealed at Snodgrass by Price (Price and Griffin 1979), where access points to the town and to a distinct neighborhood or barrio within it can be followed clearly in plan view.

To the best of our knowledge, no one has yet uncovered archaeological evidence of a gateway on the boundary of a town plaza. One could, in principle at least, walk onto the plazas from any quarter. Although these were not walled enclosures to be entered only at specific points chosen by their designers, the common Mississippian practice of constructing mounds along the edges of plazas created de facto gateways by concentrating mass along some portions of the plaza.

The most common gateways between the plaza and the mounds that flanked it were the stairways that can be traced even today in the form of ramps of earth constructed on the plaza side of mounds. Such ramped stairways were not essential to the design. Given the relatively gentle slopes of Mississippian platform mounds, which were dictated more by the physical characteristics of dirt when it is stacked in tall piles than by Mississippian considerations of aesthetics and symbolism, it would have been possible to walk up any mound from any quarter. The stairways, however, drew one onto the mound at a spot chosen by the designer (e.g., Shelby 1993:186). It is unknown whether the important consideration was that of channeling access or merely protecting the sides of the mound from accelerated erosion.

Mississippian planners also did not exploit the potential of stairways and gates to convey monumentality, or the use of mass to announce the proximity and portals of the powerful or the divine. There are no archaeological or ethnohistorical examples of wide, ramped stairways on Mississippian mounds comparable to the staircases of Greek and Roman architecture, nor is there evidence of Mississippian gateway forms that can be described as anything other than utilitarian.

Organization of What Follows

The preceding lays out some of the central ideas explored in this book. Our objective is to explore and understand the Mississippian architectural grammar as it is expressed in the remains of their towns. Our primary motivation is the belief that by doing so we can derive fresh understanding of Mississippian culture.

The book chapters are organized so that we begin our journey in Florida and proceed to central Georgia, up into eastern Tennessee, down to Alabama, westward to the Lower Mississippi Valley in Mississippi and Louisiana, up to western Kentucky, into the Lower Ohio Valley, and finally to Cahokia in southwestern Illinois.

In Chapter 2, Claudine Payne and John Scarry examine the town plan of the Lake Jackson site in northwestern Florida. Located at the periphery of the Mississippian world, Lake Jackson acted as a link or mediator between two disparate cultures—the Mississippian and the Floridian. The forms, functions, and arrangements of mounds and plazas at Lake Jackson, together with the site's overall material culture and iconographic forms, show that, despite its peripheral location, it was a Mississippian town, with little evidence of Florida influence.

David Hally and Hypatia Kelly take a look at the King site, the most extensively excavated Mississippian town in Georgia, in Chapter 3. They describe the general features of its settlement plan with emphasis on domestic households and the variability evident in residential structures. They conclude that the key to understanding the variability in these structures lies in their role as symbols of household identity and continuity and in the way households grow through time.

In Chapter 4, Gerald Schroedl reassesses our understanding of Mississippian settlements in eastern Tennessee. Although he considers several general aspects of Mississippian settlement patterning, Schroedl's chapter emphasizes the placement of mounds, palisades and their use, the internal features of dwellings and their placement within settlements, and the locations of all of these features with respect to distinct site areas.

Cameron Wesson, in Chapter 5, examines the use of architecture as a mechanism for social and ideological representation. Wesson analyzes historic Creek architecture and origin myths for clues to the social meanings of Mississippian communities in Alabama. He demonstrates how social spaces modeled the cosmos and reinforced the relationships structuring Mississippian social and political practice. He suggests that Mississippian elites manipulated these relationships by controlling those spaces with the greatest symbolic connection to the cosmological. Wesson sees such actions as instrumental in the construction and expansion of Mississippian elite hegemony.

In Chapter 6, Tristram Kidder examines Mississippi period mound centers in the Lower Mississippi Valley. The wide array of mound group and community plans within the Lower Mississippi Valley provides examples of how these settlements evolved to express changing sociopolitical, economic, and cultural values of the entire population. Variations through space and time indicate local adaptations to unique historical, social, and physical landscapes and indicate that Mississippi period "town" and community planning was fluid and dynamic.

Charles Stout and Barry Lewis explore western Kentucky town planning in Chapter 7. Mississippian towns here, as elsewhere, were more than the sum of repeated architectural traits and town plans suggested by trait list definitions of Mississippian culture. They shared architectural symbolism and standards used in the conceptualization, planning, and construction of western Kentucky Mississippian life as it is reflected in the towns.

In Chapter 8, Jon Muller considers the form and structure of Mississippian towns along the Lower Ohio River. He explores the extent to which these towns resemble the patterning described for historic settlements in seventeenth- and eighteenth-century documents and concludes that Mississippian settlement patterns in this region were socially as well as naturally conditioned.

In Chapter 9, Scott Demel and Robert Hall examine the integration of natural features and artificially created elements in the landscape of the Cahokia town plan. Looking through the lens of a dynamic system of structures, surfaces, and spaces, these authors see Cahokia as having been designed and continually redesigned to infuse a visual, social, psychological, and emotional impact on each generation of inhabitants and visitors. Demel and Hall explore how Cahokia's community, the constructed site, and the surrounding natural environment interacted with and adapted to one another; how changing economics and population growth affected its conception of itself; and how its physical manifestation reflected that conception.

Chapter 10 examines the major regional trends identified in Chapters 2 through 9. Lewis and Stout also explore the articulation of these patterns with the architectural grammar and the Mississippian cultural landscape.

2

Town Structure at the
Edge of the Mississippian World

Claudine Payne and John F. Scarry

At the far southeastern corner of the Mississippian world stands a classic Mississippian town (Figure 2.1). More than 800 kilometers from the towns of the Mississippi Valley and 600 kilometers from the geographic center of the Mississippian world, the Lake Jackson site nonetheless looks typically Mississippian. Pick it up and put it in north Georgia or western Tennessee or the Lower Mississippi Valley, and it would be immediately recognizable.

Why should this be? Reason suggests that a town at the margins of the Mississippian world would likely contain foreign (i.e., non-Mississippian) structural elements. Moreover, a marginal location, far from the great centers in the heart of the Mississippian world, implies that the town itself will be marginal—a poor and unsophisticated frontier town. But the Lake Jackson site, on the contrary, is quite wealthy. It was the capital of precolumbian Apalachee, one of the most powerful Mississippian chiefdoms in the Lower Southeast, and nearly as complex as Moundville or Etowah (although, of course, not nearly as large).

In this chapter, we examine the structure of the Lake Jackson site and address the questions of (1) why the site takes a classic Mississippian form and (2) how it became as powerful and wealthy as it did. Before discussing the site, however, a few words about the Mississippian world and what lay beyond it are in order.

The Mississippian World and Beyond

The Mississippian world stretched across the southeastern United States from northwestern Florida to the lower Illinois and Ohio valleys, and from coastal Georgia and South Carolina to eastern Oklahoma.

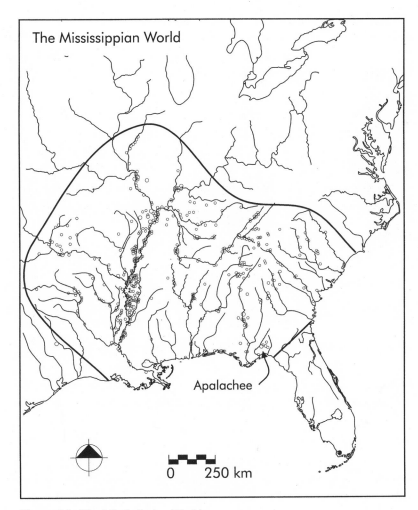

Figure 2.1. The Mississippian World.

Through links between individuals and groups, the Mississippian chiefdoms came to resemble each other in many ways. The Mississippian economy relied on cleared-field corn agriculture, although the exact subsistence strategies of individual groups varied and the mixes of crops differed from region to region (C. M. Scarry 1993). Across the Eastern Woodlands, we see broad similarities in iconographic forms; religious objects, for example, though varying in detail, clearly represent a shared cosmology (Brown 1985; Knight 1986; Muller 1989:25). And, of particular interest in this volume, the mound-plaza arrangements of major Mississippian sites

(Morgan 1980) form a distinct community plan that reflects political, social, and religious structure (Knight 1993; Payne 1994).

Beyond the Mississippian world lay other worlds inhabited by peoples with other material cultures, economies, political organizations, iconographies, and world views. The boundaries between these worlds were relatively sharp and stable. One boundary can be seen in the Ohio River Valley between the Mississippian system centered on the Angel site and the Fort Ancient groups who lived upstream. Another existed in Oklahoma between the Mississippian Spiro and Harlan phases and the Plains groups to the west. Finally, there was a distinct boundary in Florida between Mississippian Apalachee and the chiefdoms of central and southern Florida.

Florida Chiefdoms Beyond the Mississippian World

Because they play a part in this discussion, let us take a closer look at these Florida chiefdoms (Figure 2.2). Next door to Apalachee stood the western Timucuan chiefdoms of north-central Florida, known in historic times as Yustaga, Utina, and Potano (Johnson 1991; Milanich 1978). The environment of these Timucuan chiefdoms was similar to that of Apalachee.

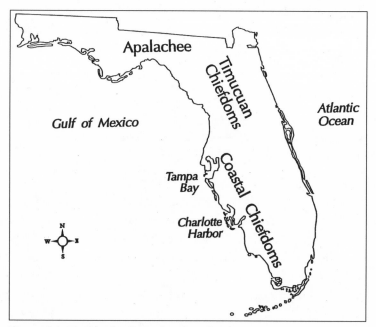

Figure 2.2. Florida chiefdoms.

All were situated in the Florida Highlands, a band of uplands that stretches across the top of the state and extends down through the center of the peninsula. The uplands, though cut by several rivers, are primarily drained by lakes, ponds, sinkholes, and marshes created by the region's karst topography. Throughout the uplands, soils are well drained and of moderate to good fertility.

Despite the similarities, the areas where the Timucuan groups lived are demonstrably less well suited to precolumbian agriculture than is the small, hilly region that was Apalachee. Soil quality, though adequate through most of the uplands, is lower than that in Apalachee. Moreover, good- or moderate-quality soils occur in less extensive tracts than in Apalachee, and their productivity is often lower because of limited water sources.

Most information on Timucuan subsistence comes from the Potano area, where there is evidence of fishing, hunting, and occasional use of freshwater shellfish (Milanich and Fairbanks 1980:172). Judging from early sixteenth-century Spanish accounts, the Timucuan chiefdoms probably relied on some corn cultivation (Bourne 1922:69, 71; Smith 1968:40), but archaeological evidence of corn is limited (Milanich 1994:339; Milanich and Fairbanks 1980:172), and farming may have been considerably less extensive than that carried out in Mississippian polities.

There are other differences as well. Timucuan material culture looks nothing like that of Apalachee; in fact, pottery styles change abruptly at the Aucilla River, the boundary between Apalachee and Yustaga. Recognizable Mississippian pottery forms and designs are present in Apalachee (see below). In Yustaga, however, the ceramics, which are poorly known, tend to be plain or brushed. Farther east, in Utina, the pottery belongs to the Indian Pond complex; surface treatment is linear marking (i.e., simple stamped/brushed/scraped), cord marking, or fabric marking (Johnson 1991; Johnson and Nelson 1990:51). In Potano, the simple bowls and cylindrical jars of the Alachua tradition are cob marked, cord marked, or fabric impressed (Milanich 1994:338; Milanich and Fairbanks 1980:176).

Limited information exists regarding Timucuan settlements, although Kenneth Johnson's (1991) surveys in the Utina and Potano areas have begun to rectify this situation. Settlements in precolumbian Utina and Potano are frequently compact villages on high ground near ponds or lakes (Johnson 1991:395, 429; Milanich 1994:339–40, 350; Milanich and Fairbanks 1980:171–72). Some villages contain plazas (Geiger 1936:115) and burial mounds (Milanich and Fairbanks 1980:176), but the platform mounds so conspicuous in Mississippian towns are absent throughout Yustaga, Utina, and Potano.

Unlike the inland Apalachee and Timucuan groups, the coastal Florida chiefdoms occupied a more typically Floridian environment: the estuaries and wetlands of Tampa Bay and Charlotte Harbor. The sheltered, nutrient-rich estuaries nurture many species of fish, shellfish, and other aquatic animals. Around the estuaries lie the unproductive and poorly drained soils of the coastal lowlands.

Blessed with a rich and productive subtropical estuarine setting, the people of southwest Florida made no effort to adopt corn agriculture (Scarry and Newsom 1992). Instead, they made use of the resources at hand and concentrated their efforts on nearshore fishing and procurement of shellfish (Marquardt 1992a; Walker 1992). Around both Tampa Bay and Charlotte Harbor, large populations lived off the bounty of the sea (Milanich and Fairbanks 1980:241).

Coastal Florida material culture shares some similarities with that of Apalachee. In the Tampa Bay area, especially, Safety Harbor pottery strongly resembles Apalachee's Fort Walton pottery (Milanich and Fairbanks 1980:209; Mitchem 1989; Scarry 1985). Forms and designs are so alike in the two areas that making distinctions between Fort Walton and Safety Harbor ceramics often proves difficult and has resulted in some controversy (Luer 1985; Scarry 1985). Much less similarity exists between Apalachee and the Charlotte Harbor area, although some Safety Harbor pottery appears around Charlotte Harbor after A.D. 1350 (Cordell 1992:168). Primarily, though, Charlotte Harbor ceramics include St. Johns Check Stamped, Belle Glade wares, and plain sand-tempered and spicule-paste wares (Cordell 1992:168; Marquardt 1992b:431). Apart from the occasional Safety Harbor designs, there are few decorations other than the impressed or "pie crust" rims of Glades Tooled (Cordell 1992:134; Marquardt 1992b:431).

Some coastal chiefdoms boasted mound centers bearing superficial resemblances to Mississippian mound centers. In the Tampa Bay area, for example, typical Safety Harbor mound centers include a rectangular platform mound with a ramp, an apparent plaza, and a burial mound (Bullen 1978:54; Griffin and Bullen 1950; Luer and Almy 1981:141; Milanich 1994:396; Milanich and Fairbanks 1980:205). In the Charlotte Harbor area, there are also large (though irregularly shaped) flat-topped mounds that may have served as platforms for important buildings (Milanich 1994:312; Milanich and Fairbanks 1980:242; Widmer 1988:6). Unlike Mississippian mounds, the coastal mounds were made of shell and earth (Griffin and Bullen 1950; Luer and Almy 1981) and, in at least some cases, are accumulations of midden (Marquardt 1989, 1992a) rather than periodically enlarged mounds. The settings of coastal mound sites also differ from those of Apalachee mound centers (which are located inland near lakes; see below). Tampa Bay mound centers generally stand on the shore of the mainland at the mouth of a creek or river (Luer and Almy 1981:141), while Charlotte Harbor mounds are usually situated on islands within the estuary (Widmer 1988:258).

Central and coastal Florida chiefdoms were clearly non-Mississippian; the precolumbian Apalachee chiefdom, where Lake Jackson stood, was, however, unquestionably Mississippian. In the next section, we review the nature of Mississippian Apalachee to provide a basis for understanding the nature of the Lake Jackson site.

The Mississippian Chiefdom in Apalachee

Mississippian Apalachee lay between the Aucilla and Ochlockonee rivers in the rolling hills of northwest Florida around present-day Tallahassee. This Fort Walton polity was a typical Mississippian chiefdom, except for one thing. Unlike most Mississippian chiefdoms, including its Fort Walton neighbors on the Apalachicola River, Apalachee was not confined to a river valley. Instead, it stretched across 65 kilometers of nearly unbroken and very fertile agricultural soils. Lakes in Apalachee may have played a role similar to that of rivers in other Mississippian polities, for the western part of Apalachee around the big lakes near the Ochlockonee River was more heavily settled than the eastern part (Figure 2.3).

Environment

Portions of two major physiographic zones (the Tallahassee Hills and the Gulf Coastal Lowlands) and several lesser ones occupy the area between the Ochlockonee and Aucilla rivers (Puri and Vernon 1964). Most important in a discussion of Apalachee is the northern zone, the Tallahassee Hills. This portion of the Northern Highlands is characterized by gently rolling hills and ridges. Broad, flat-topped hills, usually about 50 meters above sea level,

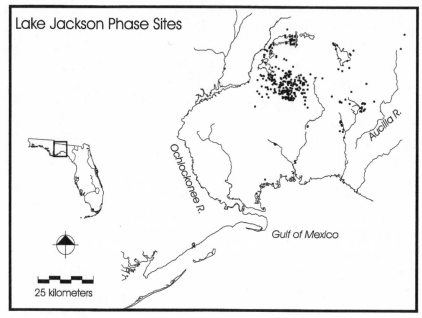

Figure 2.3. Mississippian Apalachee.

generally run east and west and alternate with boggy stream valleys (Gano 1917:340). The Tallahassee Hills drop abruptly at the Cody Scarp, and the sandy Gulf Coastal Lowlands begin a gentle slope to the Gulf of Mexico (Hendry and Sproul 1966:26).

Four large, shallow, flat-bottomed depressions interrupt the rolling countryside of the Tallahassee Hills. These lowlands occupy the courses of former streams and came about through the solution of the underlying limestone (Hendry and Sproul 1966:36–37; Sellards 1910). Three of the depressions hold shallow marshy lakes (Lakes Jackson, Iamonia, and Micco-sukee) while the fourth, once occupied by Lake Lafayette, is now largely dry (Hendry and Sproul 1966:41).

The part of the Tallahassee Hills lying between the Aucilla and Och-lockonee rivers boasts large unbroken tracts of well-drained loamy soils. These soils are among the best in north Florida and have supported fields and crops for about 1000 years with little sign of depletion. By contrast, the soils of the Gulf Coastal Lowlands are much poorer and generally unsuited for agriculture (Hendry and Sproul 1966:29–30; Sanders 1981:6–13).

Subsistence

There are few subsistence data from Apalachee. Only five precolumbian Mississippian sites (Lake Jackson, Borrow Pit, Winewood, Bear Grass, and 8LE484) have been extensively excavated, and comprehensive paleoarchaeobotanical and zooarchaeological studies were not carried out as part of these projects (Griffin 1950; Jones 1982; Jones and Penman 1973; Payne 1989; Tesar 1980; Willey 1949). Consequently, most available data consist of simple species identifications.

Despite these limitations, good evidence exists that maize was grown in Mississippian Apalachee; corn kernels have been recovered from four of the five excavated sites (Alexander 1984; Jones and Penman 1973; Tesar 1980). At the Lake Jackson site, maize constitutes 98 percent by weight of the total plant food remains (Alexander 1984:106). The preponderance of corn at Lake Jackson gives some idea of how important it was to the people of Apalachee (Alexander 1984:106). In fact, Spanish explorers entering Apalachee early in the sixteenth century described large expanses of cleared fields and the cultivation of beans and squash in addition to maize (Varner and Varner 1951:182). Additionally, a mass of corn was found in association with a high-ranking thirteenth-century burial at Lake Jackson, perhaps indicating that maize served a ritual as well as a subsistence purpose (Alexander 1984:106).

Wild food resources were also exploited by the inhabitants of Apalachee. Wild plants appearing at Mississippian Apalachee sites include hickory nuts, acorns, persimmons, water locust, and chinquapin (Alexander 1984; Tesar 1980:789, 821; Lee A. Newsom, personal communication, 1991). Information on faunal resources comes primarily from Lake Jackson. These resources include several terrestrial mammals (deer, southeastern pocket gopher, and, possibly, gray squirrel), several species of birds and turtles, snakes, freshwater fish (including catfish and bowfin), marine fish (including hardhead catfish and mullet), and mollusks (including gastropods and bivalves) (Jones 1982:20; Marc Frank, personal communication, 1991). Deer bones have also been found at Bear Grass and 8LE484 (Tesar 1980:789, 812). Given the location of many sites near lakes, waterfowl, fish, and other aquatic species undoubtedly played an important part in the Apalachee diet.

Material Culture

From its beginnings in the eleventh or twelfth century, the Apalachee chiefdom possessed a clearly Mississippian material culture. Pottery appears in typical Mississippian forms: collared jars, bottles, beakers, and carinated bowls (Scarry 1985; Willey 1949:457–66). Apalachee pottery design motifs are shared with other Fort Walton chiefdoms to the west and northwest (Schnell, Knight, and Schnell 1981:159–218; White 1982). Some designs have even more far-flung connections. For example, an arcade motif (Cool Branch Incised [Scarry 1985:214]) also appears on pottery from central Alabama (Moundville Incised [Steponaitis 1983:323–26]), the Mississippi Valley (Matthews Incised [Phillips 1970:128]), the lower Tennessee River Valley (Webb 1952:94–95), and the lower Ohio Valley (Webb and Funkhouser 1931:392–96).

Exotic items found in Apalachee also demonstrate a Mississippian identity. Some, in fact, originated in other parts of the Mississippian world. In the mid-1970s, Calvin Jones excavated burials from Mound 3 at the Lake Jackson site. The individuals buried in the mound were accompanied by artifacts that include prominent elements of the regional prestige economy. There are large repoussé copper plates, quantities of shell and pearl beads, copper and groundstone axes, carved shell gorgets, remains of costumes and elaborate headdresses, and other artifacts of nonlocal raw materials or manufacture (Jones 1982, 1994).

The Mound 3 artifacts link Apalachee to Mississippian polities in Tennessee and northern Georgia. The presence of identical copper symbol badges (headdress ornaments) at Lake Jackson and Etowah (Leader 1988) suggests close ties between the two sites. Several embossed copper plates also have unmistakable stylistic affinities to plates from Etowah (Jones 1982:16). Two Dallas bubble pipes recovered from one grave in Mound 3 are clearly not made of local clays and may have come from the Tennessee Valley (Jeffrey Brain, personal communication, 1988). Spaghetti-style shell gorgets from Lake Jackson also point to northern links (Brain and Phillips 1996; Jon Muller, personal communication, 1991). Apalachee was clearly part of a regional exchange network in which such prestige goods were circulated.

Settlement

The hierarchical political structure of Mississippian Apalachee is reflected in its settlement pattern. At the apex of the settlement hierarchy is the multimound Lake Jackson site, which is the largest mound site in Apalachee and the largest within a 200-kilometer radius.

At the second level in the site hierarchy are several smaller mound centers with one or two platform mounds each: Letchworth, Lake Iamonia, Lake Lafayette, Rollins, and Velda. Most of these mound centers, like the Lake Jackson site, lie near one of the four shallow marshy lakes (Figure 2.4). Investigations in the vicinity of the Velda Mound revealed not a dense village occupation but several small occupation areas looking remarkably like the numerous farmsteads found throughout the area. This configuration suggests that settlements adjacent to the mounds were small—probably a few houses rather than concentrated villages (Payne 1982; Scarry 1984a).

   One hamlet, the Borrow Pit site, is represented in Mississippian Apalachee (Payne 1982; Shapiro and McEwan 1992; B. Calvin Jones, personal communication, 1982). Four closely spaced circular structures arranged in an arc around the crest of a hill were uncovered at this site. One structure was substantially larger than the others and contained several burials. This may be a public building of some sort, possibly a council house (Jones 1990; Shapiro and McEwan 1992; B. Calvin Jones, personal communication, 1982), although, as Shapiro and McEwan (1992:63) note, it would thus represent "the only known example of a council house being used for burials."

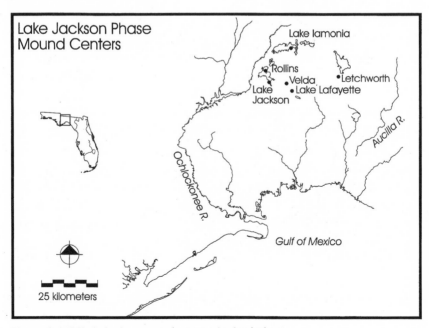

Figure 2.4. Mississippian mound centers in Apalachee.

Most Mississippian sites in Apalachee fall into the fourth category: farm-steads or homesteads. More than 200 Mississippian farmsteads have been identified in the Tallahassee Hills (Scarry 1995). The farmsteads are often located on the highest-quality soils, and 80 percent of the Mississippian sites identified during the Leon County Bicentennial Survey occur near lakes or swamps (Tesar 1980:617). The sites are small, less than 1 hectare (Louis Tesar, personal communication, 1982), and are often found within 500 me-ters of one another.

All archaeological evidence indicates that, with one exception (Lake Jackson), compact villages do not exist in Mississippian Apalachee. Instead, sites are dispersed over the landscape. Apalachee "towns" probably took the form of dispersed communities composed of groupings of scattered farm-steads, perhaps centered on a hamlet or mound center (Payne 1982).

Social Structure

The hierarchical nature of Mississippian society in Apalachee is also reflected in burial patterns. Skeletal remains in the Apalachee area are gener-ally very poorly preserved, but their locations and accompanying grave goods present a clear picture of a ranked society (Payne and Scarry 1990). Three different types of burial settings exist: (1) in platform mounds (all data for this setting come from Mound 3 at Lake Jackson); (2) below the floors of public buildings; and (3) in cemeteries or small burial plots (Jones 1982, 1990; Jones and Penman 1973). This differential treatment suggests the presence of social inequality. Additional detail is gained by ranking the buri-als by the number of artifact types accompanying them (a measure of the richness of the burials) and comparing this ranking with selected kinds of artifacts present (a measure of burial diversity; Figure 2.5). The resulting pattern suggests three general categories.

Category I individuals are usually buried in a platform mound (al-though one burial occurs below a public building) and are accompanied by three or more artifact types. Many of the Category I burials are quite rich, containing large numbers of artifact types and such elaborate or exotic items as engraved shell gorgets, marine shell beads, various kinds of copper items (e.g., celts, decorated plates, and ornaments), pearl beads, galena, mica, and red or yellow ochre. It is worth noting that mica, galena, and red and yellow ochre are found only in Category I burials with twelve or more artifact types. In addition, Category I burials usually contain copper items or pearl beads

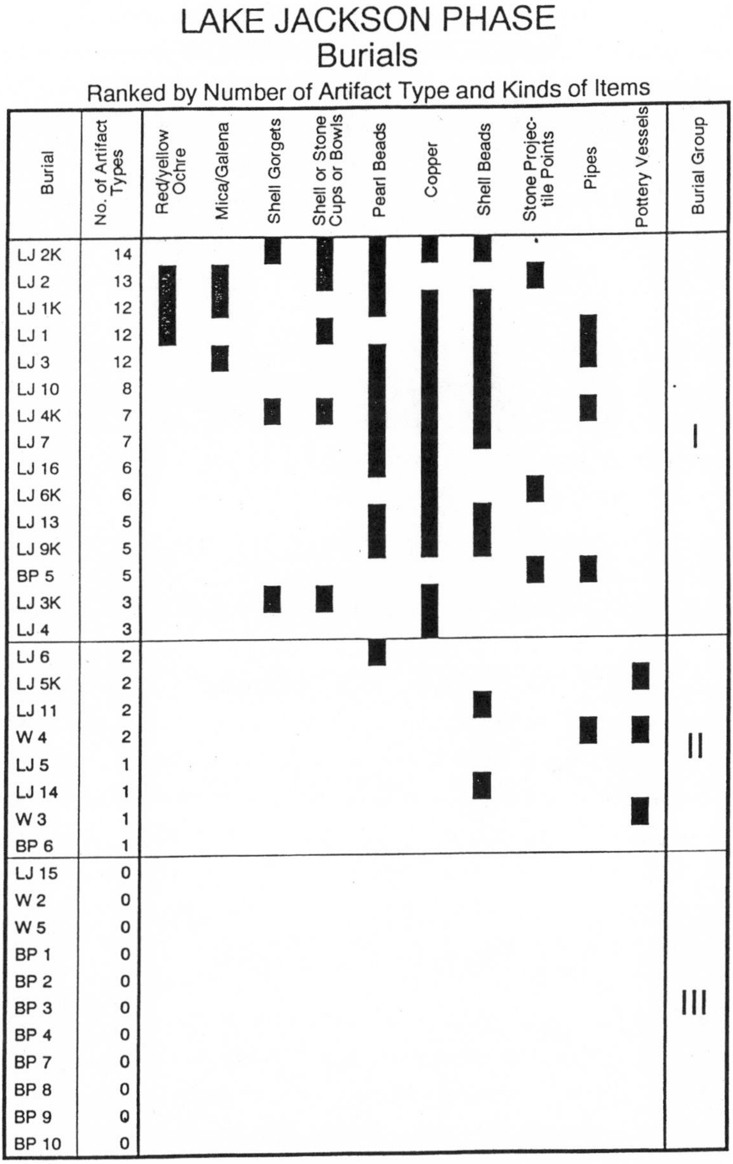

LAKE JACKSON PHASE
Burials
Ranked by Number of Artifact Type and Kinds of Items

Burial	No. of Artifact Types	Red/yellow Ochre	Mica/Galena	Shell Gorgets	Shell or Stone Cups or Bowls	Pearl Beads	Copper	Shell Beads	Stone Projectile Points	Pipes	Pottery Vessels	Burial Group
LJ 2K	14											
LJ 2	13											
LJ 1K	12											
LJ 1	12											
LJ 3	12											
LJ 10	8											
LJ 4K	7											
LJ 7	7											I
LJ 16	6											
LJ 6K	6											
LJ 13	5											
LJ 9K	5											
BP 5	5											
LJ 3K	3											
LJ 4	3											
LJ 6	2											
LJ 5K	2											
LJ 11	2											
W 4	2											II
LJ 5	1											
LJ 14	1											
W 3	1											
BP 6	1											
LJ 15	0											
W 2	0											
W 5	0											
BP 1	0											
BP 2	0											
BP 3	0											III
BP 4	0											
BP 7	0											
BP 8	0											
BP 9	0											
BP 10	0											

Figure 2.5. Apalachee burials ranked by artifact types.

or both. These two materials thus seem to be good indicators of elite burials in general. The only nonmound burial in Category I is that of a young male interred under the public building at the Borrow Pit site (Jones 1990). The lack of both pearl beads and copper in this burial suggests that there may have been some distinction between local nobles and nobles living at the capital, with the latter having better access to high-status goods.

Category II individuals are present in all three burial settings. They are accompanied by one or two artifact types, primarily shell beads, pottery, or pipes. Pottery vessels are present only with Category II burials. Only one Category II burial contains pearl beads, and none contain copper items, shell gorgets, mica, galena, or red or yellow ochre.

Category III individuals are buried mostly in small burial plots or under local public buildings and have no artifacts with them. Only one individual is buried in a platform mound.

These categories suggest three rough social groupings: (1) nobles, buried mainly in platform mounds and accompanied by many grave goods, almost always including copper or pearls (Scarry 1992); (2) important people, buried in all contexts and accompanied by one or two artifact types; and (3) commoners, buried mostly in nonmound contexts and without grave goods.

From the foregoing summary emerges the picture of a polity with almost all the hallmarks of Mississippian society: cleared-field corn agriculture; ranked society; Mississippian material culture, iconography, and world view; participation in the Mississippian exchange network; and mound-and-plaza sites. We turn our attention now to the capital of this Mississippian chiefdom.

The Lake Jackson Site

The Lake Jackson site is located in the western part of Apalachee, facing the Fort Walton chiefdoms along the Apalachicola River (Figure 2.4). The site stands on the southwestern shore of Lake Jackson in a broad flat plain that is part of the Lake Jackson Lowlands. The 15- to 30-meter bluffs immediately west of the main mound precinct mark the edge of the Tallahassee Hills. Inhabitants of the site clearly had easy access to both physiographic zones as well as to the Ochlockonee River Valley Lowlands only 5 kilometers to the west. The lake itself can be reached by walking east about 100 meters from the main mound precinct.

The site is a group of seven earthen mounds (Figure 2.6). Six of these

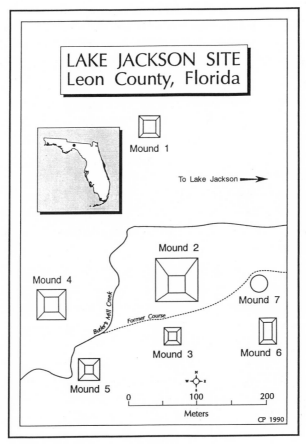

Figure 2.6. The Lake Jackson site.

mounds are pyramidal, flat-topped mounds; one is a low rounded rise. The main mound precinct consists of five large flat-topped mounds and the low mound. These are arranged on both sides of Butler's Mill Creek, which rises 30 meters above on the ridge to the west and flows east through the site into Lake Jackson. The seventh mound (Mound 1) is situated about 400 meters north of the main precinct. The entire site, including mounds, living areas, and some large cleared spaces, encompasses about 24 hectares (Jones 1982). The mound precinct itself covers 19 hectares (Payne 1994). Mound 2 is the largest mound, covering more than half a hectare and standing about 11 meters high. The other mounds at the site vary in height from 5 meters (Mound 4) to less than 1 meter (Mound 7).

Archaeological Investigations at Lake Jackson

The state of Florida owns about half of the main mound and approximately 30 hectares of land west of the mounds. The property is managed by Florida's Division of Natural Resources as the Lake Jackson Mounds State Archaeological Site.

Archaeologists have explored the Lake Jackson site for more than 50 years now, though much of the work has gone unreported. Gordon Willey (1940, 1949) was the first archaeologist to work at Lake Jackson. In the summer of 1940, Willey and Richard Woodbury dug two 3-meter by 3-meter units on either side of Mound 2. A unit south of Mound 2 yielded very few artifacts and unclear stratigraphy. A unit north of Mound 2 uncovered a 30-centimeter-thick midden and a moderate collection of sherds.

In 1947, John Griffin (1950) excavated a fairly large area between Mounds 2 and 4. Here he found midden averaging 45 centimeters deep along with many overlapping pits, postholes, and other features. A series of tests south of the main excavations, however, turned up very little. This along with the barrenness of Willey's unit south of Mound 2 led Griffin to speculate that areas between Mounds 2 and 4 and between Mounds 2 and 3 represent portions of a cleared plaza.

In the late 1960s, two salvage excavations provided data on the extent of the occupation around the main mound group. In 1968, Daniel Penton (1968; Payne 1989, 1994) placed two test units northeast and north of Mound 2 where a drainage ditch now is. The northeastern unit revealed little midden and a limited number of artifacts. In the northern unit (not far from Willey's first test pit), however, Penton found about 30 centimeters of midden with numerous features, including a possible clay floor. The following year, the Division of Natural Resources requested excavations at proposed park building construction sites. Frank Fryman (1969; Payne 1989, 1994) opened up an area about 6 meters by 10 meters in the area north of Mound 4. The eastern side of this excavation revealed midden and various features, including a portion of a wall trench. In the western side of the excavation, however, much less midden appeared and there were no features. Fryman also tested areas at the foot of the bluff just west of Mound 4, finding no features and little aboriginal material.

In 1989, Claudine Payne (1989, 1994) carried out an auger survey of part of the main mound precinct. The survey area encompassed the north and west sides of the main mound precinct, covering about 3 hectares in an L shape around Mounds 2, 4, and 5. Auger holes (20 centimeters in diameter and generally about a meter deep) were placed at intervals of 10 meters. The survey showed that the heaviest occupation occurred in the immediate vicinities and just to the north of Mounds 2 and 4. Artifact densities drop off and midden accumulation becomes shallower to the northwest and west of Mound 4 and southwest of Mound 5. The small floodplain of Butler's Mill Creek prevents much occupation between Mounds 4 and 5. Shallow midden deposits and low artifact density in the area between Mounds 2 and 4 support Griffin's view that a plaza existed between the mounds. The survey results suggest that living areas at the Lake Jackson site are not extensive but are limited in space, primarily concentrated around the mounds.

Several of the mounds have been tested. The most spectacular excavations were those of Calvin Jones (1982, 1994) in Mound 3. Faced with imminent destruction of the mound by the landowner, Jones and a small crew carried out hurried salvage excavations in the middle 1970s. They found twelve living floors and twenty-four burials, many accompanied by elaborate and beautiful items. These artifacts were described in some detail earlier in this chapter. Radiocarbon dates from Mound 3 place its use between about A.D. 1250 and 1500. The mound had been built over an earlier occupation.

Less spectacular but still informative were excavations in Mound 6 by a Tallahassee resident (Payne 1994). Ten 2-meter by 2-meter units were excavated in the mound. No burials were encountered although several possible living floors were found. The mound was built over an earlier midden, and a layer of light sand had been laid down before mound construction.

Test excavations in Mounds 4 and 5 were carried out by Claudine Payne in 1989 and 1990, respectively (Payne 1989, 1994). Test units were placed on the flanks of the mounds and yielded data on mound construction and on the nature of the premound occupations. These data indicate that the mounds were constructed over existing occupation areas. As with Mound 6, a layer of light-colored sand was spread over midden before construction on Mound 4 began. A radiocarbon date from the midden under Mound 5 suggests that its submound occupation dates to around A.D. 1050. Mounds 4 and 5 are built of various kinds of soils apparently carried in by the basketload (and sometimes including midden material). Each flat-topped construction stage is capped with a layer of orange-brown clay that dried rock hard, providing ample structural support. Forty years before Payne's tests, the summit of Mound 4 had been briefly explored by John Griffin (1950:101), who uncovered seven postholes, indicating that some sort of structure may have stood atop that mound.

Small windows into the interior of Mound 2 were provided by the profiling of a vandal's cut on the south side of the mound (Griffin 1950), a series of postholes up the slope of the north face of the mound (for the construction of stairs), and a small shallow unit on the west slope near the top (for the placement of a sign) (Payne 1994). These all indicate construction techniques similar to those of Mounds 4 and 5 (i.e., lenses or basketloads of varied soils covered with an orange-brown clay layer).

These investigations provide a clear picture of the structure of the Lake Jackson site. Occupation areas surround the mounds and extend northward 50 to 100 meters from Mound 2. The area north and west of Mound 2 contains the densest occupation known from the site so far. Artifact density and evidence of midden drop off immediately west of Mounds 4 and 5, just southwest of Mound 5, and not too far east of Mound 2. A cleared area occurs between Mounds 2 and 4. The boundaries of settlement to the south and southeast are not known. All mounds for which we have data (Mounds 3, 4, 5, and 6) are built over earlier occupations. At least two of these areas (under Mounds 4 and 6) were covered with clean sand before mound construction began. Mound construction is similar in all five of the platform mounds in the main precinct: varied types of soil were laid down in lenses suggestive of basketloads, then covered by mantles of orange-brown clay. Two mounds (Mounds 3 and 4) revealed evidence of structures on their summits, and one mound (Mound 3) contained elaborate and wealthy burials of individuals interpreted here as nobles. Radiocarbon dates and ceramic data indicate that the cultural florescence of the town occurred between about A.D. 1250 and 1500, with settlement dating perhaps as far back as around A.D. 1050.

A Classic Mississippian Town

In the previous section, we presented a description of the Lake Jackson site based on archaeological investigations there. With these data in hand, we can compare the site to other Mississippian mound centers and see exactly how Lake Jackson is a "classic Mississippian town."

Lake Jackson ranks as a medium-large site (along with twenty-three other mound sites) in Payne's (1994) recent size classification of Mississippian mound centers. It should be noted, however, that only fourteen sites are included in larger size classes. In the Lower Southeast, Lake Jackson is one of the largest mound centers. Only four sites are larger: Moundville, Etowah, Ocmulgee, and Bottle Creek. The closest site of comparable size is 200 kilometers away (Rood's Landing), and the closest appreciably larger site lies nearly 400 kilometers distant (Bottle Creek).

Mississippian mound centers contain from one to about a hundred mounds. The average number of mounds per site is about three and the median number is only two (Payne 1994). Lake Jackson, with its seven mounds, is well above average in number of mounds. In fact, in a survey of 536 Mississippian mound centers, only thirty-three sites (6.2 percent) had more than seven mounds (Payne 1994).

Several types of mounds occur at Mississippian sites, but the most frequent form is a simple truncated pyramid (Payne 1994). These truncated pyramids usually served as bases for one or more buildings. Some mounds contained burials of nobles in the floors of the buildings. Frequently the mounds were built in stages over the course of 150 to 200 years (Hally 1996). At Lake Jackson, six mounds are simple truncated pyramids; the form of the seventh is indeterminate. Archaeological investigation has revealed that buildings stood on the tops of at least two mounds (Mounds 3 and 4) (Griffin 1950; Jones 1982, 1994). Nobles were buried in at least one (Mound 3) (Jones 1982, 1994). The mounds at Lake Jackson were built in stages and periodically covered with clay mantles, as described above. Radiocarbon dates from Mound 3 indicate that its use spanned about 250 years.

The arrangement of mounds at Mississippian sites varies widely, but two common patterns can be discerned. In a survey of 103 Mississippian mound centers with adequate data on the location of the main mound, the principal mound stood at the edge of the mound precinct at seventy-six sites (73.8 percent) (Payne 1994; see also Reed 1977:35). The main mound stood at the center of the precinct at twenty-seven sites (26.2 percent). Sites with central main mounds are generally larger (median of eight mounds) than those with peripheral main mounds (median of four mounds). Central location may thus result from the addition of mounds as a site grows. The principal mound at Lake Jackson stands in a central location, perhaps reflecting its larger than average number of mounds.

The arrangement of mounds and plazas at some Mississippian centers presents a formal appearance, suggesting a deliberate plan of the builders. This formality results from the alignment of mounds with each other. At ninety-one sites with adequate data on mound alignment, forty-nine sites (53.8 percent) contained aligned mounds, fourteen sites (15.4 percent) contained mounds not aligned with each other, and twenty-eight sites (30.8 percent) had both aligned and nonaligned mounds (Payne 1994). Sites with aligned mounds appear to be larger (in number of mounds) than sites with nonaligned mounds. This pattern suggests that formal arrangements result not from a plan laid out at the beginning of a site's history but from the presence of a continuing central authority that dictated or influenced the relationships of mounds to each other. The mounds at Lake Jackson are clearly aligned with each other. This formal arrangement may reflect a strong central authority at Lake Jackson, an inference supported by other data from the site (e.g., the size of the site, the presence of numerous prestige goods).

Mississippian mound centers are often oriented with their long axes parallel or perpendicular to a water body, usually a river (Payne 1994). Because many rivers in the Southeast flow in a north-south direction, many mound centers are also thus oriented to the cardinal directions, making it difficult to separate symbolic from practical siting influences. Though not situated on a river, the Lake Jackson site is oriented to water. The main mound precinct lies perpendicular to an arm of Lake Jackson. The precinct also exhibits a clear directional orientation: the long axis is oriented east-west.

Plazas or public spaces are common features of Mississippian communities. Plazas have been identified not only at mound centers but also at other types of Mississippian sites as well (e.g., the Turner and Snodgrass sites in southeastern Missouri [Price 1978:218–19]). At mound centers, the arrangement of mounds often suggests the presence of plazas. These architectural spaces may not coincide with the boundaries of plazas, however, so plaza identification should come through subsurface survey (Payne 1994). At Lake Jackson, the site's layout suggests two plazas, one between Mounds 2 and 3 and Mounds 4 and 5 and one between Mounds 2 and 3 and Mounds 6 and 7 (the present course of the stream running through these areas is the result of historical and modern diversions and landscape alterations; the original course of Butler's Creek is uncertain). Archaeologists have identified a cleared space between Mounds 2 and 4 (Griffin 1950; Payne 1989). Subsurface data are unavailable in other likely places, so we cannot confirm the presence of additional plazas.

Many Mississippian mound centers, both large and small, were enclosed by fortifications in the form of an embankment, ditch, or wooden palisade (Lafferty 1973). In a survey of 132 Mississippian mound centers, fortifications were identified at forty-seven sites (35.6 percent) (Payne 1994). Because subsurface testing is necessary to determine the presence of palisades, this proportion could rise with additional research. Defensive earthworks (embankment and ditch) occur somewhat less frequently in peripheral areas of the Mississippian world than in central areas (Payne 1994). At Lake Jackson, no obvious embankments or ditches exist, and excavations have uncovered no evidence of a palisade.

From the above comparisons, we see that Lake Jackson is a medium-large mound center with a larger than average number of mounds. In the Lower Southeast, it is one of the ten largest mound centers. Five of the six mounds in the main mound precinct are truncated pyramids built in stages, some with structures on their summits and one containing the burials of nobles accompanied by Mississippian prestige goods. The mounds at Lake Jackson are laid out around at least one plaza in a formal arrangement and are oriented to the cardinal directions and to the nearby lake. The central location of the largest mound is a minority pattern among Mississippian mound centers but is not unusual for sites with more than the average number of mounds. No fortifications are known for Lake Jackson but subsurface testing would be necessary to confirm the absence of a palisade.

In contrast to its likeness to Mississippian mound centers, Lake Jackson does not resemble Florida towns. Timucuan towns, though sited in environments roughly similar to Lake Jackson's (in uplands, near lakes or ponds), lack platform mounds. The only mound structures described for Timucuan towns are burial mounds. Some Timucuan towns are known to have had plazas (as did some coastal towns), but plazas are a common feature of many kinds of settlements, including, of course, Mississippian towns. In contrast to the Timucuan towns and Lake Jackson, coastal towns generally stand on the shores of estuaries. Coastal towns often contain flat-topped mounds (some are even truncated pyramids), but these are built of shells and often consist largely of irregular accumulations of midden.

In summary, Lake Jackson seems to be a moderately large, well-to-do, typically Mississippian town with few structural similarities to Florida towns.

The Edge of the Mississippian World

At the beginning of this chapter, we asked why a site located at the edge of the world took a typically Mississippian form and why it was powerful and wealthy. Given its location at the interface of the Mississippian and non-Mississippian worlds, we might have expected to see characteristics of both worlds in the structure of the site, and we might have expected the site to be poor and unsophisticated. Yet, Lake Jackson looks structurally Mississippian with no Florida influences at all. Moreover, Lake Jackson is not only Mississippian, but it is also a comparatively large and clearly wealthy town. So, what is a big, rich Mississippian town doing out here in such a marginal location?

To begin to address these issues, we have to look at how Apalachee came to be settled and at the role of Lake Jackson in Mississippian exchange.

The Origins of Apalachee

Before A.D. 1000, few people lived in the Apalachee area. Only around 100 Weeden Island sites are known for the area between the rivers, and more than half of these are located on or near the coast. Fewer than fifty sites occur in the Tallahassee Hills. Throughout the Weeden Island period, the number of sites was relatively steady, even declining a bit toward the end of the period (Tesar 1980:601–2). This suggests a stable and possibly even decreasing population (Figure 2.7).

By contrast, 70 kilometers away on the Apalachicola River, Weeden Island foragers and gardeners flourished. We know of about 250 Weeden Island sites throughout the valley. Between A.D. 500 and 1000, the numbers of Weeden Island sites increased steadily (Figure 2.8), and population began to outstrip carrying capacity (Scarry 1990:234).

Sometime around A.D. 1000 or 1100 these regional trends changed (Scarry 1990:234, 243). From a relative backwater in Weeden Island times, the Tallahassee Hills rapidly became a thriving center of activity. Population increased strongly and steadily for the next 500 years. About 250 Fort Walton sites are known for the same area that held only fifty Weeden Island sites. In the Apalachicola Valley, on the other hand, population apparently stabilized and may even have dropped. About 100 Fort Walton sites are recorded where more than twice that many sites had existed earlier.

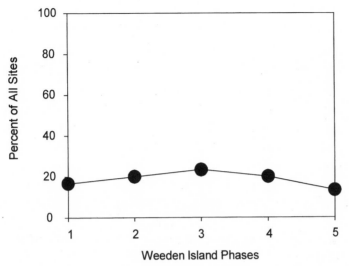

Figure 2.7. Weeden Island population trends in the Tallahassee Hills.

The shift from Weeden Island to Fort Walton occurred around A.D. 1000 in the Apalachicola Valley. This was a gradual, local development with maize assuming greater importance in the diet and simple political hierarchies appearing at the earliest Fort Walton sites alongside Weeden Island elements (Scarry 1984b:210–36, 1990). In Apalachee, however, we see little evidence of a similar gradual transition. Few sites equivalent to the earliest Fort Walton sites in the valley are known. When Fort Walton sites did appear, their ceramic assemblages contained few Weeden Island elements, suggesting little local continuity. Moreover, Fort Walton ceramics at sites in the Tallahassee Hills are strikingly similar to those in the Apalachicola Valley.

These patterns suggest that the development of the Apalachee chiefdom was not local but was spurred by the movement of people from the spatially limited territories along the Apalachicola Valley into the open, relatively unpopulated Apalachee area (Knight 1991; Scarry 1990).

The Role of Lake Jackson in the Mississippian Exchange Network

One of the most important links among Mississippian polities was an exchange network between nobles. A limited set of raw materials and finished artifacts marked by recognizable iconographies flowed through this network

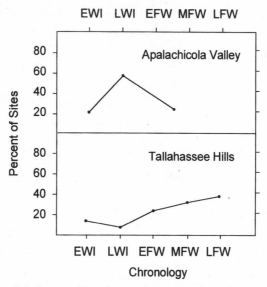

Figure 2.8. Late prehistoric population trends in the Apalachicola River Valley (*top*) and the Tallahassee Hills (*bottom*). The
chronological scale is early Weeden Island (*EWI*), late Weeden
Island (*LWI*), early Fort Walton (*EFW*), middle Fort Walton
(*MFW*), and late Fort Walton (*LFW*).

(Brown 1976; Muller 1989). This network also formed the arena in which
many of the political and social interactions of the Mississippian chiefdoms
were carried out. The artifacts marking this network form part of what has
been called the Southern Cult or Southeastern Ceremonial Complex paraphernalia. They include copper, shell, and stone items, many of which were
probably used as symbols of status or political position. Among these items
are weapons and nonfunctional representations of weapons, elaborate headdresses, carved shell gorgets, and repoussé copper plates. Other items, such
as shell cups, ceramic beakers, and pipes, may have been used in social or
religious ceremonial contexts. The artifacts that moved through this network were typically low mass/high value goods.

There is clear evidence of Apalachee participation in regional exchange
networks linking it to other Mississippian polities. The nobles buried in
Mound 3 at Lake Jackson were accompanied by grave goods that included prominent items of the Mississippian prestige economy. Recall that
the artifacts recovered from Mound 3 include large repoussé copper plates,

quantities of shell and pearl beads, copper and groundstone axes, engraved shell gorgets, pipes, and the remains of regalia and elaborate headdresses (Jones 1982).

For Apalachee nobles to obtain such valuables, they must have had something to exchange. The Mound 3 burials give a few clues about what these might have been. The burials contained hundreds of marine shell beads, pearl beads, and shark's teeth. All these items are most easily procured as by-products of subsistence fishing and shellfish gathering (Brown, Kerber, and Winters 1990:271). Small scattered fishing settlements dotted the Gulf Coast south of Lake Jackson and could have provided limited supplies of shells, pearls, and shark's teeth. The large quantities, however, suggest acquisition from a relatively large population engaged in fishing and collection of shellfish. This points to coastal societies, perhaps the coastal chiefdoms of the Tampa Bay and Charlotte Harbor areas, as the source of these items.

Another product that Apalachee could have provided to inland groups was *Ilex vomitoria*, which was used to make the ceremonial "black drink." This important plant is abundant in the coastal zone; the Apalachee were thus in a good position to supply it to inland groups. The presence of decorated ceramic beakers in submound contexts at Lake Jackson suggests that black drink ceremonialism was part of Apalachee culture from its beginning.

Apalachee could also have supplied interior Mississippian groups with knowledge gained from non-Mississippian peoples (Scarry 1991). Mary Helms (1988) notes that political and religious elites typically monopolize esoteric knowledge and use it as a source of power. She points out that geographically distant places, and the people and things found in those places, are frequent sources of such esoteric knowledge.

Support for the suggestion that the leaders of the Lake Jackson chiefdom may have linked other societies with South Florida chiefdoms may be seen in a set of elaborately decorated pins bearing the images of crested birds. One of these pins, manufactured of marine turtle shell, was found in the grave of a high-ranking man at the Etowah site in northern Georgia (Larson 1993). A second was excavated from a protohistoric Apalachee site on the Gulf Coast just south of Lake Jackson (Goggin 1947; Griffin 1947; Marrinan, Scarry, and Majors 1990). This pin was manufactured from sheet copper and gold and was associated with European artifacts. Both these artifacts were likely manufactured in South Florida. Several similar pins have been recovered from sites in the Charlotte Harbor–Lake Okeechobee area (Allerton, Luer, and Carr 1984; Goggin 1947). Most of the pins appear to date to the sixteenth century, although the Etowah example should date to the thirteenth or perhaps fourteenth century (i.e., contemporaneous with Lake Jackson) (cf. Larson 1993 for a different interpretation of the dating of the Etowah specimen).

The pins found at Etowah and in south Florida are so similar that they can be taken as evidence of the exchange either of finished artifacts or of the ideas about the styles and symbolic forms, if not the meanings, that were used to decorate such pins. In the absence of a direct cultural connection between Etowah and south Florida, artifacts or ideas must have moved somehow between the two. Individuals could have traveled directly from one to the other or ideas and/or artifacts could have been transmitted from individual to individual in a down-the-line exchange from group to group. People, ideas, or artifacts could have moved down the Chattahoochee-Apalachicola river system and across the Gulf of Mexico, through the Lake Jackson chiefdom, through interior societies in Georgia and north Florida, or through the St. Johns area of northeast Florida. Evidence for any of these is limited. More evidence for Mississippian-Florida connections exists for Lake Jackson (artifacts from Etowah at Lake Jackson, marine shell at Lake Jackson, and Mississippian-style pottery in the central Gulf Coast of Florida) than for either the Apalachicola route or the eastern routes (although Mount Royal may have held a position like that of Lake Jackson, with similar consequences).

Other evidence that points to interaction between Mississippian and Florida societies via Lake Jackson includes a repoussé copper plate found at a mound near Old Okahumpka in Lake County (Goggin 1949; Moore 1895:542–43; Phillips and Brown 1978:206–7). This plate is clearly of Mississippian origin and bears a striking resemblance to plates found in Alabama and at the Spiro site in Oklahoma (Phillips and Brown 1978:207). Sherds that can probably be classified as Fort Walton Incised were also found in the mound (Goggin 1949:36; Moore 1895:fig. 91). The closest sources of this pottery type would be either the Tampa Bay area or Apalachee.

Having explored the origins of Apalachee and the role of Lake Jackson in the Mississippian exchange network, we can now address the questions we raised earlier.

Mississippian Town at the Edge of the World

Lake Jackson's "Mississippian-ness" can be seen partly as a result of environmental and historical factors and partly as a result of its role in the Mississippian exchange network. Coastal Florida influences rarely appear at Lake Jackson because its inland environment and agricultural subsistence strategy made unlikely the adoption of structural features uniquely suited to the coast.

Moreover, the site was originally settled by Mississippian people expanding from their crowded Apalachicola River homeland. The non-Mississippian people of north Florida, with considerable space at their disposal, found no need to expand into the Tallahassee Hills. Historically, then, Apalachee's (and Lake Jackson's) ties were west to the Mississippian world, not east to the Timucuan chiefdoms.

In addition, Lake Jackson's leaders were able to provide interior chiefdoms with exotic and valuable Florida items (shells, pearls, etc.). This ability tied them firmly into the Mississippian exchange network and gave them access to quintessential Mississippian insignia, regalia, and religious items. This access, in combination with the area's historical antecedents, defines Apalachee as intrinsically Mississippian. Put simply, then, the Lake Jackson site looks typically Mississippian because it *is* Mississippian.

Wealth and Power at the Edge of the World

The other question we raised was why Lake Jackson was so rich and powerful given its marginal location. To address this we turn again to Lake Jackson's role in the Mississippian exchange network. The edge of the world offered certain advantages to groups who lived there (Scarry 1991). The location of Apalachee gave its nobles access to esoteric knowledge from beyond the Mississippian world and the opportunity to control the flow of highly valued material goods to other societies. This control increased the status, power, and wealth of the Apalachee leaders (both internally and externally) and contributed to the stability and growth of the Apalachee polity. Thus it seems that a peripheral location, far from being detrimental to a town's rise to wealth and power, may actually increase the likelihood of it. Similar processes may also have contributed to the wealth and prominence of Mount Royal and Spiro, two other sites located on the edge of the Mississippian world (see Schambach [1993] for a discussion of Spiro's role in exchange between the Mississippian world and the Great Plains).

In conclusion, we have seen that, though sited at the edge of the Mississippian world, the Lake Jackson site is a moderately large, typically Mississippian town. Indeed, it probably owes its wealth and power to that peripheral setting, a location that gave its leaders the chance to control the exchange of information and goods between two worlds. It owes its classic Mississippian structure to its development out of the Mississippian societies of the Apalachicola Valley, its lush and agriculturally productive environment, and its successful participation in the Mississippian exchange network. The edge of the world, far from being a marginal backwater, proved to be a most advantageous location for Lake Jackson.

3

The Nature
of Mississippian
Towns in Georgia

The King Site Example

David J. Hally and Hypatia Kelly

The King site (9FL5) is the most extensively excavated Mississippian town in Georgia. In this chapter, we describe the general features of its settlement plan with emphasis on domestic households and the variability evident in residential structures. The key to understanding the variability in these structures, we argue, lies in their role as symbols of household identity and continuity and in the way households grow through time.

King is located on the Coosa River in northwestern Georgia. It is one of five large sixteenth-century towns known to lie along a 20-kilometer stretch of the Coosa River (Figure 3.1). With the addition of a possible contemporary mound site (9FL162) located at the junction of the Etowah and Oostanaula rivers, this group of sites conforms closely to the settlement pattern characteristic of the sixteenth-century inhabitants of much of the upper Coosa and upper Tennessee River drainages (Hally, Smith, and Langford 1990). Throughout this region, settlement was primarily in towns (Figure 3.1).[1] These averaged 2.8 hectares in size, were occupied by 200 to 1000 people, and occurred in clusters of four to seven towns distributed along rivers over distances of 11 to 24 kilometers. Most, if not all, town clusters contained at least one mound site that probably served as an administrative center. These town clusters are interpreted as representing politically integrated societies or chiefdoms.

King covers 2.3 hectares, is square in plan, and is bounded by a ditch

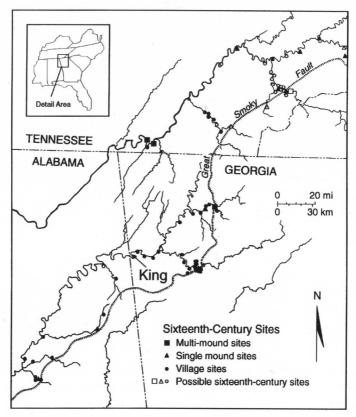

Figure 3.1. The King site and other sixteenth-century site clusters
in northwestern Georgia, eastern Alabama, and eastern Tennessee.

and palisade system on three sides and by the Coosa River on the north
(Figure 3.2). The alignment of the town, approximately 13 degrees west of
north, parallels that of the adjacent stretch of river. A large open area containing two structures and several large posts lies at the center of the town
and is surrounded by a domestic habitation zone measuring 25 to 35 meters
across.

Overbank erosion and plowing have destroyed the aboriginal ground
surface over the entire site. Modern plow zone is underlain by a sterile yellow
loam. This deposit predates site occupation and is intruded by postholes,
burial pits, house floors, and the defensive ditch. Erosion and plow damage
are least severe in the east-central portion of the site (the area above an elevation of 30 meters [98.5 feet]) and most severe in the western portion. The

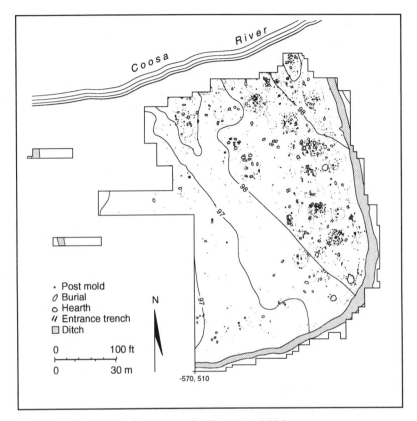

Figure 3.2. Excavated features at the King site, 1992.

floors of several domestic structures (Structures 4, 5/10, 7, 8, 9, 14, and 23; Figure 3.3) are preserved in the former area. Moving west and south across the site (and lower in elevation), evidence of house floors disappears first, followed by evidence of shallow burials, postholes, and, finally, all features except the defensive ditch.

Square Structures

Posthole patterns representing two distinct kinds of structures—square and rectangular—can be distinguished in the excavated portion of the site (Figure 3.3). There are at least twenty-seven and possibly as many as twenty-nine square structures. All but two of these (Structures 16 and 17) are located in the domestic habitation zone and are identified as domestic struc-

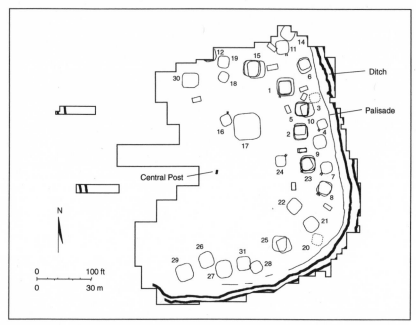

Figure 3.3. King site square and rectangular structures. Structures identified by *dotted lines* are tentative.

tures. These structures average 60 square meters in floor area and have straight walls with rounded corners. Exterior walls were constructed of vertical, single-set posts and wattle and daub (Figure 3.4). Floors were set in basins dug 30 to 50 centimeters below the ground surface; earth excavated from these basins was banked against the exterior walls. Interior features include a central hearth, four roof support posts defining a square central floor space, and low wattle-and-daub walls that divided the outer floor area into cubicles that served as work, storage, and sleeping areas. Seven structures in the habitation zone have entrance passages defined by pairs of wall trenches. Stratigraphic evidence indicates that these features would have been destroyed by erosion and plowing in the cases of the remaining structures. Presumably entrance passages were designed to prevent earth banked against outer walls from eroding into the structure. In the absence of such features, structure entrances are difficult to identify.

Square structures are identified as residences on the basis of several lines of evidence. First, all structures with excavated floors (Structures 4, 5/10,

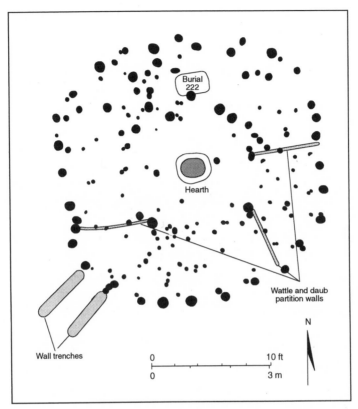

Figure 3.4. Structure 7 at the King site (adapted from Blakely 1988:12). Used by permission of the University of Georgia Press.

7, 8, 9, 14, and 23) yielded a variety of artifacts and ecofacts indicative of domestic activities. These include large quantities of animal bones and the charred remains of economically important plants; an abundance of pottery fragments representing all of the more common vessel forms found at the site; and many non–flaked stone tools such as grinding slabs, pitted stones, and hammer stones. Second, all square structures in the habitation zone are architecturally similar, differing only in floor area, number of rebuilding stages, and state of preservation. Third, except for the rectangular structures described below, no other type of building can be identified in the habitation zone.

Structure 16 is similar in most architectural features to the square structures located in the habitation zone (Figure 3.3). It is tempting to identify this structure as the residence of the town chief, but its small size, 37 square meters, does not support such an interpretation.

Structure 17, located next to Structure 16 in the plaza (Figure 3.3), resembles the pattern described above in that it is square with rounded corners and has single-set exterior wall posts, a central hearth, and interior partitions that divide the outer floor space into cubicles. It differs in being considerably larger (214 square meters) and having eight interior roof support posts. The structure probably had a depressed floor, but erosion and plowing have destroyed any evidence of the basin in which it might have stood.

Structure 17 almost certainly had public and ceremonial functions. It probably served as a meeting house for adult members of the community much like the townhouse or rotunda characteristic of eighteenth-century Creek and Cherokee towns. Unlike those found in the domestic habitations at King, burials placed within Structure 17 were, with only two exceptions, middle-aged and old men (eight of ten burials). Several of these men were accompanied by high-status grave goods, including large flint blades, flint-worker kits, and stone discoidals.

In the plaza immediately north of Structures 16 and 17 were a cluster of burials and many postholes. Although no clear pattern can be discerned among the latter, it is possible that they represent supports for the roof of an open shed. A similar group of features occurs on the summits of several stages of Mound A at the Late Mississippi period Toqua site in eastern Tennessee and includes two square structures of markedly different sizes that face a long shedlike structure containing numerous burials (Polhemus 1987).

Rectangular Structures

At least nine rectangular structures can be identified in the excavated part of the site (Figure 3.3). These range in length between 3.7 and 6.1 meters and in width between 1.9 and 2.7 meters (Figure 3.5) and were erected on the ground surface rather than in basins. They appear to have been constructed with six or more large posts placed at corners and midway along the side walls and smaller posts placed along the end walls. Overlapping posthole alignments indicate that the structures were rebuilt in many cases. Erosion and plowing have obscured or destroyed these structures except in the habitation zone on the eastern side of the site.

Polhemus (1987) recognizes similar structures at Toqua. On the basis of the occurrence of fired soil features and human burials within their walls,

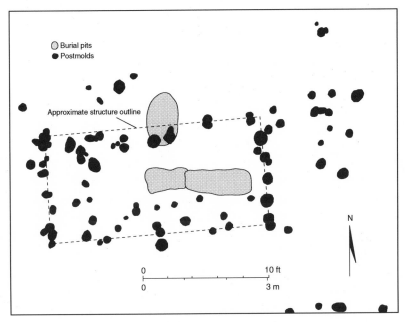

Figure 3.5. Rectangular structure located south of square Structure 2.

he suggests that the Toqua structures were open sheds or elevated corncribs beneath which cooking and other domestic activities were carried out. The same function can be attributed to the rectangular structures at King since several had burials located within or overlapping their walls. Burned floor features would have been destroyed by erosion and plowing at King.

As at Toqua (Polhemus 1987), domestic households at King are represented minimally by a square earth-embanked residence, a rectangular structure or shed, and an outdoor work area. The more substantial square structure probably served as a dwelling and work area during the colder months of the year, while the rectangular structure may have served these functions during the warmer months. The subterranean floor, wattle-and-daub walls, and earth-embanked walls would have made the former relatively efficient to heat; the presumed open sides of the latter would have permitted greater air circulation during the warm and humid summer. These seasonal associations are further supported by the artifacts excavated from two square structures at the culturally related Little Egypt site (Hally 1981, 1983). Charred plant remains indicate that one of these structures was destroyed by fire in the late fall or early winter and that the other burned in the late summer. The former contained abundant pottery vessels and stone tools, indicating it was being occupied at the time it burned. The latter contained no whole vessels and few tools, indicating that it was not being actively utilized when it burned.

The existence of separate summer and winter houses at King is further supported by frequent references to such structures in European accounts of native people in the southern Appalachian region (Swanton 1946). The earliest references appear in the Elvas and Anunciacion narratives of the de Soto and Luna expeditions in the mid-sixteenth century. Each noted the use of separate winter and summer structures. In addition, Elvas (Clayton, Knight, and Moore 1993) described winter houses as having wattle-and-daub walls, while Anunciacion (Priestly 1928:239) stated that winter houses were "covered with earth." Each description, as far as it goes, fits what is known about square structures at the King site. There is no archaeological evidence that the roofs of those structures were covered with earth, but the depressed floors and earthen embankments would have contributed to that perception.

Most human burials at King are located within square or rectangular structures and immediately adjacent to them (Figure 3.6). These burials in-

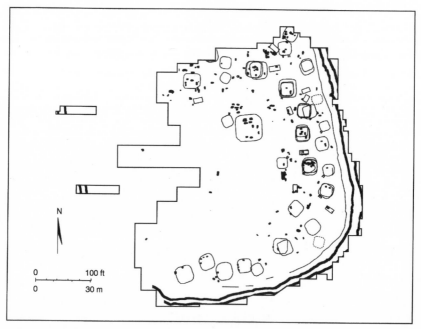

Figure 3.6. Distribution of burials (black dots) at the King site. Structure numbers are as given in Figure 3.3.

clude individuals of all ages and both sexes. It is probable that they represent deceased members of the households occupying the structures with which they are spatially associated. Indeed, several individuals interred in Structure 15 shared an inherited trait called Carabelli's cusp (Tally 1975). Sullivan (1987) identifies a similar household and burial relationship at the contemporary Mouse Creek phase sites in eastern Tennessee. It is tempting to speculate that the individuals were interred in square structures in the winter and in rectangular structure burials during the summer.

As at Toqua, we believe it is possible to identify larger household units consisting of two or more square structures facing onto a single outdoor work area and one or more rectangular structures. The latter are located in the common outdoor work area or next to the square structures. Four examples of such configurations are tentatively identified in Figure 3.7. To the extent that such multistructure household units actually did exist, it is likely that they were occupied by extended families, with each square structure being occupied by a separate "nuclear family." Unfortunately, there is no human skeletal or artifactual evidence currently available to support the

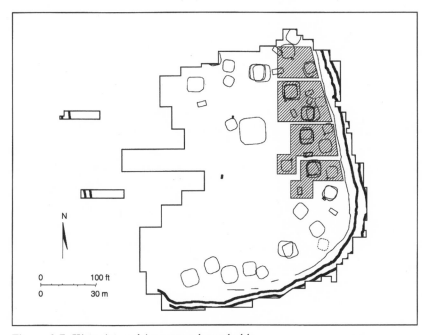

Figure 3.7. King site multistructure households.

identification of these larger household entities. The architectural and settlement plan data presented below, however, are more readily interpreted if such households did indeed exist.

King Site Development

Several kinds of evidence indicate that King was laid out in conformity with a specific settlement plan and that this plan was implemented at the beginning of site occupancy. As delineated by the defensive ditch, the town is essentially a perfect square, measuring 149 meters on a side. A large post, 1 meter in diameter (Feature 45), erected in the plaza, marked the exact center of the town. A large posthole is located west of Structures 16 and 17 in the northwest corner of the plaza. This post and the central hearth in Structure 17 lie on a line parallel to the east-west axis of the site (west 13 degrees south). This symmetry of site layout, together with the absence of multiple palisade lines and the almost total absence of overlapping square structures, indicates that the town did not grow out of an earlier, smaller settlement.

Although there is no evidence that the outline, size, and internal structure of the settlement changed significantly subsequent to its founding, the settlement did experience certain kinds of growth and change during its lifetime. These developments are the focus of the remainder of this chapter.

Households and Burials

The twenty-five measurable square structures (excluding Structures 12 and 30 and including Structures 3 and 20) located in the domestic habitation zone exhibit considerable variability in size, number of construction stages, and the number of burials contained within them (Kelly 1988). The floor areas of these structures range from 30 to 101 square meters. Most were erected only one time, but four were rebuilt one time (Structures 6, 8, 25, and 26), four were rebuilt two times (Structures 1, 2, 5/10, and 15), and one was rebuilt three times (Structure 23) (Figure 3.3). There were between zero and eleven burials per structure (Figure 3.6).

The relationships between structure size, number of construction stages, number of associated burials, and the growth of households at the King site were first explored by Hypatia Kelly (1988). Among the twenty-five structures, there is a strong positive correlation between number of construction stages and number of burials ($r = .90$, $p = .0001$). Assuming that all households experienced approximately the same death rate among their members and were interring the same proportion of their deceased in square structures, we may infer that some structures were used as residences for a longer time than others.

Larger structures also were generally occupied longer than were smaller ones (Kelly 1988). This inference is supported by correlations between the size of square structures and the number of interments ($r = .59$, $p = .003$) and between the size of square structures and the number of construction stages ($r = .47$, $p = .02$).

Sullivan (1987) reports a similar correlation in the Mouse Creek phase between the size of domestic structures and the number of burials contained within them. She attributes the relationship to differences in household size, reasoning that more populous households can be expected to experience more deaths among their members on average. We concur with Sullivan that the number of people residing in a square structure probably has an effect on the number of individuals who are ultimately interred in it. However, we do not believe that this is the primary cause of the relationship between structure size and number of burials because it does not account for the correlation of construction stage number with burial number and structure size.

Why should smaller square structures have been utilized for shorter periods of time? We can think of no reason they should have been abandoned sooner than larger structures built at the same time. On the other hand, there is indirect evidence that some small square structures were erected later in the site's life span than larger structures. Small structures tend to be situated in more marginal locations within the domestic habitation zone. Three of the five smallest primary structures (Structures 3, 4, and 20) are located very close to the palisade and, in the case of Structures 3 and 4, in rather cramped settings. The other two of the smallest structures (Structures 18 and 24) are located on the edge of the plaza. If the King site population grew through time, vacant space in the domestic habitation zone would have become increasingly limited. To accommodate this growth, structures erected late in the site's occupancy may have had to have been built smaller and placed either on the edge of the plaza where they would encroach on public space or next to the palisade in what may have been less desirable locations.

Some square structures may have been added to the King settlement as a result of the arrival of new residents. It is also likely that the addition of some structures reflects the growth of resident households. Three of the four tentatively identified multistructure households in the eastern portion of the site contain both large multistage and smaller single-stage square structures (Figure 3.7). The former may represent the residences of the families that founded the households at the time the King site was first occupied. The latter may represent the residences of children who grew up, married, and remained in the extended family household (Kelly 1988).

Interpreting Rebuilt Structures

What prompted the rebuilding of square structures? Decay of wooden wall and roof support posts is a possibility. However, the fact that the plaza structures, Structures 16 and 17, and the palisade have only one construction stage suggests that decay was not a factor. Accidental fires almost certainly took their toll of residences. That most of the nine square structures with multiple stages are of larger size, however, suggests that random house fires were also not a major factor.

We propose that square structures were destroyed and rebuilt most often as a result of the death of a significant household member, perhaps the genealogically senior member and household head. This could account for the correlation between number of burials and number of construction stages, since the longer the structure was occupied, the greater the chance that one or more of its significant residents would die. If some households at King began with a single large square structure and added smaller square structures as their membership grew, we should also expect a correlation between number of burials and size of structure. The small number of structures with multiple construction stages, furthermore, follows from the likelihood that "significant" individuals resided in the household's first-built square structure. There are several ethnohistorical accounts for the southeastern United States that describe the destruction of domestic structures at the death of an individual. Adair, writing in the late eighteenth century, states that the Choctaw formerly had the custom of burning a house when the "owner" died (Adair 1986:136). The Natchez burned the houses of their chief and war chief (Swanton 1911:102, 149). The Timucua burned the house of their chief as well as those of at least some priests (Faupel 1992:12).

Only in the case of the Natchez chief, however, is there mention of the rebuilding of the house.

If, as seems likely, households at King were organized around matrilineal and matrilocal principles (Hudson 1976:190), the "significant" member whose death occasioned structure destruction and rebuilding may have been female. We have compared the number of construction stages and number of adult female and male burials in each square structure looking for evidence of these "significant" individuals. Presumably, single-stage structures should have no such persons interred within their walls, and two-, three-, and four-stage structures should have one, two, and three such interments, respectively. Unfortunately, we have had no success in making these identifications. Even if we could distinguish "significant" individuals from other adult burials, the analysis is plagued by seemingly insurmountable problems such as differential skeletal preservation and interment of individuals elsewhere in the household complex and in public areas.

With two exceptions (Structures 5/10 and 15), square structures were rebuilt in the exact location where they were originally erected. Structure 10 was shifted 3.4 meters to the west of its predecessor, Structure 5, perhaps to make room for the construction of Structure 3 nearby. Structure 15 was shifted 2.25 meters to the east. In-place rebuilding of domestic structures may simply have been a practical response to limited space within the domestic habitation zone. We believe that it was also the physical expression of an ideological emphasis on household identity and continuity through time. Extended family households, either singly or in combination, may have constituted the core of corporate matrilineal descent groups. If this were the case, households would have had a strong interest in their own identity, perpetuation, and existence through time. In-place rebuilding of the square domestic structure, especially the structure erected by the founding family, would have served as a highly visible symbol of those conditions.

The practice of burying the dead in and around primary structures probably also reflects a concern with household identity and continuity (see, for example, McAnany 1995). As with earlier construction stages, deceased ancestors would represent the household's past. Association of ancestors and earlier construction stages with the physical location of an existing household would have served as an effective and convenient symbol of the continuity between that household and its past.

We believe the validity of these inferences is supported by what seem to be analogous practices and beliefs related to the chiefs of the Natchez, a Mississippian chiefdom located in the Lower Mississippi Valley and described by French observers in the late seventeenth and early eighteenth centuries (Swanton 1911). According to the ethnohistorical accounts, chiefs were considered to be direct matrilineal descendants of a man and woman who came from the Sun deity in the mythological past and who gave the Natchez many of their important cultural institutions. Stone statues representing this man and woman and baskets containing the bones of all former chiefs were stored in the main temple located on the summit of one of two earthen platform mounds erected in the Grand Village of the Natchez.

The French also report that the Natchez chief resided on the summit of the second platform mound. When he died, his house was destroyed, a mantle of earth was added to the mound, and the residence of his successor was erected on this "new" mound, presumably in the same location as the earlier structure.

These practices appear to have been widespread across the southeastern United States after A.D. 1000. Mississippian platform mounds were constructed in multiple stages, each consisting of a mantle of earth surmounted by one or more summit buildings. The latter probably functioned as temples and residences for the chiefs. Each construction stage, in essence, represented a new mound with associated summit structures that was erected in precisely the same location as its predecessor (Hally 1996). Human burials, often accompanied by exotic and highly crafted grave goods, are found in many of these mounds. Presumably new mound stages were added each time a new chief assumed office and at least some of the interments represent the bodies of deceased chiefs.

Among the Natchez, interment of the chief in the mortuary temple along with the remains of his predecessors clearly served to distinguish his (the chiefly) lineage from all others and to demonstrate its continuous existence through time from the mythological past. Construction of the residence of the chief above that of his predecessor would have communicated the same message.

Ethnohistorical evidence from the eighteenth century indicates that Indians of the Southeast recognized a certain degree of parallelism between the larger society and the domestic household. The Creek use of different communal structures (rotunda and square ground) during the winter and summer seasons was paralleled by the use of different domestic structures during those seasons (Swanton 1928a). Creek domestic structures were arranged in a square similar to that of the square ground. At the time of the Green Corn ceremony, the Creek extinguished and relighted both the sacred temple fire and their household cooking fires. We might expect a similar parallelism to exist in the way community leaders and household heads were conceived of and treated at the time of their death.

In conclusion, square residence structures at King vary in size, number of construction stages, and number of associated burials. We have argued that this variability is due in large part to the growth of extended family households through time and to the role played by domestic structures as symbols of household identity and continuity. Ongoing analysis of data from King site excavations should provide additional information bearing on these interpretations.

Note

1. Large-scale surveys have been conducted in three locations in northwestern Georgia and eastern Tennessee: the Etowah Valley in the vicinity of the Etowah site (Southerlin 1993), the margins of the Chickamauga Reservoir on the Hiwassee River (Smith, Weaver, and McNutt 1990), and in the flood pool of the Tellico Dam on the Little Tennessee River (Kimball 1985). These surveys recorded late prehistoric/early historic sites larger than 1 hectare and smaller than 1 hectare in ratios of 1:2, 6:7, and 5:2, respectively. While these numbers demonstrate that small, presumably habitation sites exist in the area, they also indicate that only a small percentage of people lived in farmsteads or hamlets.

4

Mississippian Towns
in the Eastern
Tennessee Valley

Gerald F. Schroedl

Mississippian cultures appear around A.D. 900 in eastern Tennessee (Figure 4.1). As elsewhere in the Southeast, their sites are characterized by platform mounds, distinct and sometimes large village complexes, elaborate mortuary patterns, and evidence of intensive corn agriculture. In general, the Mississippian archaeological record traces the development, maintenance, and eventual demise of the complex social, political, and religious organizational patterns of chiefdoms. In eastern Tennessee, these patterns are archaeologically distinguished as the emergent Mississippian Martin Farm phase (A.D. 900–1000), the early Mississippian Hiwassee Island phase (A.D. 1000–1300), the late Mississippian Dallas phase (A.D. 1300–1600), and the late Mississippian Mouse Creek phase (A.D. 1400–1600). The Cherokee and other historically documented native American groups represent terminal Mississippian cultures in the region after A.D. 1600. These groups are excluded from consideration here because they represent fundamental cultural reorganization initiated by European contact. Comparisons of the household and community patterns of late prehistoric Mississippian cultures and those of the historic Cherokee have been presented by Sullivan (1995).

I consider three aspects of Mississippian settlement patterns in this chapter: settlement location and spacing relative to local topography and physiography, variability in settlement size and probable use, and internal settlement organization. I am particularly concerned with the placement of earthen mounds and their number of construction episodes; the occurrence

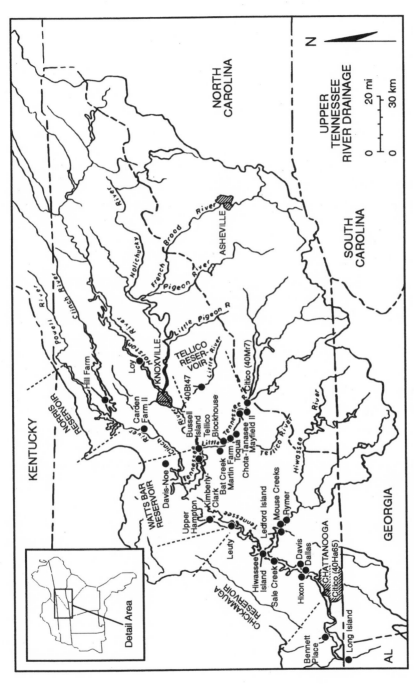

Figure 4.1. Location of major sites discussed in the text.

and characteristics of palisades; variability in the size, kind, and internal features of domestic and public dwellings and their positioning within settlements; and the placement of these features with respect to open or plaza
areas, work or disposal areas, and mortuary areas.

My examination of settlement patterns also assesses two differing perspectives on Mississippian settlement in eastern Tennessee. The first perspective is that palisaded villages were the primary mode of settlement in late
Mississippian times, while small hamlets and isolated households were infre-
quently utilized. This view, which comes from an emphasis on the excavation
of large village and mound complexes in eastern Tennessee, with a corresponding underrepresentation of small settlements in archaeological survey
data, is clearly articulated by Polhemus (1987, 1990) and is evident, for example, in the work of Lewis and Kneberg (1946), Lewis and Lewis (1995),
and Kneberg (1952).

The second perspective assumes that all spatially clustered sites of the
same archaeological culture were occupied contemporaneously and that they
represent multiple, coherent sociopolitical entities or chiefly polities (e.g.,
Hally 1994a; Hally, Smith, and Langford 1990). This position largely derives
from the inability to detect or to consider as significant occupational hiatuses
at individual village sites or to examine more closely intraregional variability
among sites. Compounding this situation, only six radiocarbon dates (all
from Toqua) exist for the late Mississippian Dallas phase (Kimball 1985:table
70). Although both of these views regarding settlement variability or contemporary village occupations have gone unchallenged until recently (Baden
1987; Davis 1990; Smith, Weaver, and McNutt 1990), I argue that neither
is warranted or substantiated by the archaeological evidence.

The Emergent Mississippian Martin Farm Phase

The Martin Farm phase (A.D. 900–1000) was first described from evidence recovered at the Martin Farm site (40Mr20) (Salo 1969a). Additional
work at this site and systematic survey in the lower Little Tennessee Valley
provide the data for reconstructing settlement variability for this phase
(Schroedl, Boyd, and Davis 1990; Schroedl, Davis, and Boyd 1985).

The emergent Mississippian occupation at Martin Farm covers about
0.5 hectare and represents a degree of site size, complexity, and probable
permanency not previously represented in the archaeological record of east-

ern Tennessee. It is the earliest documented village site with dwellings (including both single-post wall and wall-trench buildings) comparable in form and permanence to those of later Mississippi period phases (Schroedl, Davis, and Boyd 1985). A platform mound, which was constructed in two stages, is also associated with this component. The first mound stage was built over the remains of a structure; no evidence of a structure was detected on the mound summit. Adjacent to the mound was a possible palisade trench segment measuring 16 meters long, 1.75 meters wide, and 0.5 meter deep. No other possible palisade was detected here or elsewhere in the excavations (Schroedl, Davis, and Boyd 1985:77, 80). No distinctive village plaza was detected in the small and widely spaced excavations, but the mound was situated at the edge of the most densely occupied area. No human burials were associated with the residential occupation and the use of isolated conical burial mounds surely was the preferred pattern of interment (Schroedl and Boyd 1991).

Elsewhere in the lower Little Tennessee Valley, emergent Mississippian villages and early mound use also may be present at Bat Creek (40Ld24) and Bussell Island (40Ld17) (Schroedl, Boyd, and Davis 1990). The additional fourteen sites where emergent Mississippian occupation is documented are residential bases of limited extent and eleven are located on first alluvial terraces (Schroedl, Davis, and Boyd 1985). Emergent Mississippian occupations also likely occur at the Hiwassee Island (40Mg31), Dallas (40Ha1), Hixon (40Ha3), and Sale Creek (40Ha10) sites along the main course of the Tennessee River. Recent surveys of the Watts Bar (Cannon 1986) and Chickamauga reservoirs (Smith 1988a; Smith, Weaver, and McNutt 1990) along the main course of the Tennessee River have also identified additional sites that could represent Martin Farm phase occupations, but their positive identification from small sherd samples is ambiguous.

The Early Mississippian Hiwassee Island Phase

Hiwassee Island phase (A.D. 1000–1300) sites are both more abundant and more easily identified than Martin Farm phase components. For example, seven Hiwassee Island sites were investigated in the Norris Basin (Webb 1938), twenty-nine are documented for the lower Little Tennessee River Valley (Davis 1990), and more than sixty probable sites are known from the Watts Bar and Chickamauga reservoirs (Cannon 1986; Lewis and

Lewis 1995; Smith, Weaver, and McNutt 1990; Whiteford 1952). Village sizes, however, are difficult to estimate because site excavations have not been sufficient to expose entire components or because site features are difficult to distinguish from those of subsequent occupations at multicomponent sites. Important exceptions are the Bat Creek (40Ld24) site and 40Bt47, where the early Mississippian occupations are well defined and each site covers about 1.5 hectares (Bentz and Greene 1991; Schroedl 1975). The Hiwassee Island phase village occupation at the Martin Farm site may have included as many as 4.5 hectares (Schroedl, Boyd, and Davis 1990).

The Carden Farm II site (40An44), which covers slightly more than 0.5 hectare, was enclosed by a circular, single-post wall construction palisade approximately 200 meters in circumference (Figure 4.2) (Polhemus and Simek 1996). At 40Bt47, a 30-meter segment of a 1-meter-wide by 50-centimeter-deep palisade trench with a single-post wall was investigated. The palisade was situated on the interior side of the trench (Bentz and Greene 1991). At Bat Creek, individual dwellings at the village periphery were linked by single-post-construction walls or fences (Schroedl 1975:fig. 4.39). No palisade was detected for the Hiwassee Island occupation at Martin Farm. Evidence of Hiwassee Island phase occupations occurring before the construction of the initial early Mississippian palisades is found at Toqua (40Mr6),

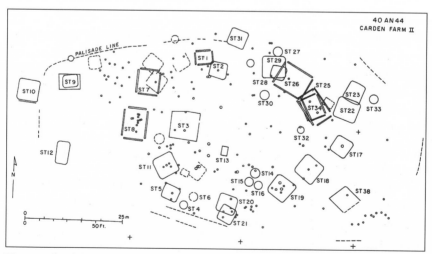

Figure 4.2. Plan of the Carden Farm II site (40An44) (courtesy of Richard Polhemus).

Hixon, and Hiwassee Island (Lewis and Kneberg 1946; Neitzel and Jennings 1995:393; Polhemus 1987).

Six early Mississippian village sites with associated mounds occur in the Tellico Reservoir on the lower Little Tennessee River, and their locations show a distinctive shift of village settlements to higher river terraces during the Hiwassee Island phase. Another twenty-three sites are hamlets of two or more households, individual households, or perhaps special-purpose locations (Davis 1990:244). These sites are found on first, second, and higher alluvial terraces and along more remote tributary streams. Excavated dwellings at hamlets often show several rebuilding episodes along with small numbers of associated processing and storage pits.

For example, a single structure and three associated features were recorded at the Tellico Blockhouse site (40Mr50) (Polhemus 1979:100–105), and a single isolated structure was found at Chota-Tanasee (40Mr2/40Mr62) (Schroedl 1986:234). Similar sites have been investigated along the main channel of the Tennessee River and some of its tributaries. The Kimberly-Clark site (40Ld208), for example, consists of two superimposed structures, a third possible building, and two refuse-filled pits (Chapman 1990). The Davis-Noe site (40Re137), located on a small tributary stream of the Clinch River, is interpreted as a salt procurement/processing station (Hood 1977). Data from the Mayfield II site (40Mr27) (Salo 1969b), the Leuty site (40Rh6) (Schroedl 1977), and Hill Farm (Webb 1938:63), indicate that platform mounds may have been constructed in locations well away from village sites. The Carden Farm II and 40Bt47 sites also indicate that mounds may never have been constructed at some Hiwassee Island villages. It is not clear whether this is related to length of occupation, socioideological considerations, or the simple fact that some early Mississippian mounds, such as the one at Martin Farm, which was only 25 centimeters high, are very difficult to detect (Schroedl, Davis, and Boyd 1985:46).

On the basis of their size, internal characteristics, or association with a platform mound, certain Hiwassee Island phase structures undoubtedly represent community buildings. In general, these buildings were either single-post wall or, more often, open- or closed-corner wall trench constructions with a single central hearth. In some structures there are two large roof support posts. Structures measure 8 to 10 meters wide by 12 to 15 meters long (Lewis and Kneberg 1946; Polhemus 1985). At sites such as Carden Farm II, where no mound is present, and at sites such as Mayfield II and Bat

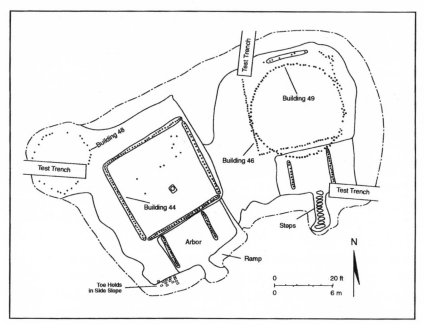

Figure 4.3. Paired structures on mound summit (Level E2) at Hiwassee Island (from Lewis and Kneberg 1946:plate 16). Used by permission of University of Tennessee Press.

Creek, where mounds are present, only single community buildings have been identified. At other sites, such as Toqua (Mound A, Phases A-1 and A-2) and Hiwassee Island (Mound Levels E through G), there are pairs of structures with accompanying porches or arbors (Lewis and Kneberg 1946:75–76; Polhemus 1987:133, fig. 3.35).

At Hiwassee Island, these buildings sat on two separate mounds built just 2 meters apart (Lewis and Kneberg 1946:75–76) (Figure 4.3). Also associated with Levels E1 and E2 were single, small, poorly defined buildings located at the edge of the mound, near a corner of one of the primary structures. The function of these buildings as storage or residential structures is undetermined (Lewis and Kneberg 1946:75 and plates 16, 17). Lewis and Kneberg (1946:fig. 8) indicate that these buildings were found on a lobe or terrace of the primary mound or on what was originally a separate mound.

Internal partitions, as well as clay benches or seats and prepared clay hearths, are found within the primary community buildings (Lewis and Kneberg 1946:64–68; Polhemus 1985). Similar features were associated with mound structures in the Norris Basin (Webb 1938). In village contexts at the Hixon (Polhemus 1985:71) and Mouse Creeks (Sullivan 1989a:48, 54) sites, single structures that have clay seats were built in shallow basins. These too may represent community buildings, albeit an infrequent form of such structures.

Community buildings and platform mounds were typically situated at the edge of a village plaza. At Hiwassee Island, Lewis and Kneberg (1946:26) note that the plaza area was relatively free of refuse and that the early Mississippian inhabitants had intentionally added sediments to it. At Carden Farm II, two small, partly superimposed, rectangular structures, measuring approximately 2 by 3 meters, were found near the plaza center. These structures were flanked on either side by large postmolds (Polhemus and Simek 1996).

Hiwassee Island domestic structures duplicate community buildings in both plan and method of construction. Small, circular, single-post wall buildings, 2 to 3 meters in diameter, were also present at a few sites. At 40Bt47, each example of these small buildings was next to a domestic dwelling (Bentz and Greene 1991:figs. 12 and 43). Whether these small structures served as storage buildings or were used for some other purpose is unknown (Figure 4.4). Shallow, refuse-filled pits and deeper pits that may have been used for storage are present near most structures. There is a distinctive spatial pattern to these features only at Bat Creek, where they form a row parallel with the long axis of three structures (Schroedl 1975:fig. 39).

No human burials are found in Hiwassee Island village or platform mound contexts, and the probable mortuary pattern was mound burial (Schroedl and Boyd 1991). The contemporaneity and association of specific burial mounds and residential sites, however, have not been established. Hiwassee Island villagers possibly utilized burial mounds located close to their settlements. At the Hiwassee Island site, for example, the burial mounds reported by Lewis and Kneberg (1946:map 1) are within a few hundred meters of early Mississippian occupation areas. Similarly, two burial mounds at Bat Creek are situated less than 100 meters from the Hiwassee Island phase village (Schroedl 1975:102–3; Thomas 1894:391–93).

On the other hand, many conical burial mounds in eastern Tennessee are found remote from early Mississippian residential sites (e.g., Cole 1975; Davis 1990; Schroedl 1990; Schroedl and Boyd 1991; Thomas 1894). On the basis of evidence from Moore's (1915:338–51) work at Bennett Place

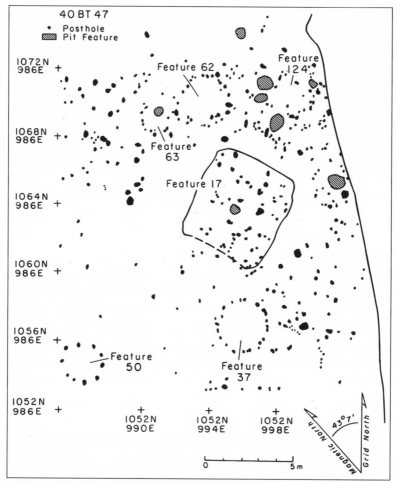

Figure 4.4. Domestic structures and small circular structures at 40Bt47 (adapted from Bentz and Greene 1991:fig. 43). Reproduced courtesy of Tennessee Department of Transportation.

(40Mi7) near Chattanooga, where burned matting and artifacts were associated with human burials in a substructure mound, Lewis and Kneberg (1946:38–39) argue that the absence of burials in Hiwassee Island phase villages is best explained by the use of charnel houses. However, no excavations since Moore's work, including Lewis and Kneberg's investigations at Hiwassee Island, have produced evidence for Hiwassee Island phase charnel houses. Although Lewis and Kneberg also noted the possibility that Hiwassee Island phase people buried their dead in cemeteries outside village areas, no such cemeteries have been identified.

Hiwassee Island phase village planning is difficult to interpret. In some cases, villages gradually formed from hamlets of a few houses. The Toqua and Hiwassee Island data, for example, suggest that, sometime after the beginning of these villages, each deliberately organized the community around three essential elements: a plaza, one or more community buildings with or without a platform mound, and a village palisade. Using comparative data from Norris Basin (Webb 1938) and their own observations at the Hiwassee Island, Sale Creek, Hixon, Davis, and Mouse Creeks sites, Lewis and Lewis (1995:10) indicate the presence of public buildings at both the north and south ends of the plaza with the more important building situated at the north end facing south-southeast. At Martin Farm, and perhaps elsewhere, this organizational pattern may have been established as an emergent Mississippian feature. In other cases, Hiwassee Island villages apparently were planned communities built in locations where there had been no previous Mississippian occupation. A process of village fissioning brought about by increased population and agricultural expansion could produce such a situation. Judging from the number of pit features, their contents, and the number of structure rebuildings, occupations were short lived at some sites, such as Carden Farm II. At other places, such as 40Bt47 and Bat Creek, the patterns indicate successive or continuous occupations that spanned several generations. Subsequent Dallas phase village patterns generally follow the Hiwassee Island phase and show even clearer evidence of conscious and deliberate village planning and construction.

The Late Mississippian Dallas Phase

In the upper Tennessee River Valley, thirty-three late Mississippian Dallas phase village sites with mounds have been identified (Polhemus 1987:fig. 13.5). It is not clear whether there are Dallas villages of comparable size that have no associated platform mounds, although Lewis and Lewis (1995:15) indicate that initial Dallas phase public buildings in some instances were "built upon the original land surface." Four sites—Toqua, Citico (40Ha65; Hatch 1976 [Citico is also the name for 40Mr7, see Figure 4.1]), Hiwassee Island, and Long Island (40Mi69; Ball, Hood, and Evans 1976)—are multiple-mound centers, and Smith (1988b) suggests that the Hixon and Dallas sites were functionally equivalent to such centers. Smith (1988b) and Smith, Weaver, and McNutt (1990:226–50) suggest, furthermore, that these centers are paired with nearby single-mound centers and that together they were the largest settlements in a Dallas chiefdom. Hally, Smith, and Langford (1990) reconstruct different estimates of the number and distribution of polities from sites and site clusters from those found in Smith's study because they focus on the period of the de Soto entrada (ca. A.D. 1540) and include both Dallas and Mouse Creek phase sites (see discussion of Mouse Creek below).

Polhemus (1987:1240–46, 1990:134–38) proposes that the Dallas phase settlement pattern is best modeled as a four-tiered hierarchy consisting of households, household aggregates, towns, and town aggregates. He also suggests that towns or local centers were the characteristic settlements, indicating "few isolated homesteads [minimal settlement units] or hamlets [Level II household aggregates] appear to exist outside of local centers [compact Level III towns]" (Polhemus 1987:1246). Although Dallas phase mound centers are unquestionably larger and more complex than those of the Hiwassee Island phase, the evidence shows that, contrary to Polhemus's interpretation, hamlets and homesteads remained important components of the settlement pattern. Comprehensive examination of the Tellico Reservoir settlement data from the lower Little Tennessee Valley yielded three Dallas phase hamlets and twenty-one isolated households (Davis 1990). At least ten hamlet or household sites have been documented for the Chickamauga Basin (Smith 1988a). There are an additional eighteen sites in the Chickamauga Basin (Smith, Weaver, and McNutt 1990:table 8) and twenty-two sites in the Watts Bar Reservoir (Cannon 1986:appendix D) that could represent Hiwassee Island or Dallas phase hamlets or households.

The primary source for describing Dallas phase town planning and village organization is the work conducted at the Toqua site in the 1970s (Polhemus 1987, 1990; Schroedl and Polhemus 1977) (Figure 4.5). These data are complemented by the important descriptions of the Hiwassee Island site (Lewis and Kneberg 1946) and the Davis, Dallas, Hixon, and Sale Creek sites (Cooper, Jennings, and Nash 1995; Nash et al. 1995; Neitzel 1995; Neitzel and Jennings 1995). At Toqua, three critical elements in the settlement plan were established early in the site history, and they remained conceptually important to the site's inhabitants throughout its occupation. These elements were the primary platform mound, Mound A; Mound B to the south-south-

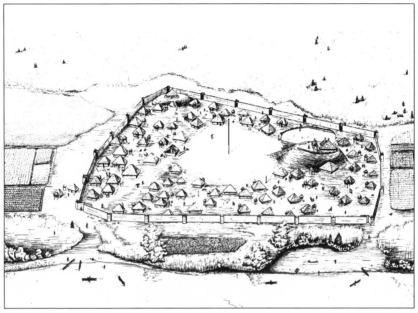

Figure 4.5. Artist's reconstruction of the Toqua village (from Polhemus 1987:fig. 13.4). Courtesy of the McClung Museum.

east; and a probable charnel house to the north-northeast (Figure 4.6). An equilateral triangle approximately 70 meters on a side is formed by these three features, and a line from Mound A bisecting the triangle is oriented approximately 121 degrees east of north. Throughout the occupation of the site, there was a strong tendency for both domestic dwellings, as well as human interments, to have this same orientation, which approximates the alignment of the winter solstice. Much of the interior area of this triangle is occupied by the village plaza, which at one time was enlarged by removing structures along its north periphery and paving the surface with small river pebbles (Polhemus 1987). Immediately south of Mound A is a large depression where fill was borrowed for the construction of the earthwork and for the building of domestic and public structures. A smaller soil borrow area was dug next to the east side of Mound B. In comparison, a probable borrow area at Hiwassee Island, which may have been used throughout the site's occupation, was located over 100 meters south of the primary mound (Unit 37). Investigations at Hiwassee Island and at other multiple-mound centers were not extensive enough to identify other village area community struc-

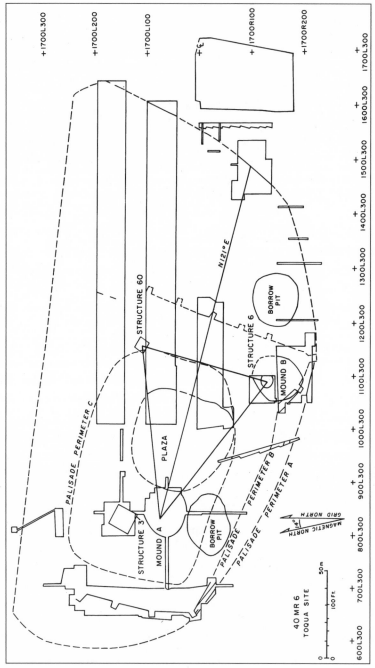

Figure 4.6. Plan of major site features at Toqua (adapted from Polhemus 1987:fig. 13.1).

tures, such as charnel houses and the residences of high-status individuals, or to determine their relationship to mound and plaza areas. Presumably, a variety of public structures existed at many Dallas sites in the vicinity of the village plaza. Nearby stream banks, rather than large pits excavated in villages, may have been used for borrow areas.

Multiple palisade segments representing at least three major construction episodes are identified at Toqua (Polhemus 1987:216–18). The earliest palisade, Perimeter A, enclosed about 3.9 hectares with large posts set at close intervals in a trench (Figure 4.6). This feature and much of the village was destroyed by fire. The second palisade, Perimeter B, enclosed approximately 2.0 hectares and had 3- to 4-meter-square bastions, two of which held towers or platforms. This palisade was repaired, replaced, and relocated several times, especially in the vicinity of Mound B. Although the Perimeter B palisade was smaller than Perimeter A, it enclosed all major elements of the village. The third palisade, Perimeter C, intrudes village midden deposits as well as the plaza area, leaving Mound B outside the enclosure and further reducing the village to about 1.7 hectares. Each perimeter shows evidence of rebuilding and repair.

Although not as well documented as at Toqua, multiple palisades also are known from the Hiwassee Island, Dallas, and Hixon sites (Lewis and Kneberg 1946; Nash et al. 1995; Neitzel and Jennings 1995) and the Loy site (40Je10) (Sherwood 1991:37). Their placement has been used to argue for episodes of village expansion (e.g., Hixon, Hiwassee Island, and Loy) as well as reduction (e.g., Toqua). Lewis and Kneberg (1946:38) suggest that the palisaded portion of Hiwassee Island was 1.6 hectares. Comparable areas were enclosed at Upper Hampton (40Rh41; ca. 4.4 hectares) (Smith 1987:table 5.4), Hixon (the small palisade encompassed about 0.5 hectares and the large palisade about 1.0 hectare), Dallas (ca. 1.6 hectares), Citico (40Mr7; 1 hectare), and Loy (2.5 hectares). These data suggest that the enclosed areas of Dallas palisaded villages ranged between 1 and 5 hectares; at most sites there also was contemporaneous occupation immediately outside the palisade lines. The Dallas phase village size estimates are consistent with northern Georgia and eastern Tennessee village sizes reported by Hally, Smith, and Langford (1990), but their figures are based on surface artifact distributions rather than palisaded areas.

The plan of public structures associated with Mound A at Toqua is comparable to that found at Hiwassee Island. Associated with twelve major construction phases at Toqua are paired primary structures on the west mound summit (Figure 4.7). These structures, one of which is generally larger than the other, have well-defined, prepared clay hearths, and in some there are clay partitions and benches (Figure 4.8). Polhemus (1987:237) believes the larger structure (mean floor area 91.3 square meters, $n = 6$) was for ceremonial purposes and the smaller building (mean floor area 41.4 square meters, $n = 5$) was the residence of a high-status individual. It is also possible that one or both of these structures were used as public storehouses for the display of economic surplus. Such structures were observed by the Spanish in the sixteenth century and are recorded widely for southeastern Indian groups (Hudson 1976:311; Smith and Hally 1992:102; Swanton 1946:372–81, 386–420). At Hiwassee Island, Lewis and Kneberg (1946:41) think that paired buildings separated sacred and secular activities, and they suggest that this might be related to the dual organizations of historic southeastern Indians. In front of each structure pair on the west mound summit at Toqua is an associated porch or arbor. In the later stages of mound construction high-status burials are associated with the porch or arbor and only a single primary structure was erected on the west summit. At other sites, such as Dallas and Hiwassee Island, only a single primary structure with or without an arbor was used during the final occupations. On sites at which initial mound use dates to the Dallas phase, Lewis and Kneberg (1946:41) also note that only single community buildings were constructed.

At Toqua, in addition to the structures located on the primary and secondary mound summits, a "large rectangular building [Structure 3], 11.6 m on a side, was situated on a rectangular platform adjoining the north face of Mound A" (Polhemus 1987:257). A succession of hearths associated with the structure suggested as many as twelve rebuilding episodes and indicated that a building had been maintained at this location throughout the Dallas occupation (Polhemus 1987:257; Schroedl and Polhemus 1977:26). Given the building's size and location and its architecture and floor contents (Bogan and Polhemus 1987; Roberts 1987; Shea, Chapman, and Polhemus 1987), Polhemus (1987:258) infers that it represented a public building or the residence of a high-status individual. No structures of comparable size and location have been recorded at other Dallas sites. This pattern, however, resembles the small secondary structures found on the Hiwassee Island mound summit in Levels E1 and E2, and occurring with the ancillary structures dating to the Barnett phase (A.D. 1500–1650), recorded by Hally

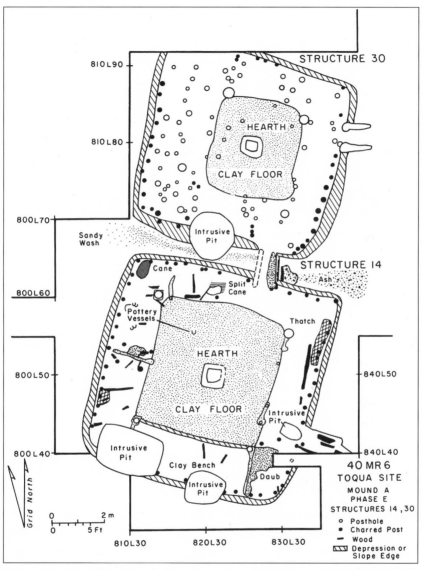

Figure 4.7. Mound A, Phase E, Structures 14 and 30 at Toqua (adapted from Polhemus 1987:fig. 5.27).

Figure 4.8. Artist's reconstruction of Structure 14 at Toqua (from Polhemus 1987:fig. 5.32). Courtesy of the McClung Museum.

(1980:93–197) for a mound terrace or lobe at the Little Egypt site (9Mu102) in northern Georgia. It is unclear how the use of Structure 3 at Toqua relates to the structures found on the summit of Mound A. The number of rebuilding episodes shows that the replacement of Structure 3 was closely synchronized with the replacement of buildings on the mound summit.

Mound B at Toqua was constructed in three stages, each of which was capped by a building placed on the mound's summit. Mound B also served an important mortuary function with thirty-six and sixty-nine interments, respectively, recovered from the final two stages. Two mounds (Units 73 and 81) located near one another about 100 meters south-southeast of the primary mound (Unit 37) represent generally comparable features at Hiwassee Island. One of these (Unit 73) contained both Late Woodland and Dallas phase burials, but no structural remains (Lewis and Kneberg 1946:24). The second mound (Unit 81) contained superimposed single Hiwassee Island and Dallas phase structures, but no burials (Lewis and Kneberg 1946:33). Two secondary mounds also occur at Long Island (40Mi69), but their contemporaneity with each other and the primary mound is undetermined (Ball, Hood, and Evans 1976). At Citico (40Ha65), many burials, but no struc-

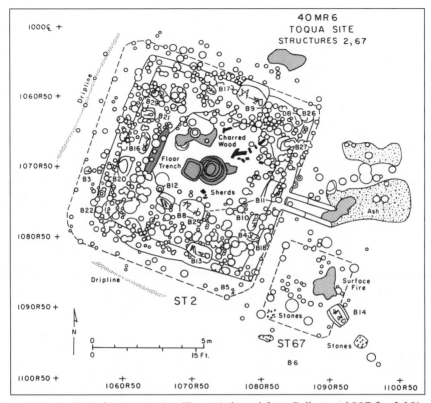

Figure 4.9. Plan of Structure 2 at Toqua (adapted from Polhemus 1987:fig. 2.18).

tural remains, are identified with the secondary mound first reported by Moore (1915) and analyzed by Hatch (1976).

Including mound-associated buildings, eighty-seven structures are attributed to the Dallas phase occupation at Toqua. The predominant structure form here and at other Dallas sites is a rectangular building measuring 4 to 12 meters on a side with parallel trench entrances, a central prepared clay hearth, and four major roof support posts separating a central floor area from bench and storage areas along the interior walls (Figure 4.9). The structures are often built in a shallow depression (10 to 30 centimeters deep). Small rectangular (0.75 by 1.0 meter) pit features, probably used for storage, occur within some structures. Burials frequently occur within and outside these buildings (Polhemus 1987:177–78). Although identical in plan, structures of this type associated with Mound A have nearly twice as much floor area (ca. 70 square meters) as those found in the village areas (ca. 36 square meters), and both their size and amount of interior floor space increased over time. As with the construction of nearly identical buildings on successive mound additions, village structures often were rebuilt at the same locations, in some cases five to eight times. Adjacent to domestic dwellings were small (7 to 26 square meter) rectangular, open- or semiopen-sided structures, which were perhaps used for food storage and processing and which have been compared to ethnographically known summer houses (Polhemus 1987:1221, 1990). Burials also occur within these buildings. Large, shallow pits, presumably used to obtain soil, are generally found aligned with the exterior side of the palisade rather than adjacent to a structure (Polhemus 1987:173). Similarly, large, deep storage pits are rarely found in the vicinity of domestic dwellings or summer houses. Domestic structures and their associated summer houses sometimes are found in groups of two or more clustered around an open area, and these groups are interpreted as kin-related household aggregates at Toqua (Polhemus 1987:1240, 1990) (Figure 4.10).

Taken as a whole, Toqua was an extraordinarily well-planned, well-organized, and well-maintained settlement. Although the village size enclosed by the palisade was substantially reduced over time, the placement and probable function of the village elements remained essentially unchanged for much of its occupation. The exclusion of Mound B by the final palisade is the strongest evidence for a major disruption to this plan. It is also possible that additions to Mound A were curtailed or halted and that only a single building was used on the northwest summit. The details of village planning

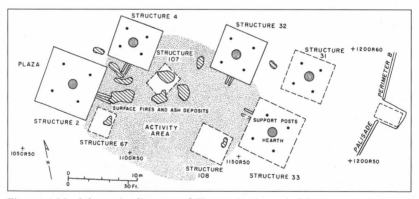

Figure 4.10. Schematic diagram of Toqua site household aggregate (adapted from Polhemus 1987:fig. 13.3).

and organization at other Dallas sites are more difficult to document than at Toqua, but there is no evidence at Dallas, Hixon, Hiwassee Island, or elsewhere that these villages were any less well-conceived, constructed, and maintained.

The Mouse Creek Phase

Settlements of the Mouse Creek phase (A.D. 1400–1600) are known primarily from the Mouse Creeks (North and South Units; 40Mn3), Rymer (40By11), and Ledford Island (40By13) sites, located within 3 kilometers of each other on the lower Hiwassee River. Throughout this section, "Mouse Creeks" refers to the south and north units of the Mouse Creeks site, which are located approximately 300 meters apart, while "Mouse Creek" refers to the archaeological phase that includes the Mouse Creeks, Rymer, and Ledford Island sites.

These sites, which were first described by Fairbanks and Neitzel (1995), Lidberg et al. (1995), and Neitzel and Fairbanks (1995), have been the subject of intensive analysis in recent years (Sullivan 1986, 1987, 1989b, 1989c, 1995; see also Boyd 1984, 1986; Boyd and Boyd 1991). Lewis and Kneberg (1946) and Kneberg (1952) believe that ethnicity accounted for the differences between Mouse Creek and Dallas archaeological patterns and that the Yuchi were responsible for the former while Creeks had created the latter. Others (e.g., Schroedl 1986) consider Mouse Creek a protohistoric culture created by the collapse of Dallas chiefdoms, while Sullivan (1995) suggests that Mouse Creek and Dallas may represent contemporary but distinctive regional variants within late Mississippian culture. Furthermore, Hally, Smith, and Langford (1990) include the Mouse Creek sites and selected Dallas sites in their analysis of sixteenth-century polities constituting the Coosa chiefdom.

Mouse Creek settlements, although similar to the general community plan of Dallas villages, differ from them in several important ways. First, burials associated with domestic structures in the Mouse Creek phase are almost exclusively adjacent to the exterior walls of the less-substantial shed or warm-weather buildings. Furthermore, most Mouse Creek individuals were buried extended rather than semiflexed as in the Dallas phase. Generally, grave associations, age, sex, and location suggest less pronounced social differentiation in Mouse Creek culture (Boyd and Boyd 1991:83; Lewis and

Kneberg 1946; Lewis 1995:table 11.2; Sullivan 1995:118–20). There is no suggestion that the Mouse Creek structures form larger aggregates or clusters as at Toqua, and Mouse Creek rebuilding episodes are less frequent. The Mouse Creek villages cover 1.9 to 6.0 hectares, and both Rymer and Ledford Island have palisades, which were probably associated with initial village settlement since later structures and features intrude them. Platform mounds are not found at the Mouse Creek sites.

At Ledford Island, the village plan is especially evident (Sullivan 1986, 1987, 1989b, 1989c) (Figure 4.11). There is a central plaza area covering

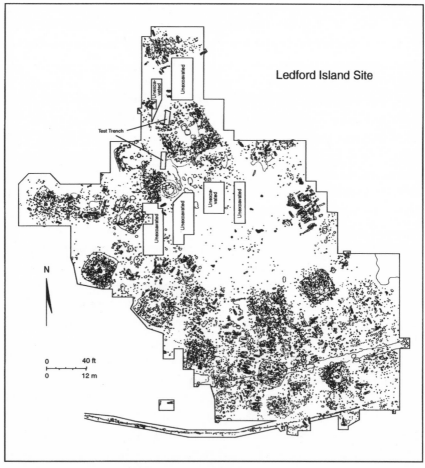

Figure 4.11. Ledford Island site plan (from Sullivan 1987:fig. 5). Reproduced courtesy of *Southeastern Archaeology*.

approximately 1200 square meters. In the middle of the plaza is a single large posthole. At the plaza's north end, there is a large community building, identical in plan to a domestic dwelling except that it measures 15.25 meters on a side. On the opposite side of the plaza, there is a domestic dwelling that, because of its slightly larger size, prepared clay floor, and density of associated ceramics, was perhaps occupied by a high-status individual. Cemetery areas are found on the northeast and southwest sides of the plaza. The northeast area is distinguished for the predominance of adult males and for containing both greater numbers of grave goods and kinds of artifacts uncommonly found in household interments. The other cemetery is distinctive for the absence of grave goods. Sullivan (1989c) argues convincingly that the relationship of the plaza, community building, and cemeteries adheres, merely on a larger scale, to the model of spatial organization for domestic household units.

Discussion

The organizational framework that resulted in the Mouse Creek and Dallas phase settlement plans began to appear in the Martin Farm phase. Aggregates of permanent domestic structures forming small villages took shape during the latter phase. Plazas, if present, were perhaps no more than small open areas set aside for ritual purposes adjacent to a community building or platform mound. Only the shallow ditch at the Martin Farm site suggests the presence of palisades. There is no doubt that emergent Mississippian settlements and the complexity they exhibit are correlated with developing agricultural economies and sociopolitical elaboration.

The essential village elements of platform mounds, plazas, and palisades are clearly represented in the Hiwassee Island phase. Once villages were established, the dedication of specific locations to these particular elements was maintained. Some villages appear to have developed from household clusters or hamlets or directly from emergent Mississippian settlements, such as at the Martin Farm site. The establishment of other Hiwassee Island phase villages, such as at Carden Farm II, may have happened as a short-term event. Some village locations, such as Bat Creek and 40Bt47, eventually were abandoned, while others, as at Toqua and Hiwassee Island, were superseded by the development of Dallas phase villages.

In the lower Little Tennessee Valley, there was a shift in settlement to higher river terraces during the Hiwassee Island phase. This shift is surely linked to the use of first terraces and floodplains for agricultural production. The creation of more substantial village architecture and increased village permanency also would have favored the occupation of more stable land surfaces such as higher river terraces. As in the Martin Farm phase, household clusters and hamlets remained abundant and important in the overall settlement pattern of the Hiwassee Island phase.

Dallas phase and, presumably, Mouse Creek phase settlement patterns also included hamlets and outlying households. Given the greater size and complexity of villages, however, it is likely that some of these, especially those located in areas of limited or marginal agricultural potential, were stations for obtaining or processing commodities for village use rather than simply kin-related farmsteads.

In comparison with the Martin Farm and Hiwassee Island phases, a major change in Dallas and Mouse Creek cultures is the inclusion of mortuary activity in village contexts. With the movement of burials into villages the spatial dimension of social status encompassed both the living and the dead. In the Dallas phase, mortuary patterning is accompanied by the increased definition of ritual or ceremonial space associated with mounds and its separation from domestic space. The division of ritual space from domestic space magnified and reinforced social differences. Access to ritual, power, and knowledge were restricted spatially as well as culturally.

What probably led to this dramatic change in mortuary behavior were differences in economic, social, political, and ritual power that developed among extended lineages and their individual members. The performance of burial ritual and interment inside villages became one means to define, reinforce, legitimize, and add longevity to differences in status among individuals in competing lineages. Village burial, and perhaps other ostentatious behavior such as the construction of platform mounds, also represented competitive exclusion among towns and chiefdoms (see Dunnell 1989). These activities served as mechanisms of group self-identity and as measures of success in both secular and supernatural realms. Since death and mortuary ritual assumed such importance among the living, village burial also was a practical solution to the protection of the dead from desecration by rival groups (DePratter 1991).

The interpretation of the placement of dual, primary community buildings on platform mounds at some, but not all, Dallas sites remains ambiguous. The number of buildings may be a regional phenomenon related to the size of the territory and degree of influence towns exercised on surrounding areas. Toqua and Hiwassee Island were unquestionably large and influential towns, and as their power grew, they had greater ability to increase the size of their mounds while maintaining sufficient surface area on the mound summits for the erection of multiple ceremonial structures, residences for elites, or public storage buildings. There are insufficient data to determine the degree to which other Dallas towns, especially those with multiple mounds, shared in the pattern of dual structures.

Late in the Dallas occupation at Toqua and Hiwassee Island, only a single large primary structure was placed on the mound summit. At other towns, some of which are contemporary and others of which may be later, only single primary structures, often with an adjacent portico or shed, occur on mound summits. In the Mouse Creek and historic Cherokee cultures of eastern Tennessee, the size of these buildings was increased, and they were no longer constructed on mounds. The change to a single large building and the termination of mound use are not solely related to technological or spatial restrictions placed on lateral mound expansion needed to increase mound height while enlarging or keeping summit surface area constant. Mouse Creek and Cherokee buildings were likely increased in size and placed on the ground surface to permit greater public access, allowing greater public participation in community ritual and ceremonial activities. The social distance between individuals was diminished and more individuals gained access to sacred knowledge. The fact that single community buildings occur on Dallas mounds also raises the possibility that late or terminal occupations at some Dallas sites are better classified as Mouse Creek, as suggested, for example, at Hiwassee Island by Kimball and Baden (1985:240). For now, Mouse Creek can be distinguished with certainty only when it occurs as a single component such as at Ledford Island, Rymer, and Mouse Creeks.

Enclosing villages with palisades and devoting public and domestic space to human interments also reduced the amount of space that could be used for below-ground storage and for soil acquisition in the vicinity of domestic structures. Public borrow pits, such as those documented at Toqua and Hiwassee Island, must have served a domestic function as well, and additional pit features adjacent to palisade lines also may have served domestic as well as public purposes. Storage pits are rare or infrequent in Dallas contexts at Toqua and elsewhere. Granaries or cribs, as well as baskets and large jars, probably were used to store food. Both Ward (1985) and DeBoer (1988) recognize the general absence of below-ground storage in late prehistoric cultures of the Southeast and correlate this with the ascendancy of corn agriculture and the use of elevated structures for corn storage. DeBoer also suggests that below-ground storage is designed to hide resources because of periods of site abandonment or to express resistance to social change. In either case, the storage pit "misrepresents resource abundance or surplus through concealment" (DeBoer 1988:1). Of further importance, as also recognized by DeBoer (1988:1), is that above-ground storage facilities misrepresent abundance through ostentation. At Toqua and other Dallas sites, cribs and granaries and their locations adjacent to houses may have served as status markers for the public display of social and economic wealth. Small rectangular storage pits found within some Dallas structures at Toqua may have concealed ritual or ceremonial paraphernalia that were displayed and used in only carefully controlled private or public contexts (Polhemus 1987:187).

Culture historical sequences like those of the Martin Farm, Hiwassee Island, Dallas, and Mouse Creek phases treat the constituent sites of each phase as contemporary regardless of the actual time they were occupied. Although greater time resolution is desirable, current sociopolitical and economic interpretations of the Martin Farm and Hiwassee Island phases do not suffer for having their constituent sites treated as contemporary. Viewing the Dallas phase in this way, however, fosters interpretations that are difficult to sustain. As presently conceived, the Dallas phase sites form four or five contemporary geographical polities, each consisting of a multimound center; at least one lesser mound center; and additional villages, hamlets, and households, all spread along the Tennessee River and its tributaries at 40- to 60-kilometer intervals. Each was theoretically occupied through the duration of the Dallas phase. The Mouse Creek phase sites, if treated as showing contemporary regional variability in late Mississippian culture, would further increase the number, complexity, and density of settlements.

An important question not often considered in this perspective is: Was there sufficient agricultural land that, when cultivated with the available technology, could sustain even moderately large populations at this settlement density? The correlation of large Mississippian village sites with highly productive soils has been long recognized (Ward 1965). Until recently, however, the ability of these soils to sustain high yields over long periods of use with the methods of aboriginal technology had not been evaluated. Similarly, the implications of soil exhaustion on settlement longevity have not been considered in the modeling of Dallas settlement patterns. Baden's (1987) detailed quantitative modeling of eastern Tennessee agricultural production in the Mississippi period strongly suggests that soil exhaustion and crop failures would have forced some large Mississippian towns to considerably reduce and disperse their populations or to relocate their towns at 50- to 150-year intervals. Village abandonments as a response to land-use patterns would tend to have archaeological visibility, like the kinds of episodic patterns of palisade rebuilding, major changes in mound construction, and multiple structural placements such as those seen at Toqua and elsewhere. Series of proximally located and sequentially occupied villages, such as the three Mouse Creek sites and the Dallas-Hixon-Davis sites, also are potential outcomes of these land-use dynamics, as are the paired sites tentatively interpreted as primary and secondary mound centers of chiefly polities.

Such a view does not detract from the sophistication with which Dallas societies planned, executed, and maintained large palisaded villages. The number and density of contemporary Dallas sites, however, are reduced when soil depletion and other variables are considered, such as competition for political or ideological power among individuals and social groups within villages, threats from external groups for access to environmental resources, and the danger posed by the environment from natural disasters or the depletion of firewood. As a result, the presumption of sustained occupation of Dallas villages for long periods is diminished and so is the argument for multiple, contemporary Dallas polities at close intervals in the upper Tennessee River Valley (Schroedl 1993). This does not mean one or more hierarchies of contemporary sites constituting chiefdoms never existed in the upper Tennessee River Valley, for they surely did. That they were as numerous and distributed across the landscape as currently envisioned (e.g., Hally, Smith, and Langford 1990; Smith 1988b) requires reconsideration.

Conclusion

Martin Farm and Hiwassee Island phase villages seldom covered more than 1 hectare and probably averaged ten to twenty domestic dwellings. One or two community buildings were situated at opposite ends of a plaza. One of these buildings was placed on a platform mound at some villages, and some, but not all, villages had palisades. Below-ground storage and soil borrow pits were associated with individual households. Contemporary villages were probably comparatively close and evenly distributed in major river valleys. Associated isolated households and small hamlets also were found in agriculturally suitable locations in river valleys, tributary streams, and upland areas. Some settlements surely served as extractive or processing stations. Earthen mounds, located in a variety of topographic situations, were used for mortuary purposes.

Although the Dallas phase retained the general hierarchy of sites established in emergent Mississippian times, a few villages grew into large palisaded towns, some of which surely were the paramount settlement of a chiefdom. Dallas towns occupied 2 to 5 hectares, with thirty or more houses and populations of 200 or more individuals. The residences of certain social elites were placed on mound summits. The replacement of these and other buildings devoted to community activities was synchronized with the enlargement of platform mounds. Patterns of mound building, construction of multiple palisades, and structure replacements are compelling evidence that towns were periodically abandoned and reoccupied. A reduction in agricultural yields probably was the major contributing factor for these occurrences. Platform mounds, fences, screens, plazas, and other features, such as the charnel house and burial mound at Toqua, distinguish sacred or ritual space from domestic and public or secular space. Above-ground storage, burials within villages, and community soil borrow areas also are characteristic of Dallas phase village organization.

Mouse Creek phase villages follow the same general pattern as Dallas villages. However, there are no platform mounds and there is a single, large community building at the edge of the village plaza. The differences between the structures and spaces associated with social elites and those associated with other members of the society are less sharply defined. Villages of the Mouse Creek phase are presently best known from the lower Hiwassee River Valley. The presence of satellite hamlets, isolated farmsteads, and special-purpose sites seems likely but has not been firmly established. Although the Mouse Creek and Dallas phases are partly contemporary, their sociopolitical and sequential relationships in general and at specific sites remain important research questions.

With these characteristics in mind, the picture that emerges for Mississippian villages in eastern Tennessee includes a number of patterns:

1. The idea of a village plan consisting of a community building, with or without a mound, a palisade, a plaza, and an associated group of domestic structures and their associated facilities, including their arrangement and orientation, became fixed at an early date.

2. The size, elaborateness, precision of placement, and redundancy of these features from village to village in the Dallas phase reflect the greater economic need to regulate access to and control of agricultural land and crop production, which was sanctioned in socioideological terms. At this time, specific spaces and spatial arrangements became dedicated to particular social positions, and the partitioning of space into public, ritual, and domestic domains was magnified.

3. When burials were added to villages and mounds, this connected the sociopolitical and socioideological dimensions of Dallas society and gave both sacred representation within settlements. This is correlated with increased use of community soil borrow areas, first as a practical consideration and second as a means, albeit subtle, to reinforce group cohesion and cooperation. Increased use of above-ground storage had its practical considerations and may have contributed to the recognition of social positions and wealth.

4. The relationship of the number and arrangement of buildings on platform mounds to patterns of social, economic, and ritual organization remains equivocal.

5. In the Mouse Creek phase, community buildings were larger and were not on platform mounds, a pattern suggesting that status differences were less rigorously defined and that there was greater public access to ritual space. This pattern began to emerge late in the Dallas phase when only a single large community structure was placed on the summit of platform mounds.

6. Including burials within village areas and moving ceremonial buildings off mounds were the two greatest changes in village organization during the Mississippi period in the eastern Tennessee Valley.

Acknowledgments

I thank Barry Lewis and Charles Stout for all their help, suggestions, and encouragement in preparing this chapter. I also thank my colleagues Brett Riggs, C. Clifford Boyd, Jr., R. P. Stephen Davis, Jr., Lynne Sullivan, Marvin Smith, Amy Lynne Young, Zada Law, and Michael Logan for their comments, suggestions, and editorial assistance. I particularly appreciate the data for the Carden Farm II site provided by Richard Polhemus and the materials from 40Bt47 contributed by Lance Greene. All the above-mentioned individuals helped me sharpen my ideas and polish my prose, and for this I am grateful. J. Bennett Graham, Tennessee Valley Authority, kindly provided several unpublished reports for the Chickamauga Reservoir. Original figures depicting the Toqua site and Hiwassee Island were provided by the Frank H. McClung Museum, University of Tennessee, or the Tennessee Valley Authority. Figure 4.4 is courtesy of the Tennessee Department of Transportation. I am grateful to Terry Faulkner for drafting the map and most of the site plans used here.

5

Mississippian Sacred Landscapes

The View from Alabama

Cameron B. Wesson

*Culture must be understood as meaningfully constituted, where
individuals are seen as not only inhabiting, but also creating, the
meaningful universe of their existence.*

Kus 1983:278

In general we may say that man "builds" his world.

Norberg-Shulz 1980:51

Archaeologists have long recognized architecture as a potent cultural
expression. Traditionally, archaeologists have turned to architecture for information on issues such as construction technologies, settlement patterns,
social organization, and structure use. Although such studies provide valuable additions to our knowledge, most are incapable of fully assessing the
inherent social and ideological meanings of architectural remains. Recent
research departs from these approaches by addressing these remains with
theoretical models designed to reveal aspects of their social, political, and
ideological meanings (Bender 1993; Benson 1985; Cosgrove 1993; Leone
1984, 1988; McGuire 1991; Mrozowski 1991; Schele and Miller 1986;
Tilley 1994; Wesson 1996). Borrowing liberally from the intellectual traditions of architecture, philosophy, sociology, linguistics, and geography, these
studies search for an improved understanding of the cultural importance of

architecture and social space. Among the most important contributions of
these approaches is the recognition that architecture and social spaces are not
merely material remains but, like all aspects of culture, contain various levels
of social meaning (Beaudry, Cooke, and Mrozowski 1991; Donley-Reid
1990; Fletcher 1989; Leone and Potter 1988; Miller 1982; Tilley 1989).

One of the most common meanings expressed in architectural form is
the representation of cosmological order. By structuring architecture and
social spaces as replicas of culturally specific cosmological ordering systems,
a culture translates abstract notions of social, political, and historical order
into physical forms. Thus, the built environment becomes a cosmogram,
signifying connections between society, the supernatural, space, and time.
Architectural theorists refer to this as concretization, a process whereby abstract concepts are expressed in physical form (Norberg-Shulz 1971, 1980).
Through concretization, ideologies are made explicit, acting and being acted
upon in new and creative ways. As a result, ideologies become more easily
manipulated in the production and reproduction of social power (De Marrias, Castillo, and Earle 1996; McGuire 1991; Orser 1991; Pearson 1984).
Thus, space becomes an active medium for both the inculcation and alteration of cultural practices.

This chapter assesses Mississippian public architecture, not for clues to
construction phases or regional settlement structure, but as an important
conveyor of social meaning. I adopt a theoretical approach similar to that
pioneered in contemporary phenomenology and spatial theory, arguing that
public architecture translates the cosmos into material form. Architecture
and social spaces, taken collectively, are shown to represent powerful 'sacred
landscapes', physical expressions of the cosmic forces structuring Mississippian cosmological and social worlds. These representational schemes are
demonstrated to have met the existential, psychosocial, and sociopolitical
needs of Mississippian peoples through the creation of meaningful physical
and social environments. In addition, I illustrate how Mississippian social
groups manipulated sacred landscapes to advance their positions in local
status hierarchies and counter the claims of their social rivals. Such efforts
resulted in the alteration of meanings and symbolism in both the sacred landscape and cosmological order. In particular, ascendant elites are shown to
have engaged in the co-optation of positions of power within these representational systems, attempting to represent themselves and their ideologies
as necessary, inevitable, natural, and justified.

Data used to assess these claims are taken from the Mississippian site of Moundville. Because of its size and uniqueness, Moundville cannot be argued to represent a prototypical Mississippian community in Alabama or, for that matter, any other part of the Mississippian world. What it does provide, however, is an opportunity to assess the importance of architecture and social space in Mississippian communities and their role in translating cultural meanings into physical form.

I contend that Moundville was designed as a cosmological referent, making it a powerful sacred landscape. Furthermore, I propose that certain positions within Moundville's sacred landscape formed central components in elite strategies for social aggrandizement. Attempts were made at conflating elite-centered ideologies with traditional sources of supernatural power by establishing close associations between elites and elements of the sacred landscape. These strategies are shown to represent efforts designed to establish, consolidate, and expand social position and legitimate emergent social inequalities.

Sacred Landscapes

Whether houses, palaces, marketplaces, or ceremonial precincts, the spaces in which people live and interact are socially meaningful. This social space is not a homogenous cross-cultural entity, but represents the unique cultural milieu within which it is created and used, with both spaces and meanings open to alteration through continued social interaction and use (Bender 1993; Giddens 1979; Kleppe 1989; Pearson 1984; Tilley 1994). Tilley (1994:10) contends that "space does not and cannot exist apart from the events and activities within which it is implicated," which makes space an integral component of all social interactions. Social spaces are not merely containers for action, backdrops upon which lives take place; they are instead fundamental elements of social praxis, capable of influencing the form, direction, and meaning of social activity (Bourdieu 1977; Foucault 1977; Giddens 1979, 1981, 1984). But how do meaningful spaces come to exist? How do cultures impart meaning to their mundane, local surroundings?

Although the architecture and social spaces of each culture are self-representative, there are similarities in the ways in which spaces are created and given meaning. Phenomenologist Christian Norberg-Shulz argues that humans 'symbolize' their understanding of nature and the cosmos in built form by creating social spaces that form "an *imago mundi* or *microcosmos*" (Norberg-Shulz 1980:17, italics in original). In this view, the built environment is seen as a cosmic model, replicating the order and divisions structuring the universe, society, space, and time. Kus supports this idea, stating that the "creation of a meaningful context of existence involves, in part, the recognition and the assignation of order in society and in the universe. Thus space, as one of the most immediate dimensions of order as perceived and conceived, must play a critical role in the self-definition of society and the meaning it assigns to an *order* of physical nature" (Kus 1983:278, italics in original). All architecture can therefore be seen as a translation of a culturally defined cosmological order into a physical form. These acts of translation establish built environments and social spaces that serve as existential centers, producing a meaningful context for human action and social life (Bourdieu 1977:87–95; Norberg-Shulz 1980:17–18).

Built environments that double as cosmograms transcend cultural, temporal, and hierarchical boundaries, forming an essential component of all architectural endeavors (Norberg-Shulz 1980).[1] Although sacred landscapes require planning, it is unnecessary to propose that any individual or social group is singly responsible for their construction and the attribution of their meanings. Sacred landscapes do not require hierarchical social systems, or elites, to dictate their form and meaning. Instead, they rely upon a vernacular knowledge of architecture, space, time, and the cosmos. The structure and meaning of these systems are expressions of a shared identity, a concretization of culturally specific knowledge. This is similar to Bourdieu's (1977:87–95) concept of the dialectic of objectification and embodiment. For Bourdieu, the social world is full of cultural messages that shape our experience and reinforce a social rationale for our actions. These messages are transmitted in a diverse array of phenomena: "[in] verbal products such as proverbs, sayings, maxims, songs, riddles, or games; in objects, such as tools, the house, or the village; or again, in practices such as contests of honor, gift exchanges, rites, etc." (Bourdieu 1977:88). Through the assimilation of these various messages, individuals come to understand their culture and reproduce these systems of meaning in their action. Architecture, like other communicative systems, becomes a culturally expressive medium, conveying information necessary for social reproduction (Cunningham 1972; Eco 1976, 1984; Eco, Santambrogio, and Viola 1988; Glassie 1975; Leone 1984, 1988; Sanders 1990).

Cultures empower architecture and natural landscapes through a dialectical process that links abstract social meaning to concrete local situations (e.g., Cunningham 1972; Eliade 1959; Fritz and Michell 1991; Heidegger 1972; Norberg-Shulz 1971, 1980; Tilley 1994; Wheatley 1971; Zuidema 1964). Unlike language, however, the messages of material culture are more easily misinterpreted, reinterpreted, or unheard altogether. Because both the signifier (architecture and social space) and the signified (cosmological order) can be altered, material messages are not unambiguous or inalterable (Derrida 1976; Fletcher 1989; Hodder 1985; Leone 1986; Palkovich 1988; Tilley 1989).[2] Such ambiguity leads to a continual shifting of meanings and a reinterpretation of the entire symbolic system, allowing the meanings of architecture and social space to change to meet current sociocultural needs.

Cultures act to limit changes in the meaning of architectural signs through the linkage of language and space. Most commonly, the key metaphors that unite the built environment to supernatural contexts are narrative myths. These are stories that connect people and social spaces with their local environment and the structure of the cosmos. Narratives act as cultural messengers, reinforcing social roles and giving instruction on socially acceptable behaviors. As Tilley (1994:33) illustrates in his study of European Mesolithic and Neolithic landscapes, "narratives establish bonds between people and features of the landscape . . . creating moral guidance for activity. Both land and language are equally symbolic resources drawn on to foster correct social behavior and values. In narratives geographical features of the landscape act as mnemonic pegs on which moral teachings hang. The landscape is full of named locations that act so as to fuse time and space." The same process is identified by Kleppe (1989:198) in North African chiefdoms, where creation myths are given material form to reinforce socially appropriate behavior and reify the social order. Through the use of narratives, structure and meaning are imparted to the supernatural, the natural environment, the social body, and architecture.

Narratives not only establish a link between people and their environment, but they also serve the important task of mapping the cosmos onto the natural world around them. Stories of cosmogenesis and ethnogenesis are grounded in the physical environment, with local physiographic and topographic features serving as representations of the powerful primordial locations. Hills, rivers, valleys, caves, and other natural features become repositories of cosmological powers, resulting in a powerful sacred geography

(see Bradley 1996). Heyden (1975, 1981) identifies this process at Teotihuácan, where caves are seen as representations of the place of origin—the
source of supernatural power. Thus, caves (and architectural constructions
that mimic their structure) become powerful "other-worldly" spaces serving
as interfaces between the world of humans and that of the gods. This process
does not end with the assignment of cosmic order to the natural landscape,
but finds expression in architecture and social space.

Architecture becomes powerful sacred space by translating these same
narratives into built form, resulting in human-built 'sacred landscapes'.
Through this process of concretization, cultures project cosmological order
into the everyday lived experience of individuals by modeling architecture
and social spaces as cosmic representations (Heidegger 1972; Norberg-Shulz
1971, 1980). As Eliade (1959:29) states, "all territory with the objective of
being inhabited or of being utilized as 'vital space' is necessarily transformed
from 'chaos' into 'cosmos'." Through the process of narrative representation
social spaces become cosmograms, possessing powers synonymous with those
residing in the elements for which they are referents. These architectural cosmograms are not merely backdrops for the stage of cultural action, but are
active participants in the social drama, informing and shaping social praxis.
Thus, cultural action (or inaction) resides within the overarching frameworks of social and cosmological spaces, what Giddens (1979, 1981, 1984)
refers to as 'locales', which inform and shape social interaction.

An example of this process is found in Paul Wheatley's (1971) classic
study of Chinese site planning, *The Pivot of the Four Quarters*. Wheatley
(1971:417) argues that Chinese religion and cosmology played a central role
in the development and planning of Chinese cities: "those religions which
hold that human order was brought into being at the creation of the world
tend to dramatize the cosmogony by reproducing on earth a reduced version
of the cosmos. Sacrality . . . is achieved through the imitation of a celestial
archetype, as a result of which such religions can be powerful transformers
of landscape, sometimes to an extreme degree." Wheatley demonstrates that
ancient Chinese communities were structured in relation to their cosmic order, such that a powerful dichotomy between the realms of the sacred and
profane was created. He contends that this is an essential division for Chinese
religion and architecture: "The sacred space delimited in this manner within
the continuum of profane space provided the framework within which could
be constructed the rituals necessary to ensure that intimate harmony be-

tween the macrocosmos and microcosmos without which there could be no prosperity in the world of men" (Wheatley 1971:418).

Although defined social hierarchies are not prerequisites for sacred landscapes, these symbolically charged systems are often employed by social groups in complex struggles for social power, what Gramsci (1971:229–35) refers to as hegemonic wars of position. Since these cosmological associations yield power to not only buildings, but also those individuals or social groups who are most closely associated with them, these spaces become potent resources in struggles for political advantage. Who sits at the center of these cosmological representations, the *axis mundi*, ensuring the safe continuance of both the microcosmos and macrocosmos? The elite, of course. These places are potent seats of power, legitimizing social positions by representing their holders as essential components of both social and cosmological universes (Earle 1990; Eliade 1959; Schele and Miller 1986; Wheatley 1971). Elites commonly engage in ideological manipulations that justify their positions in the social order (Tilley 1982:26). As Schele and Miller (1986:103) reveal for the Maya, "The function of public art and architecture was to define the nature of political power and its role as a causal force in the universe. Maya imagery explains the source and necessity of kingly authority, by which the ancient Maya defined social order and expressed their perception of how the universe worked." Public architecture and sacred landscapes thus provide a link between the cosmos, political power, and elites, often representing elite social positions as divinely instituted.

This process can be seen in Maya architecture, where structures and architectural spaces were often constructed as referents to cosmological and social orders. Places of cosmological power were seen to permeate the Maya natural landscape, with architecture concretizing this power in built form and social space. Although deities resided in the natural landscape (hills, rivers, and caves), Maya buildings were constructed as metaphorical referents to these key features. Maya elites co-opted much of this symbolic power by adding elements to architecture that materialized their ideological claims, thereby linking their social positions and political power to the sacred order of the cosmos. As Benson (1985:188) argues, "The ruler, housed in a cosmos-defined environment, either in architecture or sculpture, is the pivot of a focused, integrated world view. The god, the ruler, and the people are in control of the forces of nature, the universe as conceived, believed in, and presented by that people; the monumental pyramid not only defines the cosmos, but proclaims this power in a public statement to the world." This incorporation of both the concretization of cosmic order and the materialization of elite-centered ideologies resulted in increased power for dominant social groups based on their close association with places thought to be empowered by the supernatural. Ultimately, Maya architecture and Maya elites superseded metaphorical association with the cosmos, becoming essential components of this order (Benson 1985; Schele and Miller 1986).

Attempts at expanding elite social control are best done ideologically, rather than through brute force. Pearson (1984:61) argues that people respond best to social controls that are not "directly coercive," but that are essentially ideological in nature: "The position of a ruling class might be legitimated in several ways; by misrepresenting the inequalities between the surplus-producing and the surplus-consuming groups; by representing the interests of the elite as universal for the whole society; and by justifying the status quo through hierarchical conceptions of the supernatural which 'explain' the hierarchical nature of social existence." The use of architecture as a means of materializing elite ideologies follows all of these rules (De Marrias, Castillo, and Earle 1996), with elites attempting to conceal their ultimate goals by representing themselves as cosmologically essential and divinely guided.

This process was not limited to Mesoamerican and Asian elites, but is arguably a major source of legitimization for elite interests in numerous cultural contexts, including those of the Mississippian peoples of the southeastern United States. Research by Knight (1981, 1986, 1990a) indicates that Mississippian platform mound architecture was linked to cosmological order and the social performance of religious ritual, a concretization of supernatural power. These sources of power appear to have been quickly usurped by elites; Smith (1992:11) has advanced the idea that Mississippian elites used architecture and social spaces not only to increase their roles as social coordinators but also as "structures of domination—containers of authoritative resources involved in the control of social time-space that provided powerful levers of social inequality." Thus, elements of the Mississippian built environment allowed elites the opportunity to enhance their social power and increase their political dominance over society and potential rivals.

The recovery of the cosmologies and ideologies empowering such systems is a difficult task. Carlson (1981:144) states that "the task of approaching an understanding of the 'world-view' or cosmology of a vanished civilization from its material remains ultimately requires nothing less than a holistic approach that includes the examination of the 'hard' archaeological data, on the one hand, balanced by an attempt at understanding the mind and spirit of the people, their ritual and religion." Through assessment of archaeological data from Moundville in concert with analogies drawn from ethnographic and ethnohistorical contexts, it is hoped that something of the "mind and spirit" of Mississippian peoples will be revealed.

Moundville as Sacred Landscape

One of the largest and most important Mississippian centers, Moundville has long been of interest to archaeologists (Knight 1992, 1993; Knight and Steponaitis 1996; Moore 1905, 1907; Peebles 1971, 1978, 1981, 1991; Powell 1988; Scarry 1986; Steponaitis 1983; Welch 1991). Located along the Black Warrior River in west-central Alabama, Moundville contains at least twenty-nine earthen mounds and encompasses approximately 75 hectares in total area (Knight and Steponaitis 1996). The site's core comprises a central plaza flanked by fifteen mounds, with a large central mound (A) and two smaller interior mounds (Figure 5.1, Mounds S and T). It is within this plaza-periphery group that Moundville's sacred landscape is most fully expressed.

The earliest occupation at Moundville is thought to date to the Moundville I phase (A.D. 1050–1250) (Knight and Steponaitis 1996), although pottery from the preceding West Jefferson phase (A.D. 900–1050) has been recovered from portions of the site (Steponaitis 1983) (Figure 5.2). Traditional views of Moundville's development stress an accretional expansion of the plaza-periphery group, with the mounds flanking the plaza appearing over an almost five-hundred-year period (Peebles 1987, 1991; Steponaitis 1983, 1991) (Figure 5.3). However, recent excavation and analysis suggest that the construction of Moundville's major mounds began at roughly the same time, between A.D. 1200 and 1250 (Knight 1992, 1993; Knight and Steponaitis 1996). This interpretation of Moundville's architectural history means that the basic organization of the plaza-periphery group was present very early in the site's development, rather than developing over a prolonged period of time. This supports a view of Moundville's spatial arrangement as symbolically meaningful, since the arrangement of architecture and social spaces did not develop as the result of centuries of prolonged use but as a

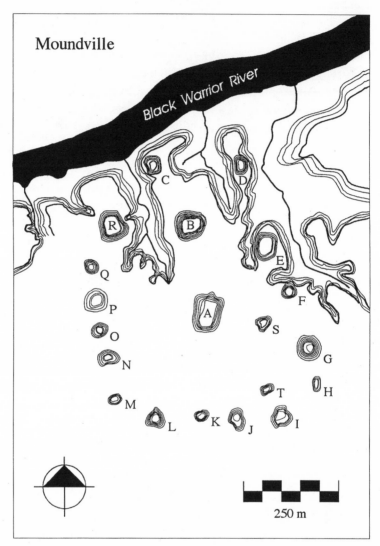

Figure 5.1. The central plaza–periphery mound group at Moundville (from Scarry and Steponaitis 1997:111). Used by permission of The University of Alabama Press.

PHASE	A.D.	POLITICAL DEVELOPMENTS
	1650	
Moundville IV Phase	1600	
	1550	Virtual Abandonment of Center.
Moundville III Phase	1500	Limited Residential Population at Center. Continued Mound Construction in Some Areas. Evidence for Gradual Atrophy of Centralized Control.
	1450	
	1400	
Moundville II Phase	1350	Elaboration of Chiefly Cult Symbolism. Beginning Out-Migration of Populace from Center. Transfer of Chiefly Iconography to Service Pottery.
	1300	
	1250	
	1200	Height of Traffic in Exotic Minerals, Marine Shell, Copper, and Non-Local Pottery
Moundville I Phase	1150	Political Consolidation of Region. In-Migration to Center. Evidence of Town Planning.
	1100	
	1050	Emergence of Small, Independent Chiefdoms
West Jefferson Phase	1000	Intensification of Maize Agriculture.
	950	
	900	

Figure 5.2. Moundville's chronological and political development (after Knight 1997:233, 236). Used by permission of University of Nebraska Press.

preordered system imposed upon the local landscape from Moundville's beginnings as a community.

Knight (1993) has convincingly argued that Moundville represents a diagrammatic ceremonial center. He defines these centers as "central places in segmentary societies in which the layout of public architecture or monuments calls deliberate attention to key social and cosmological distinctions, in a map-like manner" (Knight 1993:1). Although the definitions of sacred landscapes and diagrammatic ceremonial centers are very similar, there are significant differences in the levels of sociopolitical organization and intentionality they suggest. Knight (1993:6) states that "the creation of a diagrammatic ceremonial center is, in part, an effort to insure the intergenerational stability of a particular arbitrary vision of social reality. The

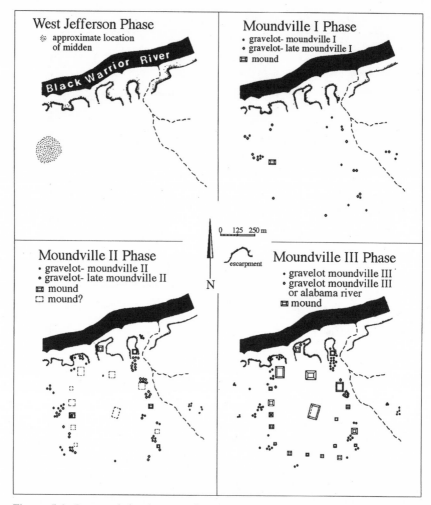

Figure 5.3. Proposed developmental sequence at Moundville. Reproduced from Peebles (1991:118) by permission of Leicester University Press, Cassell Academic, Wellington House, 125 Strand, London, England.

dimensions of that reality—its hierarchies, levels, oppositions, contrasts, and polarities—once designated and monumentalized in public architecture, from that point onward contribute to the re-creation of that reality, as ordinary people participate in the center as a part of their everyday environment."

Although sacred landscapes represent visions of social reality, their principal role is not ensuring the intergenerational stability of those visions but concretizing them to begin with. Support for this view is found in Eliade's (1959) concept of hierophany, the act of manifestation of the sacred. Eliade (1959:20–24) contends that by mirroring the cosmos, sacred spaces form essential hierophanies. These spaces provide existential footholds that provide human beings a center from which all actions and thoughts emanate. The spatial hierophany, for Eliade (1959:22), "is equivalent to the creation of the world." In the act of building, cultures produce architecture and social spaces that mimic the initial creation of their world. However, there is, most certainly, a dialectical relationship between social and cosmological orders. In and of themselves, sacred landscapes reflect, and are derived from, cosmological *and* social order. They are simultaneously cosmograms and sociograms. Sacred landscapes, as spatial hierophanies, meet basic religious and psychosocial needs for their creators. Once produced, they may be used to support the social status quo or be manipulated by interest groups, but their initial expression is not primarily political, but existential.[3]

The most visible Mississippian architectural features, earthen mounds, are found throughout the Southeast at a variety of sites. There is a good deal of spatial similarity in these mound centers, and Wahls (1986:25) suggests that this likeness is the result of a shared culture and ceremonial system. Although there is a good deal of similarity in Mississippian mound architecture, there is a great deal of spatial variation as well. Wahls (1986:26) attributes this variation to local topographic conditions, with Mississippian centers demonstrating consistent spatial relationships but illustrating adaptations to local constraints. It is important to recognize that these local constraints are not confined to geography but extend to local social environments as well, with individual communities producing built environments and sacred landscapes that reflect their unique cosmological and social visions. This explains both the spatial similarities in Mississippian communities and their individualities. What are needed are ethnographic analogies that can give us the ability to determine the nature of the shared culture and ceremonial system of Mississippian peoples and detailed archaeological data that can reveal the individual features of each site's unique sacred landscape.

Creek Architecture as a Mississippian Analog

To attempt to interpret the meanings of Moundville's sacred landscape, it is necessary to use ethnographic analogies that can shed light on the potential social meanings of space and earthen architecture. Creek architecture and cosmology have become traditional sources of analogies for Mississippian lifeways and together with historical documentation have helped form widely accepted views of Mississippian culture (Howard 1968; Knight 1981, 1986, 1990a; Moore 1994; Swanton 1912, 1922, 1928a; Waring 1968; Waring and Holder 1945). By using the Creek as a source for ethnographic analogies for Moundville's sacred landscape I am in no way suggesting that the site's occupants were ancestral Creeks. Given the abundant information recorded on Creek cosmology and social organization, they provide a point of departure for interpreting Mississippian culture, yielding tantalizing clues to the possible meanings of Moundville's sacred landscape.

The connection between the Creek and Mississippian peoples was originally supported by scholars who proposed that Mississippian peoples colonized the Southeast rapidly and replaced, assimilated, or acculturated the previous occupants of the region, with the Creek seen as the most likely candidates for this cultural invasion (Caldwell 1958; Corkran 1967:4; Hawkins 1971:19 [1848]; Swanton 1922:192, 1928a:34–40). Evidence for this view was found in Creek myths that seemed to show that they were relatively recent occupants of the Southeast. John Swanton (1922, 1928a) attempted to show continuity between the historic Creek and their prehistoric Mississippian antecedents by using these myths, along with the physical and cultural geography of the Southeast, to demonstrate that these were indeed accurate descriptions of their migration to the region. Swanton additionally sought to refine our understanding of Mississippian ceremonial centers through an analysis of Creek architectural practices, ethnohistorical documents, and ethnographic data (Swanton 1928a). He demonstrated that the spatial arrangements of Mississippian ceremonial centers were similar to those of the Creek, with the "uniqueness of many such arrangements . . . simply due to spatial recombination of a smaller number of essential elements," thus strengthening the link between the Creek and Mississippian groups (Knight 1981:11).

Additional research by Waring and Holder (1945) expanded the use of Creek analogies for Mississippian culture by addressing similarities in religious ceremonialism and ritual paraphernalia. Much of this research drew parallels between Creek myths and the archaeological remains found at Mississippian sites, arguing that there was a high degree of cultural continuity between the historic Creek and Mississippian peoples. As with Swanton,

Waring (1968) was interested in trying to connect what was known about Creek symbolism and architecture with the archaeological remains of Mississippian sites across the region. By analyzing Creek architecture and cosmology, Waring hoped to recover cultural meanings and enhance existing interpretations of the Southeastern Ceremonial Complex, an approach also adopted by Howard (1968).

Archaeological research does indicate a link between the historic Creek and Lamar Mississippian groups in Alabama and Georgia, supporting the view that the historic Creek developed out of Mississippian antecedents (Fairbanks 1952; Hally 1994b; Mason 1963; Moore 1994; H. Smith 1973; Williams and Shapiro 1990). However, contrary to the earlier view of prehistoric Creeks as migrating bearers of Mississippian lifeways, most archaeologists now see Mississippian culture spreading through the exchange of ideas and material items rather than through the wholesale relocation of populations (Pauketat 1994; B. Smith 1990; M. Smith 1987). Thus, the historic Creek may have in fact descended from groups that occupied the Southeast well before the time proposed by Swanton and others, predating the introduction of Mississippian material culture and lifeways. Regardless of the Creek relationship with the "original" Mississippians, they are a productive source for analogies concerning at least local manifestations of Mississippian culture.

Research by Knight (1981, 1986, 1990a) demonstrates the value of analogies drawn from the Creek for understanding elements of Mississippian culture. Through an analysis of the Creek Chekilli migration myth, Knight (1981) shows how Mississippian platform mounds were related to, and empowered by, mythic structures. His primary focus is the reading of Mississippian social space as an expression of cosmological associations in an attempt to construct links between religion, cosmology, and social action. By reading a Creek migration myth onto Mississippian architecture, Knight reveals Mississippian architecture as a series of powerful ritual stages, replete with meaningful social, historical, and cosmological references. Power generated through cosmological references in these structures not only served the communal, ceremonial, ends but also provided a potent source for the establishment and support of Mississippian elite political dominance.

Our ability to use the Creek *talwa* as a model for Mississippian towns is limited, but we can recognize many similar spatial themes in both Creek and Mississippian architecture. More important, we can begin to understand these spaces in a cultural context and interpret much of their social meaning. Research by Stout and Lewis (Chapter 7) supports this view by indicating that there was a basic Mississippian spatial and architectural grammar that "transcended linguistic and regional boundaries." Using architectural evidence from Mississippian sites in Kentucky, they show that many of the spatial relationships present at these sites are "culturally prescribed" even when site size and form appear to be different (Stout and Lewis, Chapter 7). It is these differences in the combination of constituent elements that give Mississippian ceremonial centers much of their architectural and spatial uniqueness. An examination of the architectural elements from which Creek towns were constructed illustrates similarities between Creek and Mississippian built environments, with both ordered by powerful sacred landscapes.

During the eighteenth and nineteenth centuries, several myths were collected from the Creek that relate to the structure of the cosmos and sacred landscapes. Although some details of these myths vary, they share a great many similarities. Most of these myths relate not only to the movement of peoples across the land but also to the process of Creek ethnogenesis. Several recurring spatial elements are found in these legends, with the most common consisting of an earth mouth (or cave), a sacred mountain, and a sacred tree. The mythical first people are said to have completed a journey that gave them the vital social and cosmological information needed for survival. The ancestors are believed to have escaped from within the earth, journeyed east toward the rising sun, ascended a large mountain where they received knowledge and culture, and finally descended to begin life as a people. These myths establish a narrative bond between the natural and social worlds, creating dichotomies between "nature" and "culture," "upperworld" and "underworld." These places of power exist not only in myth and the natural environment but are also given physical expression in architecture and ritual space. The concretization of cosmic order did not begin or end for Creek or Mississippian peoples with the construction of temple mounds but is present in all aspects of architecture and social praxis. Both public and domestic architecture are filled with cosmological references, working to establish the entire built environment and social world as a powerful sacred landscape.

At the beginning of the Chekilli legend, and several comparable myths, people are said to have originated inside the earth and emerged from the earth's mouth (Swanton 1928a:53–58). These first people lack clothing, fire, medicine, and other vestiges of culture, all elements used by later groups for self-definition. Several myths tell of hollow mounds with people living inside, including a Coweta-Kashita myth in which a hollow chamber, referred to as the "bowels of the earth," is made inside a mound so that the people can "fast and purify their bodies" there (Swanton 1928a:54–55). This supports Knight's (1981) contention that Creek and Mississippian social worlds were placed in constant tension by the forces of nature and culture, with spaces for ritual purification necessary for establishing balance in the physical and social bodies. These hollow mounds represent the primordial earth mouth or earth cave and are replicated in architectural form in the southeastern earthlodge and in the Creek council house. The council house was a semisubterranean structure, similar to Mississippian earthlodges identified across the region (Hally 1994b; Rudolph 1984). The low, narrow entrance of the council house forced individuals to crawl upon entering and leaving, mirroring the emergence of human beings from the mouth of the earth.

A Creek myth records how, after emerging from the earth, the people traveled to a mountain from which they could see the rising and setting of the sun (Swanton 1928a:53). Other myths record the importance of a mountain for these first people, telling of a thundering mountain where they received the sacred fire and the knowledge of edible plants and herbs. One account indicates that one of the first things the original people did after emerging from the earth was to construct two mounds designed to protect and help them (Swanton 1928a:57–58). The Creek have a long history of mound building, with small mounds still constructed today as a part of sacred squares in Creek communities in Oklahoma. The prehistoric Creek built supportive mounds for chiefly residences, council houses, square grounds, and possibly charnel houses, and these structures were a major element of the sacred landscape of the towns in which they were constructed.

Using Creek myths, Knight (1981:47) interprets Mississippian platform mounds as representative of the earth, with their construction seen as an effort to "control, defeat, or remove Earth from Society, as Society aspires for purification." These structures also served as sacred mountains, replicating and symbolizing the point where the Creek received the elements that made them unique and gave them a cultural identity. By constructing mounds, the Creek were giving physical form to an important element of their ethnogenesis. This is supported by Knight's (1981:51) contention that the earth used to construct these mounds was "not ordinary, unadulterated earth but instead village midden. It is earth full of cultural debris, and it is therefore in a sense 'compromised earth', belonging fully neither to the realm of Society nor to Earth." Since the sacred mountain provided the original people with the knowledge of all things cultural, it is only fitting that its representation be constructed with a mixture of earth and cultural materials. Since culture did not originate from within the earth in the primal state of human beings, but was acquired in a migration across its face, a reconstruction of the earth in mound architecture becomes a powerful cosmological and cultural metaphor and an essential element in Mississippian and Creek sacred landscapes.

After human beings received the necessary elements of culture, the Chekilli myth states that a dispute arose among various factions concerning which group was the oldest and thus the most revered. Four divisions were formed, with each having a distinct social identity (Swanton 1928a:53). This four-part division of society is expressed in Creek architecture in the form of the sacred square. Consisting of four rectangular buildings (clan beds) arranged in a square around a central courtyard, the sacred square served as the major ceremonial and political center for Creek towns. Seating within the clan beds was divided along lines of kinship and social status, replicating the social order in spatial terms, informing and reinforcing each individual's existing social position in a spatial medium (Hawkins 1971:70–71 [1848]) (Figure 5.4). Thus the Creek possessed the ability not only to recognize social divisions but also to replicate them in sacred space and social action.

The most important Creek ceremony, the busk, took place within the sacred square. Through this ritual the Creek spiritually renewed themselves and reestablished their ties to their deities through acts of ritual purification. At the center of the square was the Creek sacred fire. Given to them by the primordial "King of Mountains," and representative of their chief deity, the sacred fire was the most visible symbol of the Creek cosmos, representing the origin and migration of the Creek people as well as their connection with the supernatural. One of the essential elements of the busk was the extinguishing of the old sacred fire and the lighting of a new fire; but the busk not only rekindled the sacred fire, it also renewed the Creek social world and its connections to the cosmological. In this way the Creek reenacted essential elements in their ethnogenesis, translating myths into prescribed ritual action.

Through these supernatural associations, the Creek sacred square not only became a repository for sacred power but also served as a social and

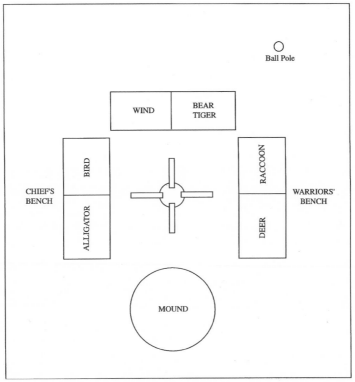

Figure 5.4. Spatial arrangement of seating in the Creek sacred square (after Howard 1968:89).

cosmological map as well. By reflecting the social order in its seating, the square reified existing social divisions, clearly demonstrating an individual's appropriate place (or space) in Creek society. Given the cosmological and symbolic associations structuring interactions within this ritual space, social divisions were represented as natural and divinely established. This process was furthered through the ritual actions that took place within the sacred square and their strong association with powerful, cosmologically sanctioned social elites. Through all these means, the Creek sacred square became a cosmological referent and a significant component of the Creek sacred landscape.

There is evidence that sacred squares existed during Mississippian times, functioning in much the same way as their Creek counterparts. Howard (1968:130) contends that during the Mississippi period the public square was not divided into four separate buildings as with the historic Creek but was instead a unified structure possessing a single roof. He identifies references to public squares in early Spanish chronicles at the Mississippian sites of Casqui, Ucita, and Atahahaci, with others possibly existing among the Calusa (Howard 1968:133–38). This suggests that Mississippian public squares may have topped platform mounds, much as Bartram (1853) argued. If the public square was represented by a single structure during Mississippian times, it may be difficult to assess the presence of this important cosmological referent. There is, however, archaeological evidence of buildings that approximate the size and structural relations of the public square.

One of the best potential examples of a Mississippian sacred square is from the Bessemer site, excavated during the 1930s by the Civil Works Administration and the Alabama Museum of Natural History (DeJarnette and Wimberly 1941). On Mound Three, identified by DeJarnette and Wimberly as the "Domiciliary Mound," two structures appear to be nondomestic in size and function (Figure 5.5). These structures, each encompassing a floor area of approximately 40 square meters, far exceed the average domestic architectural pattern at the site (DeJarnette and Wimberly 1941:40). Although there is little evidence to indicate the function of these structures, one appears to have been divided into two distinct halves, which were apparently constructed over two previously separate structures. This is similar to the pattern identified by Howard (1968:134) as the possible precursor of the four-structure public square: "They are usually divided into two rooms by a partition. The anterior chamber consists of a square room with a central fire pit and a bench running around the four walls. The entrance is usually off center in the eastern wall or may be in the corner. The rear structure has a prepared floor but no evidence of a bench or hearth." Although the evidence at Bessemer is difficult to interpret, it is possible that these structures represent corporate structures rather than simply domestic habitations.

Although these architectural elements are representative of individual aspects of the cosmos, taken together they are a concretization of the Creek migration myth. The structure of the Creek built environment is seen to follow the course of their ethnogenesis, progressing from an unstructured underworld, represented by the council house, to the highly structured social positions of the upperworld, as exemplified by the public square. Ethnographic information concerning contemporary Creek and Yuchi rituals indicates that several contemporary dances follow this same progression, originating outside the public square, progressing to a mound, and then ending

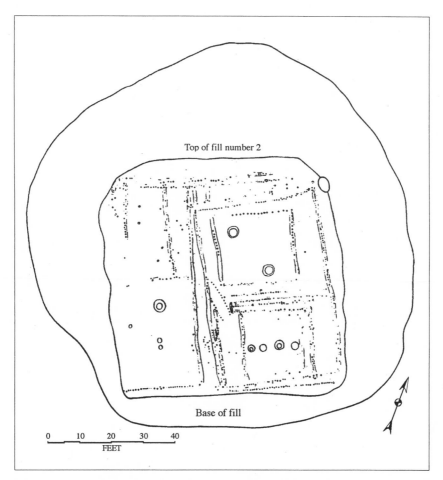

Figure 5.5. Architectural remains from the domiciliary mound at the Bessemer site (from DeJarnette and Wimberly 1941). Used by permission of the Geological Survey of Alabama/Alabama Museum of Natural History.

at the sacred fire (Ballard 1978). Through similar rituals the Creek were constantly reminded that their architectural and social landscapes were not separate from the order of the cosmos but were essential components of its order.

The Politicization of Sacred Landscapes

Creek elites were also aware of the power inherent in sacred space, acting to promote their sociopolitical agendas through close association with these cosmological elements. The council house was an essential component of elite power strategies. During the historic period, chiefs had to accommodate the views of their council, but when chiefly power was at its height during the Mississippi period, it is argued that the chief's power was not placed in check by a council. In fact, many scholars see council houses developing during the protohistoric and historic periods out of the large chiefly mound-top residences. DePratter (1991:165) contends that council houses were extremely rare between A.D. 1000 and 1600 and that mound structures from this period actually represent chiefly residences. This suggests that as chiefdoms in the Southeast began to form out of less complex social organizations, council houses began to decline in number. Coinciding with this greater centralization and complexity was an increase in the size and prominence of chiefly residences. DePratter (1991:165) states that "councils which advised the chief or controlled his decisions may have been present during the early stages of the development of a chiefdom, but as the chief grew stronger, the councils apparently grew weaker and eventually disappeared all together in most Southeastern chiefdoms."

The accounts of Hawkins, Taitt, Bartram, and Fitch suggest that the chief's house continued to play a semipublic role in Creek society. This is understandable if it replaced a communal building form. It is possible that in some cases chiefly mounds were constructed on top of previous council houses, providing a powerful symbolic termination of a village government based on consensus and the imposition of a more centralized and powerful chiefly elite. Although the presence of council houses in Mississippian contexts appears to be limited (DePratter 1991; Steponaitis 1986), the idea that the chief's residence replaced this communal structure would have meant increased cosmological power for chiefly elites, as they co-opted a sacred communal form to advance their social positions.

Steponaitis (1986:386) and others have argued that one of the ways emerging elites in Mississippian society could legitimize their authority was to construct mounds and chiefly residences on top of what would have previously been communal centers of power. Often chief's houses are not merely domiciles but serve semipublic functions as well (Anderson 1994; DePratter 1991; Pauketat 1994). Tilley (1994:34) states that architecture "is invested with powers, capable of being organized and choreographed in relation to sectional interests, and is always sedimented with human significance . . . "; thus the imposition of elite hegemony over not only social power but also traditional structures endowed with human significance would have only heightened the power of an elite desirous of expanding its sociopolitical control. Thus, it is possible that chief's houses during the Mississippi period fulfilled many of the roles later represented in the public square.

The social order represented in the public square certainly represents the interests of the chiefly elite as central to communal success as well. In the sacred square, chiefly elites were intimately linked with the most sacred Creek ritual paraphernalia. These sacred items were kept in a small room to the rear of the *mico's* cabin and consisted of both items of a communal religious nature and emblems of chiefly authority (Bartram 1853:53). By maintaining these items in the *mico's* cabin, a strong link was established between chiefly power and the sacred, supernatural power of the cosmos, helping to expand and consolidate elite political control. This position of power was recognized in the seating of the sacred square, with all seating positions structured in relation not only to the sacred fire but also to the *mico* as well.

It is important to note that along with the loss of many cultural traditions, the contact and historic periods brought diminished political and social power for Mississippian elites. As much recent research has shown, the prehistoric Southeast was home to a number of paramount chiefdoms that encompassed enormous territories and multiple communities. In such large-scale political formations, chiefly power was not only exemplified in the civic ceremonial center where the paramount resided but also replicated in the architecture of surrounding subject towns as well. Smith and Hally (1992) indicate that it was normal for paramounts to tour the territory under their control, with such visits probably occurring at least once a year. Although there are few documentary sources that address this point, there is reason to believe that such visits not only would have been enacted in economic and political spheres (checking up on local accounts) but also would have formed a significant symbolic act in the ritual life of these surrounding towns. Sahlins (1981) indicates a similar process at work in the Hawaiian Islands, where, during certain rituals, paramount rulers personified the god Lono and were honored accordingly. These Hawaiian rituals involved a progression from one village to another, following a defined mythic narrative. Mississippian paramount tours may have been accompanied by similar pomp and circumstance, enacted in a supernatural or mythic form.

Just as the built environment is empowered through cosmological references and mythic narratives, elite movements in many cultures are thought
to mirror those of supernatural beings, including the sun, moon, and stars.
Such movements are not haphazard but follow a precise ritual program. This
may be glimpsed in the treatment given to Hernando de Soto and his party
on their journey across the region. Smith and Hally (1992) argue that there
are strong indications that the treatment his party received was commensu-
rate with that of a paramount being toured through the territory under his
control or of a paramount visiting from another chiefdom. Such practices may also partially reveal the meaning and importance of Mississippian single-mound towns, which as a group are more abundant than major
multiple-mound centers. Smaller communities would have represented a
local representation of the cosmos, but they may have also formed constituent elements in the larger sacred landscape of the chiefdom. Such smaller
communities would not have been merely political satellites of larger towns
but would have formed an essential part of the larger cosmic representation
of the chiefdom as a whole—a point in a larger narrative.

This is possibly seen in the relationship between the Mississippian center of Moundville and smaller contemporary sites along the Black Warrior
River. As Peebles (1991) indicates, Moundville was the preeminent center on
the Black Warrior River for over 300 years, with multiple secondary towns
possessing mounds and supportive populations (Figure 5.6). Over time,
Moundville came to exploit larger areas and more of these centers in an effort
to fuel its prestige-goods economy. In exchange for these alliances and support, local elites were given additional items of a ritual and symbolic nature,
expressing their connection to the main center and the power of established
elites (Peebles 1971; Steponaitis 1983; Welch 1991). Perhaps part of this
process involved visits by paramounts to these villages to reenact important cosmologically charged myths and perform acts of ritual purification,
strengthening local sacred landscapes and elite connections to the cosmos.

To have a paramount figure visit one's site would have meant an inun-
dation of supernatural power and a symbolic reaffirmation of the alliance
between local and nonlocal elites, resulting in a strengthening of power for
local decision makers. Not only would the sacred landscape and periodic visits
by a paramount lend cosmological support to local elites, but also the ritual
paraphernalia associated with chiefly office would have been an additional
source of legitimization for these rulers. Smith and Hally (1992) propose

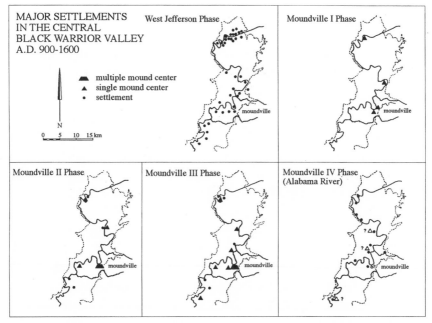

Figure 5.6. The growth of Moundville phase settlements in the Black Warrior Valley from A.D. 900 to 1600. Reproduced from Peebles (1991:116) by permission of Leicester University Press, Cassell Academic, Wellington House, 125 Strand, London, England.

that the distribution of Citico style gorgets corresponds with the political boundaries of the Coosa chiefdom, suggesting that they were possibly political badges distributed among elites at towns allied with Coosa. Just as paramounts would have served as the personification of mythical deities during certain religious rituals essential to the chiefdom as a whole, it is possible that elites in smaller communities served as representatives of the paramount during times when he was not present and thus would have assumed the role of deities during local ritual activities. Peregrine (1992:5–6), following the work of Frankenstein and Rowlands (1978:75), Helms (1979, 1988), and Clark (1986), argues that "elites in any social system display and maintain their social status through the control of exotic goods and esoteric knowledge." Such powerful sacra would have represented this transference of power from paramounts to their elite allies in subject towns and would have helped them to materialize their ideological positions within local communities and social hierarchies. Blitz (1993:23) supports this claim by arguing that "ideological legitimization of leadership within a ritual format" is central to the success and expansion of elite social control.

Interpreting Moundville's Sacred Landscape

Using ethnographic analogies similar to those described above, primarily the social and spatial structure of Chickasaw house groups, Knight (1993) views the arrangement of mounds at Moundville as a sociogram, with their positions organized by the relative status of kin groups. This structural arrangement is also very similar to the divisions of seating in the Creek sacred square, with each individual positioned in relation to both the sacred fire and the chief. In his reconstruction of Moundville's historic development, Peebles (1974, 1991:118) suggests that much of Moundville's spatial form was present long before earthen mounds were constructed, representing social and spatial divisions stretching to earlier in the Moundville I phase (ca. A.D. 1100). If the distribution of gravelots from the Moundville I phase represents discrete kin groups, then much of the site's eventual form was derived from long-standing systems of social organization.

Once mounds began to be constructed, these structures not only acted as a reification of existing cosmological and social divisions but also represented potent seats of power for both competing social groups and the Moundville site as well. Knight and Steponaitis (1996:12) contend that "a fixed rank ordering had been imposed on these kin groups by incorporating that order into a sacred landscape, an act which implies considerable power at the center. Such power, vested in the office of a paramount chief, would also have been necessary to enforce this undoubtedly contested view of social reality once it had been imposed." They explore the political implications of these developments, noting that during this period we see the first evidence for the intensification of acquisition of nonlocal goods, elite craft production, increases in the number and diversity of high-status burial goods, and the construction of secondary centers elsewhere in the Black Warrior Valley (Knight and Steponaitis 1996:11–12). These factors are believed to represent the consolidation of the region into a single polity centered at Moundville.

By the late Moundville II or early Moundville III phases (A.D. 1300–1450), with the enlargement of plaza-periphery mounds, the introduction of materials bearing Southeastern Ceremonial Complex symbolism, and a marked reduction in the local population, the consolidation of sociopolitical power at Moundville appears to have been complete (Knight and Steponaitis 1996:12). By co-opting the symbolism of mound groups, elites demonstrated their centrality in the social and political worlds and their connection to the supernatural, materializing an ideology of elite domination and privilege. As Bruce Smith (1992) has argued, architecture, and particularly in this case earthen mounds, became powerful levers of social inequality, expanding the divisions between supernaturally sanctioned elites and commoners.

Not only was Moundville's sacred landscape controlled by elites at this time, but also by A.D. 1300 a process of population dispersal had begun as well, "leaving only the elite and their retainers as permanent residents" (Knight and Steponaitis 1996:13). Knight and Steponaitis (1996:13) suggest that this outmigration was possibly a result of "a conscious decision by the elite to enhance the sanctity of the center by emptying it, by which action they could further distance themselves from the affairs of commoners." These actions represent an even tighter control of ritual space and the local sacred landscape, with Moundville's elite becoming masters of not only individual nodes in the system but also the system in its entirety. If, in the founding of spatial hierophanies, cultures create existential centers that ground human experience and give direction to social action, the complete domination of these centers by elites would have given them tremendous power in the control of space, time, and ritual. It is just such a pattern that we see at Moundville, with the gradual co-optation by elites of a powerful sacred landscape.

Another interpretation of this pattern is that as elite control of sacred space increased, an increasing number of individuals opted out of the system and either established individual farmsteads or moved to other communities. With the imposition of greater elite control at Moundville, perhaps people grew dissatisfied with their increasing physical and existential distance from the hierophanous center and went out to create new sacred landscapes. As Eliade (1959:43) states, "the religious man sought to live as near as possible to the Center of the World," and it was the center of the world that Moundville's sacred landscape represented. By vacating Moundville, nonelites became more distant from the existential center, a counterintuitive movement if the local built environment continued to represent a potent, and necessary, sacred landscape. Perhaps continued elite manipulation of the plaza-periphery group and the alienation such actions imposed on nonelites led

Moundville to become primarily a necropolis during the period from A.D. 1300 to 1450 (Knight and Steponaitis 1996:14). As Knight and Steponaitis (1996:13–14) state, "it is evident that the fixed rank order of social groups imposed upon the landscape in the initial layout of the site, some two centuries earlier, was not immune to disagreement. Those that had the least to gain from such a fixed arrangement were the lower-ranked groups, assigned spaces on the opposite side of the plaza from the shrines and temples of the ruling elites. And as these ruling elites consolidated their power, engaging in ritual activity and continued enlargements of mounds on the north end of the site, others stopped contributing. It is perhaps, the first sign of troubles that were to come."

Conclusions

This is but a brief introduction to the concretization of cosmological and social órder in Moundville's sacred landscape, but it illustrates the presence and importance of architecture and social spaces empowered with supernatural connections. Unfortunately, there are no perfect, unbroken analogical or direct historical links between Mississippian and historic southeastern peoples, making the interpretation of these remains much more difficult than that of their ethnographically known counterparts. Elite power was significantly attenuated in the late protohistoric and historic Southeast, with the dissolution of paramount chiefdoms across the region (Anderson 1994; DePratter 1991). This process had an impact on many aspects of previous Mississippian lifeways, including architectural and social spaces. Although we lack the specific mythic narratives that would have empowered such spaces, I believe that Moundville's architecture was empowered by processes similar to those identified for the Creek.

The reconstruction of Mississippian sacred landscapes is a daunting task. The effects of interactions with Euroamericans during the contact and historic periods severely impacted Mississippian communities across the region, most certainly terminating many long-standing cultural practices. As previously advanced, however, Mississippian sacred landscapes were formed through concretization and materialization, both of which processes leave archaeological signatures. Although we lack the specific narratives that would have structured complete Mississippian built environments, Knight (1981) has shown that there are close structural relationships between Creek myths and Mississippian ritual space, connections that would have concretized their cosmological order in built form. We may not have a complete picture of Mississippian cosmology and how its structure was replicated in architecture, but we can attempt to read in the reverse order, trying to reconstruct the structural relationship of these myths without knowing their actual oral or written form.

My intention is not to present the definitive statement on Mississippian sacred landscapes but to demonstrate their presence at Moundville and, by extension, all other Mississippian sites. Moundville's plaza-periphery group was shown to represent a concretization of cosmological and social orders, resulting in potent seats of power for Mississippian elites. Such spaces provided Mississippian elites with sources of power and legitimacy, allowing them to expand and consolidate their control of society. There are limitations to this power strategy, however, and as the case of Moundville illustrates, stretched too far from their original meanings, sacred landscapes lose their cosmological connections and cease to serve the needs of all members of society.

Acknowledgments

I must first thank Barry Lewis and Chuck Stout for inviting me to contribute to this volume and for patiently awaiting the completion of my chapter. I would also like to thank María Avilés, Helaine Silverman, Mark Rees, and two anonymous reviewers for their comments on previous versions of this chapter. In addition, I would like to thank Jim Knight for permission to cite several of his unpublished works.

Notes

1. Eliade (1959:20–65) argues that every construction is a form of cosmogony, expressing cosmic order in physical form. Through the act of building we sepa-

rate the cosmic from the chaotic, the meaningful from the meaningless (Eliade 1959:29–32).

2. The principal ways in which material messages can be altered are through polysemy and recursivity. Since all messages contain multiple layers of meaning, variations in these meanings can lead to the reinterpretation of the intended message or a change in the relationship between the signifier and its sign. This ambiguity of meaning does not apply only to language, but is easily seen in material culture (Derrida 1976; Fletcher 1989; Hodder 1985; Leone 1986; Palkovich 1988; Tilley 1989).

3. Although not directly contrary to these views, Foucault (1984) proposes that architecture and ritual space are tied to structures of political dominance. In particular, he makes mention of the way in which architecture was used as a means of oppression and manipulation in early modern Western societies. Although he does not specifically address the implications of these ideas for non-Western architecture, the general impression is that he views all architecture as a means of domination.

6

Mississippi Period Mound Groups and Communities in the Lower Mississippi Valley

Tristram R. Kidder

Archaeological summaries of the later prehistoric periods of the southeastern United States naturally tend to generalize about the organization of native American cultures. Based on a combination of ethnohistoric accounts (which tend to lump diachronic variation into synchronic unity) and spatially scattered archaeological data, a picture of the Mississippian town has emerged in the literature to be adopted as the paradigm of late prehistoric social, economic, and political behavior. This vision of the Mississippian town is one of a centralized, often palisaded community, dominated by one or more square-sided, flat-topped, earthen mounds. These towns were generally ruled by a kin-based group of chiefs, warriors, and priests. The central places were supported by agricultural products, notably maize, beans, and squash, produced by a widely dispersed population in the surrounding hinterland.

As typifies all such generalizations this picture is composed of elements of fact mixed with interpolations from existing data and colored by modern projections. A "truth" emerging today in southeastern archaeology is that the nature of Mississippian community organization is highly varied. This seems true as regards how native Americans used space, the nature of their settlement distribution, the social and political structure and makeup of communities, and even their economic behavior. The paradigm of a singular Mississippian world gives way on closer inspection to a fluid, regionally distinct, and particularistic group of settlements incorporated through local historical contexts and linked through shared cultural tendencies and widely diffused technological innovation. In this view Mississippian does not carry a specific cultural connotation but takes its place as a designation of shared generic cultural characteristics.

The Lower Mississippi Valley provides an instructive case study for examining the nature of Mississippian towns and communities. This region is geographically circumscribed on the east and west but is linked by the broad floodplain and actual course of the Mississippi River. It offers an opportunity to explore the themes and variations in Mississippian town and community organization and to examine the underlying variables that shaped these patterns. In order to illustrate the nature of Mississippian towns and communities in the Lower Mississippi Valley, I wish to explore the notion of community planning and its relation to the organization of settlement and society through time.

To anticipate my conclusions, I offer no revelations; rather, I demonstrate that variation is locally significant and regionally extensive. The diversity of Mississippian community organization emphasizes the historical circumstances that gird these developments. Despite the magnitude of variation that existed in these communities, especially from a parochial point of view, thematic unity is evident and too obvious to dismiss. Local content cannot be separated from regional context, for perhaps it is in the interplay of theme and variation that we can recognize at least some of the significant aspects of Mississippian towns and communities.

Space and Time

Since the focus of this chapter is on the localization of behavior during the late prehistoric period, it is necessary to familiarize the reader with the geographical and cultural terms that follow. Although the Lower Mississippi Valley can be viewed, at least from afar, as a single ecological and geographical entity, from close up it consists of a number of subregions marked by peculiar or, perhaps better said, particular variations that make each part of the valley different from its neighbors (Fisk 1944). Similarly, the cultural terminology used by archaeologists working in the Lower Mississippi Valley has its peculiarities, especially in the way late prehistoric cultures are identified and characterized.

Geologists define the Lower Mississippi Valley as beginning at Cairo, Illinois, where the Ohio River joins the Mississippi River and where the river leaves the entrenched confines of the upper part of the valley (Autin et al. 1991; Fisk 1944; Saucier 1974). To limit my discussion to a manageable geographical and prehistoric cultural scope, I will restrict my definition of the Lower Mississippi Valley to an area less than that recognized by geologists. The focus of the ensuing discussion will be the Yazoo and Tensas basins of west-central Mississippi and northeast Louisiana, respectively (Figure 6.1). These areas are well known to me, and there is a considerable body of published data on Mississippi period communities.

The culture history of the central portion of the Lower Mississippi Valley is also well known and has been the subject of extensive investigation beginning in the 1940s and continuing through today (Ford, Phillips, and Haag 1955; Phillips 1970; Phillips, Ford, and Griffin 1951; Williams and Brain 1983). On the basis of Phillips's culture historical framework, the later prehistory of the region is divided into three temporal periods and many distinct archaeological cultures (in the sense offered by Willey and Phillips 1958:51–55), which, in turn, can be subdivided into phases (Phillips 1970; Williams and Brain 1983). The Baytown (A.D. 400–700) and Coles Creek (A.D. 700–1000) periods represent what are traditionally thought of as the two temporal units of the Late Woodland stage, and the Mississippi period (A.D. 1000–contact) marks the temporal unit associated with Mississippian in most other regions of the Southeast. Figure 6.2 presents a graphic representation of the culture history of the area, depicting both spatial and temporal variations. It is important to observe that the cultural and temporal units used here are not always concordant. Thus, for example, the Coles Creek *culture* crosses the temporal boundary of the Mississippi *period* and can be traced, as a ceramic cultural entity, up to at least about A.D. 1200. Similarly, the Plaquemine culture of the Mississippi period "moves" through time, largely if not wholly as a reflection of the encroachment of shell tempering (the sine qua non of Mississippian) from the north (Hally 1972). The distinction between Mississippian and Plaquemine is often only a technological one, but it serves a useful purpose in this area because there may in fact be other, more important differences between the cultures of the Lower Mississippi Valley and other Mississippian communities in the Southeast.

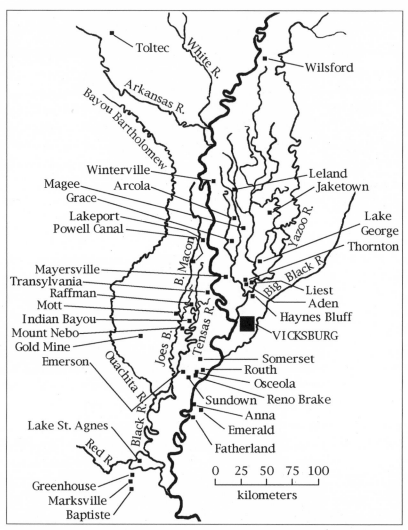

Figure 6.1. Map of the central portion of the Lower Mississippi Valley showing locations of sites mentioned in the text. The Yazoo Basin encompasses the region from the Yazoo River west to the Mississippi. The Tensas Basin is generally considered to take in the alluvial lands east of Bayou Maçon, Joes Bayou, and the Black River. The Natchez Bluffs follow the east bank of the Mississippi River from Vicksburg south to the mouth of the Homochitto River.

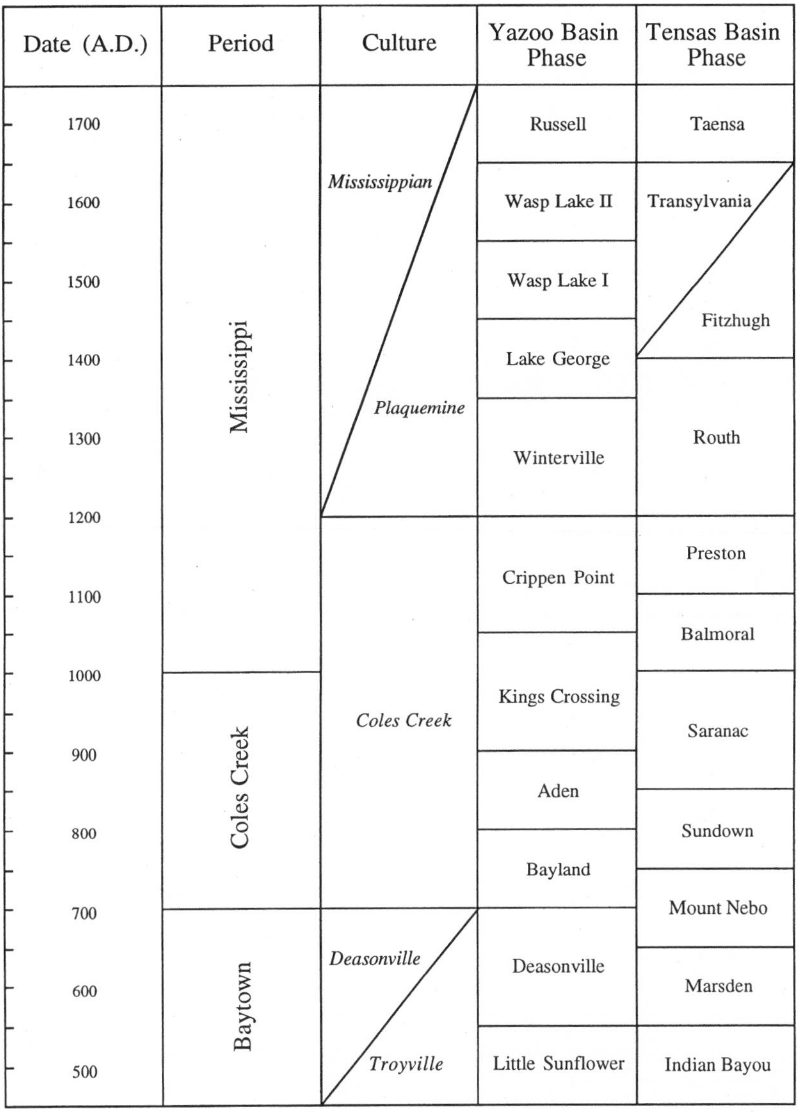

Date (A.D.)	Period	Culture	Yazoo Basin Phase	Tensas Basin Phase
1700	Mississippi	Mississippian	Russell	Taensa
1600			Wasp Lake II	Transylvania
1500			Wasp Lake I	Fitzhugh
1400		Plaquemine	Lake George	
1300			Winterville	Routh
1200				
1100		Coles Creek	Crippen Point	Preston
1000	Coles Creek			Balmoral
900			Kings Crossing	Saranac
800			Aden	Sundown
700	Baytown		Bayland	Mount Nebo
600		Deasonville	Deasonville	Marsden
500		Troyville	Little Sunflower	Indian Bayou

Figure 6.2. Chronological chart of the later Neo-Indian periods, cultures, and phases in the Yazoo and Tensas basins.

Baytown Period

The settlement pattern of the Baytown period appears to be made up of two elements: small, probably highly dispersed, hamlets or family dwellings, and larger, often mounded, communities of considerably greater size than other contemporary settlements. There is also considerable spatial variation. In the Yazoo Basin, Deasonville culture settlements are small and spatially homogeneous. The basic community plan is manifested archaeologically in circular arrangements of midden, sometimes found in discrete clusters, with empty, open spaces in the middle of the circles (Phillips 1970; Williams and Brain 1983:364–66). Comprehensive controlled surface collections of these small sites have not been undertaken and it is thus not possible to say what this pattern indicates about aboriginal behavior.

In some areas mounds were constructed at this time, both as living platforms and for the interment of the dead (Belmont 1980, 1984:81–83; Kidder and Wells 1992). This is especially true of the Troyville culture area of northeast Louisiana. The burial pattern consisted of group or mass secondary interment in bunches (Belmont 1980:17–22, 1984:83–86; Bitgood 1989). Grave goods were rare, though occasionally spectacular (Jones 1979), but do not seem to have marked individuals as having a status apart from others (Belmont 1984:90). Evidence from the mode of mass burials suggests that there was a focus on community-wide mortuary activities (Kidder 1992a; Kidder and Wells 1992). This speculation may be reinforced by the common presence of the so-called bathtub-shaped fire pits found at some Troyville culture sites (Belmont 1980, 1984; Bitgood 1989; Ford 1951). These pits are hypothesized to have been the focal point of social interaction that integrated family-sized groups into the broader society (Belmont 1980; Kidder and Wells 1992). Presumably interments in mass burials and the associated (?) feasting would have been periodic events that brought together populations living in smaller sites, possibly on an annual or semiannual basis (Belmont 1980).

The Baytown subsistence base is poorly understood but seems to have consisted of a broad-spectrum hunter-collector pattern (Belmont 1980:41, 1984:90–91; Fritz and Kidder 1993; Kidder and Fritz 1993; Mariaca 1988). Both plant and animal food sources and acquisition practices seem to indicate a strong continuity from the preceding Late Marksville period. Deer often predominate in faunal assemblages at excavated burial mound sites, and this information has been taken as further confirmation of the use of these sites as centers for community-wide feasting and ceremonialism (Kidder and Wells 1992; Rolingson 1992; Steponaitis 1986:385–86). There is at present no firm evidence for horticulture or agriculture (Fritz and Kidder 1993; Kidder and Fritz 1993; Rose, Marks, and Tieszen 1991); however, few focused attempts have been made to understand Baytown period subsistence patterns in the Lower Mississippi Valley. Consequently scholars do not have a firm appreciation of the relationship between diet, health, and cultural complexity.

The late Baytown period appears to mark a series of transformations in the cultures of the Lower Mississippi Valley. The period between about A.D. 650 and 750 represents a time of notable shifts in local and regional behaviors on a number of different levels. Changing burial practices seem to indicate a greater emphasis on individuals and their achievements or accomplishments, and evidence for communal mortuary ritual ceases or is deemphasized. Settlement patterns continue to represent a dichotomy between mound centers and what are presumed to be single-family or possibly extended-family settlements. Some nonmound communities appear to become larger and may represent the evolution of larger group "villages." The extant data suggest a broad-spectrum subsistence base exploiting the many varied and diverse environments in the Lower Mississippi Valley (Belmont 1983), although specific subsistence data are as yet unavailable or unstudied.

Coles Creek Period

The Coles Creek period marks a significant change in the culture history of the Lower Mississippi Valley. Population seems to increase dramatically, and there is now strong evidence of a growing cultural and political complexity. As a result of excavations at the Osceola site, archaeologists now have a reasonably good picture of Coles Creek subsistence practices, at least in the Tensas Basin (Kidder and Fritz 1993). At present there is no evidence for the use of domesticated or cultivated plants until near the end of the Coles Creek period, although this is certainly possible given the presence of such crops elsewhere in the eastern United States (Fritz 1990; Fritz and Kidder 1993; Kidder and Fritz 1993). Acorns are the dominant plant food resource, followed by fleshy fruits, such as persimmon, palmetto, and grape, and starchy seeds, especially maygrass. Coles Creek populations of the Tensas Basin may have encouraged or loosely "managed" certain plant food resources, especially acorns and maygrass, in order to promote better or more consistent yields (Fritz and Kidder 1993). Corn is found initially in restricted contexts, most notably mound flank middens. By about A.D. 1000–1200 we see more corn in the archaeological record, but the amount is still low, both in terms of number of remains found per unit of soil in flotation studies and in comparison with that in neighboring regions (Fritz 1990; Fritz and Kidder 1993; Kidder 1992b).

The typical Coles Creek site plan, consisting of at least two, and more commonly three, mounds arranged around a central plaza, begins around A.D. 800. This pattern is evident at the Sundown site in Tensas Parish and is likely to have been the case at Osceola as well (Kidder 1992a). Similar site plans seem to emerge across much of the Lower Valley at this time (Williams and Brain 1983:figs. 12.12, 12.13), indicating perhaps the development of incipient elite populations. In some (most?) cases these Coles Creek period mounds are constructed over terminal Baytown period (Mount Nebo and Bayland phases) platforms. At Mount Nebo (Giardino 1984), Lake George (Williams and Brain 1983), and Lake St. Agnes (Toth 1979), these Coles Creek mounds were erected over earlier mortuaries, leading several researchers to speculate that emerging elites were physically and symbolically appropriating dead ancestors to emphasize and project their own authority (Kidder 1992a; Kidder and Wells 1992; Steponaitis 1986). Material wealth is minimal in burial or midden contexts. Long-distance trade goods or exotic objects are extremely rare in Coles Creek sites.

The late Coles Creek settlement pattern appears to be an evolved form of that witnessed in earlier times. Smaller centers of the kind first noted as early as the Sundown phase appear to increase in number and also in size. The standard three-mound Coles Creek site plan is often enlarged to include up to three more mounds (Williams and Brain 1983:fig. 12.13). Nonmound communities are not well explored but are present in some numbers (Kidder 1993; Phillips 1970; Williams and Brain 1983:figs. 11.13, 11.14, 11.15). These communities are frequently of moderate size, suggesting something on the order of a village as opposed to a couple of houses. By about A.D. 1100, there are some moderately large nonmound communities scattered throughout the region (Kidder 1993).

Mississippi Period

The Mississippi period in the Lower Mississippi Valley is divided into two cultures, Plaquemine and Mississippian. Late Coles Creek *culture* also intrudes into the Mississippi period as normally defined in the Southeast. The Plaquemine culture is often identified as "Mississippianized" Coles Creek (Brain 1989; Weinstein 1987; Williams and Brain 1983). The implication of this designation is that local cultures (Coles Creek) received their impetus and stimulus for cultural evolution as a result of diffusion of Mississippian ideas and material traits from outside of the Mississippi Valley. Included in this "Mississippian" package are supposed to be ideas concerning site plans and architectural patterns, settlement organization, ceramic decorative techniques and styles, subsistence practices, and especially social and cultural values and ideals (Brain 1978, 1989; Williams and Brain 1983). Jeffrey Brain and Stephen Williams advocate actual contact with Cahokia or Cahokia-related peoples as a potential causal agent in the advent of Plaquemine culture in the Lower Mississippi Valley (Brain 1978, 1989, 1991; Williams and Brain 1983).

While the notion of Mississippianization by diffusion has its advantages, it fails to explain many of the significant elements of Plaquemine culture. Furthermore, emerging analyses of the Coles Creek to Plaquemine transition in the Tensas Basin indicate that there are clear evolutionary differences between the Yazoo Basin, where Brain and Williams conducted the bulk of their research, and the Tensas, where Plaquemine is more fully entrenched (Hally 1972; Kidder 1993). These differences appear to be especially notable in basic cultural characteristics, including subsistence and social organization. The same point evidently applies to the Natchez Bluffs region, although the data have not yet been published in full (Brain 1978; Brown 1985a). I view Plaquemine as the logical outgrowth of Coles Creek cultural evolution, which may have, in some cases, been influenced by Mississippian groups from outside of the Lower Mississippi Valley. There is, however, a clear trend toward the southern diffusion of certain Mississippian traits, especially ceramic technology (shell tempering) and perhaps domestic architecture (although the trend is equivocal at best [Brown 1985b]).

The use of crushed shell as a tempering agent is thought to characterize the break between Plaquemine and Mississippian, although few have questioned the fundamental relationship between this trait and how groups are assigned to either culture. Mississippianization per se is thought to begin earlier in the north than in the south because shell-tempered pottery spreads downriver through time. This type of pottery appears at sites such as Winterville and Lake George between about A.D. 1200 and 1400 and in the

Tensas Basin by about A.D. 1500, or even later. The historically documented Taensa may have been the last "Mississippian" peoples in the Tensas Basin, solely on the basis of their ceramic assemblages (Hally 1972; Williams 1967). Typically, however, what are identified as Taensa ceramic assemblages demonstrate Plaquemine designs on shell-tempered (Mississippian) wares (Jones and Kidder 1994; Williams 1967). Thus these ceramics serve to emphasize the artificial dichotomy between Mississippian and Plaquemine cultures and gloss over some obvious similarities.

Community Planning

The notion of a mound-and-plaza community structure is evidently very old in the Central Mississippi Valley, with examples of mounds surrounding plazas extending as far back as the Late Archaic (Gibson 1994; Saunders, Allen, and Saucier 1994). At sites from both Poverty Point and later Early Woodland times, mound-and-plaza groups have been documented in a number of instances (Gibson and Shenkel 1988; Webb 1982). For example, evidence from the Pinson site shows that flat-topped mounds were erected during the Middle Woodland (Mainfort 1986:15–17); similarly, Mounds 2, 6, and 7 at Marksville are likely to be Middle Woodland flat-topped structures (Toth 1974, 1988), and Mound C at Liest may also fit in this mold (Phillips 1970:367–73). We know too little about these mounds, however, to say much about them beyond the fact that they were not built to serve as the foundations for perishable structures (Mainfort 1986). Despite the presence of large mound communities at this time, archaeologists hypothesize that the bulk of the population was living in dispersed, nonnucleated communities and practicing a fisher-hunter-collector pattern of subsistence (Fritz and Kidder 1993; Steponaitis 1986).

Mound construction and the notion of a mound-and-plaza arrangement of community planning appear to reach a nadir in the period between the end of the Hopewellian-influenced Marksville period and the beginning of the Baytown period. There is still continuity, however, in mound construction during this time. Late Marksville mounds have been documented at Thornton in the Yazoo (Greengo 1964; Phillips 1970:581–87, figs. 253, 254), Indian Bayou in the Tensas (Bitgood 1989:47), Lake St. Agnes (Toth 1979), and possibly Baptiste in the Lower Red River area (John Belmont, personal communication, 1992). At Thornton and Indian Bayou, the basic site plan is mounds arranged around a plaza, but this plan is not evident at Lake St. Agnes, and the Baptiste site data are still unpublished. Furthermore, at both Thornton and Indian Bayou the available evidence suggests that the mounds were erected to provide a level surface but did not support perishable structures. At Lake St. Agnes the mound construction at this time was associated with the interment of at least five bodies in a pit excavated into the surface of the flat-topped structure (Toth 1979:25, 28). The plan and organization of Issaquena nonmound communities are poorly understood. No site plans have been exposed and our knowledge is limited to test excavations in deeply stratified sites. There does not seem to be evidence for any obvious community plans at nonmound sites; most of these settlements appear to be relatively small (less than 0.5 hectares), and habitation features consist principally of hearths and fire pits. No houses or other construction features have been excavated at any of these communities.

In the succeeding Baytown period we begin to see a clearer picture, in part because the archaeological data are richer. At this time community patterns show a clear shift toward the common adoption of mound-and-plaza arrangements and the emergence of a new mortuary pattern focused on multiple interments in low mounds surrounding an empty plaza. The renewed emphasis on mortuary practices centered in mound sites gives Troyville a distinctive cast when compared with the neighboring Deasonville culture centered in the Yazoo Basin. Unlike Troyville occupations, Deasonville sites do not commonly support mounds. Deasonville sites are abundant, but largely consist of small shell middens on the levees of small streams or bayous (Williams and Brain 1983:364–66, figs. 11.9, 11.10). In some instances Deasonville sites appear to be arranged in circular or semicircular patterns of discrete freshwater shell midden accumulations (e.g., Phillips 1970:figs. 77, 80, 133, 149). We cannot discern at present, though, whether these sites were occupied by one group over some period of time or whether they represent seasonal or annual refuse accumulations. In the southern Yazoo Basin south of Greenville, Mississippi, Troyville-like ceramics are more frequently encountered, and sites such as Manny and Thornton may have mound constructions dating to this time (Greengo 1964; Phillips 1970). Deasonville deposits are found underlying the Lake George site (Williams and Brain 1983), which would later become one of the largest communities in the Lower Mississippi Valley. The evidence suggests, however, that the populations identified with Deasonville culture were not embarking on any ambitious or obvious community-level construction projects and that they were evidently content, at least for the moment, to continue the previous Issaquena life-style of hunting, fishing, and gathering.

Troyville peoples in the Tensas Basin undertook to construct mound communities and to use these mounds to inter their dead. Unlike some earlier Marksville burial mounds, however, the Troyville mounds were locations where virtually all members of society were interred. Grave goods are rare at Troyville sites and are mostly effigy figurines and effigy vessels. At two Troyville mortuary sites, Gold Mine and Greenhouse, the mounds were flat-topped platforms on which or in which burials were interred. At the Reno Brake site, a flat-topped platform mound was identified but could not be positively associated with the adjacent interments (Kidder 1990; Kidder and Fritz 1993). At both Gold Mine and Greenhouse, and probably at Reno Brake as well, large, deep, bathtub-shaped pits were excavated outside of the mound complex but near the mounds. Midden deposits were found on the outside of the mounds, and the plaza areas of both Greenhouse and Reno Brake were evidently fastidiously clean. The presence of bathtub-shaped pits at the perimeter of the mounds, the sterility of the plazas, and the deposition of midden on the outside of the mound groups at these sites suggest that the focus of the behaviors was to the outside of the mounds. That is, there is no evidence that the community plan of mounds around a plaza was a means of one group's excluding or metaphorically turning its back on the community. In fact, the totality of the Troyville community plan and its functions suggests an attempt to include the broader community.

Various forms of bundle and flexed burial practices have been recorded at these Troyville sites, and the commingling of bone appears to have been a common result of the various interment processes. Mortuary goods were associated with burial groups or clusters, not with specific individuals. Mounds lack approach ramps, which is in contrast to later earthen structures of the Coles Creek and Mississippi periods when mounds could only be accessed from within the plaza. In short, I suspect that mound communities were the center for community-wide mortuary activities and associated rituals. These sites were geographically separated and served regional populations. The size and structural variability of these mortuary centers probably reflect the nature, density, and organization of local communities and regional historical circumstances. Most mortuary areas were covered over, frequently by later mound stages, and often these Baytown period burial areas were incorporated into later Coles Creek mound features, suggesting a strong degree of continuity.

Not all Troyville sites were burial localities. Small hamlets or dwellings were widely distributed and may reflect seasonal or short-term occupations. Although many sites contain Troyville components (Belmont 1985; Gibson 1984), few have been adequately investigated and, with the exception of Powell Canal, none have been excavated. The few apparently single-component Baytown period sites that have been identified are small and show little evidence of structural variability. At Powell Canal the distribution of features does not appear to be patterned (House 1982:figs. 13, 15, 1990), and although there is a mound, it may not date to the Baytown period. Given their small size, we suspect that these components represent either a seasonal pattern of movement or a highly dispersed settlement organization consisting of single (or possibly extended) family units.

The clearest evidence for cultural change occurs at the end of the Troyville sequence at the point at which the Baytown period gives way to Coles Creek. Unlike the situation at earlier sites, such as Gold Mine and Greenhouse, where mounds were constructed to cover burials, at Mount Nebo and Lake George platform mounds were constructed first and burials were later deposited in them. Burial patterns also change at this time. For example, at Lake George, one interment, Burial 49, an extended, prone adult male, was accompanied by the bodies of thirteen infants (Williams and Brain 1983:figs. 3.15, 3.26, table 3.1). At the Mount Nebo site, Individual 1 from Burial 39 is of particular interest (Giardino 1977:48–49, 1984:120). Chronologically, this burial was the earliest interment at the site (Giardino 1977:49), and it was centrally located within the Stage F platform (Giardino 1984:120). A male, between 35 and 45 years old, was interred on his back with "a deer jaw placed at his feet [and] deer antlers were located near his skull"; an isolated human cranium was found resting as if it had been placed on his abdomen (Giardino 1984:120). He was interred with two adult females on either side and three children. One of the females (Individual 4) had a quartzite projectile point embedded in her right tibia (Giardino 1977:49–50). These inclusions and the special treatment might be taken to indicate a relatively high status, and the method of interment appears to differ from that of earlier Troyville burials.

These later mortuary contexts do not reflect the same level of community-wide participation seen at earlier Troyville sites. Bathtub-shaped pits are absent, as are effigy vessels or figurines, and burial offerings are rare. Extended interments of individual adults (usually male) with associated multiple individuals (often children or women) give a different cast to the burial activities. For example, Barker (1993) observes that of the 180 burials reported from Mound C at Lake George, seventy-nine were infants (Egnatz 1983:421; Williams and Brain 1983:table 3.1), an example of either very high infant mortality or phenomenal population growth or, possibly, differential representation in the existing burial population. If we exclude infants, the remaining burials "fall neatly along the mortuary demographic profile we would expect for a small population (ca. 30 individuals or a single lineage) exhibiting moderate intrinsic growth (ca. 0.25%) over a 100-year span" (Barker 1993:7–8). Although the Lake George burials that could be reliably aged and sexed do not demonstrate any statistical bias toward mound burial for one sex or the other (Egnatz 1983:423), adult males are slightly more common (Egnatz 1983:table A.2), a pattern consistent with data from late prehistoric southeastern mound communities, such as Chucalissa and Etowah (Barker 1993:8; Powell 1992:89, table 5.2). Barker (1993:8) concludes that these burial data "are consistent with the interment of all individuals from a select portion of society, with the inclusion of additional infants from the remaining sectors of the population that did not qualify for mound inhumation." The mortuary sample from Mount Nebo, however, does not reflect a similar pattern. Here, infants are underrepresented and juveniles appear more frequently than expected, although the sample is smaller and the preservation considerably poorer than at Lake George (Giardino 1977).

The use of preexisting Baytown period mortuary facilities for later burial activities, accompanied by limited evidence of social differentiation among the burials, leads us to believe that high-ranking individuals or lineages may have occupied sacred places in order to emphasize or reinforce their status. We infer from these data that mounds not only were physical symbols of elevated status, but also served to legitimize power by symbolically connecting rulers with their ancestors (Knight 1986:678–81; Steponaitis 1986:385–86). These large mounds ultimately served as the foundations for a hierarchically organized settlement pattern involving competing mound centers ruled by emerging political and social elites (Kidder 1992a; Nassaney 1992; Steponaitis 1986:386; Williams and Brain 1983:405–8).

The shift from community-oriented to more individually focused burials is but one of many transformations occurring during the Coles Creek period in the Lower Mississippi Valley. One of the most notable shifts is the trend toward more and larger mounds and toward greater restriction of access to the mounds. Unlike Troyville burial mounds, Coles Creek and later Mississippi period earthen constructions give the appearance of introversion and isolation from the wider community. Mounds may only be approached from within the plaza, and, through time, access to the central plaza areas is physically and architecturally barricaded. The architectural features are more imposing as monuments on the landscape but they are less accessible and open to the community. Perhaps one of the most significant trends in the "Mississippianization" of the Lower Mississippi Valley is the restriction placed on the participation in what had formerly been communal ceremonies, rituals, and practices.

Chronologically, the pattern begins quite early in the prehistoric sequence. At both Mount Nebo and at Lake George in Mound C, the shift in burial practices occurs at roughly A.D. 700. In the Tensas Basin, the earliest flat-topped mound groups were constructed in the Sundown phase at about A.D. 750–800. At the Sundown site in Tensas Parish, Louisiana, three mounds arranged around a central plaza appear to have been built at this time. The two largest mounds at this site appear to have had an access ramp facing into the plaza. These early mound communities typically supported one large, flat-topped structure and one or more lower, probably flat-topped, mounds arranged to form a rectangular or triangular plaza (Williams and Brain 1983:fig. 12.12). Too few of these sites have been adequately investigated to allow us to speak confidently about the organizational processes underpinning these early mound communities. None of the mounds at sites of this period can be said to support perishable structures, but, on the other hand, the presence of buildings on the summits of these mounds cannot be positively ruled out. Furthermore, at many mound communities there is considerable evidence that the mound sites supported at least some portion of the population above and beyond those living on the mounds. Midden deposits are frequently encountered beyond the mound flanks and often ring the mounds themselves (Steponaitis 1986).

The emerging picture suggests that the mounds themselves were increasingly becoming the focus of interest within the community. Their size and complexity seem to increase, and their function changes from encompassing public ritual to accommodating more restricted segments of society.

The segregation of the whole society is not evident, however, since it appears that many people were living around the mounds and access to the mounds and the plazas was relatively open, at least at first. Beyond the mound communities, we assume that the bulk of the population was scattered across the landscape and that their subsistence base was nonagricultural, perhaps supplemented by horticulture and even the tentative exploitation of maize.

At the Osceola site in Tensas Parish, for example, the site history demonstrates a pattern of increasing spatial exclusion and restriction of access to the interior plaza spaces. The earliest occupations date to the late Marksville period, and mound construction began during or immediately after the Mount Nebo phase (Kidder 1990; Kidder and Fritz 1993). The initial pattern of mound construction focused on Mounds A and B, which were located at the northern end of the site and were closely spaced. By the later Sundown phase Mound C was added to form an elongated plaza with its axis parallel to the relict channel on which the site was constructed. Mound F was added to the eastern edge of this mound cluster sometime in the Saranac or Balmoral phase. Finally, Mound E was constructed during the Balmoral phase. The addition of this last mound formed a bounded plaza that was also complemented by a low earthen midden mound identified as Mound D. The plaza created at this time (ca. A.D. 1000) had a new axis of orientation. No longer was the plaza confined to the edge of the natural landscape, but it was shifted roughly 90 degrees so that access from the south (the only route available along the natural levee of the relict channel on which the site was situated) was no longer open. The bulk of vertical accretion was also accomplished during the later Saranac and Balmoral phases, so that Mound A appears to have had at least 3 to 4 meters of construction fill added to it, and Mound E was built in a single or brief series of efforts.

At the Lake George site, a similar process seems to have been taking place during the same interval. Mound C, which had been the locus of earlier Bayland and early Coles Creek construction activities, was added to and expanded both vertically and horizontally (Williams and Brain 1983). Excavations at the site suggest, but were unable to prove conclusively, that mound construction was initiated near or beneath Mound A at this time, indicating the formation of a plaza consisting of two mounds at opposite ends of the open space (see Williams and Brain 1983:fig. 2.1). Evidence also indicates that Mounds E, F, and F′ were constructed or added to at this time, forming the northern boundary of a well-defined plaza (Williams and Brain 1983:334–35, figs. 10.3, 10.4). No excavations were undertaken in Mound B at Lake George, but I suspect that this structure was begun during the later Coles Creek period and completed a wholly enclosed plaza.

The Greenhouse site in Avoyelles Parish, Louisiana, duplicates the pattern seen at Osceola and Lake George (Belmont 1967; Ford 1951). During the Baytown period, a midden ring was complemented by several low rises. A cluster of bathtub-shaped pits was found along the southern edge of the midden ring. During the early to middle Coles Creek period two mounds were erected at opposite ends of a plaza (Belmont 1967:29). Excavations through the plaza area indicate that it was largely sterile (Ford 1951:29–32). The plaza was bounded at its northern end by a third mound added during the later Coles Creek period. During the site occupation midden deposits along the southern edge of the site accumulated to form notable rises, labeled mounds. These rises capped house floors and burial areas. A bounded plaza surrounded by mounds or by cultural features (houses, cemeteries) was in place at or before the beginning of the Mississippi period (Belmont 1967:28–29).

By about A.D. 900–1000, the pattern becomes clearer. Mound communities are increasingly bounded and differentiated from surrounding contemporary populations. During this time we see the emergence of peoples living on the mounds themselves, and there is decreasing evidence that populations are living in the immediate vicinity of the mounds. Mound groups continue to expand in size and in their restriction of access. At sites such as Lake George, Greenhouse, and Osceola mounds effectively enclose the entire plaza, thus symbolically shutting out access. At these larger mound communities, the largest mounds tend to be opposite one another, with flanking structures being lower in height and less complex in their architectural features.

We cannot confidently speak of a regional or valley-wide pattern that emerges at this time. Mound size, the numbers of earthen structures, their individual arrangement, and plaza dimensions are variable. Furthermore, mound communities are common, and rather than thinking of each mound site as supporting a set number of earthworks and a mound-and-plaza arrangement, it is perhaps more accurate to characterize the situation as variable and flexible. There are, no doubt, far more single mound than multimound communities in the Lower Mississippi Valley, and it should be emphasized that our data base is heavily biased toward the larger mound communities.

The social and political situation at around A.D. 1000 suggests some interesting and important trends. The number of multimound communities is relatively high, and there does not seem to be strong evidence that any particular mound community achieved absolute preeminence in its particular region. There are clearly different sizes of mound communities, and some sites are absolutely larger than others in numbers of mounds and mound volume. But, as noted by Barker (1988), some communities were primus inter pares. For example, the Winterville site seems to be the largest community in its immediate region at this time, but it is not especially larger than its surrounding contemporaries (Brain 1989). Similarly, Lake George is bigger, but not much bigger than, say, Aden or Crippen Point or other mound groups in the southern Yazoo Basin (Phillips 1970; Williams and Brain 1983). The Osceola and Mott sites appear to be the largest contemporary mound communities in the Tensas Basin, but they do not dominate the physical (and hypothetically then) the political landscape (Kidder 1992a).

The only significant exception is the Toltec site in the Arkansas River Valley, which between A.D. 800 and 1000 rose to be the largest mound community in the Lower Mississippi Valley and along the tributaries of the Mississippi; clearly it was the dominant mound site in the Arkansas River lowlands (Nassaney 1991, 1992, 1994, 1996; Rolingson 1982, 1990). Here we seem to have a good example of a community that, by its size and presumably authority, eclipsed its nearest neighbors (or competitors) in virtually every measure of power, wealth, and status (Nassaney 1991). Mound construction began at Toltec by at least A.D. 750; the earliest mounds were evidently flat-topped platforms and were not surmounted by perishable structures. At Mound S, dated to about A.D. 700–800, mound flank deposits of deer bones that were buried soon after butchering have been used to suggest that this was the locus of some sort of ceremonial feasting event or events (Rolingson 1992). By about A.D. 800–900 Toltec supported at least nineteen mounds, arranged in a double plaza and surrounded by a ditch. The largest mound at the site (Mound A) is 15 meters tall, but it is not clear whether it supported any structure on its summit. Nassaney (1991, 1992, 1994) argues that Toltec was the center for a widespread trade network extending up and down the Arkansas River and its relict tributaries. On the basis of an analysis of artifacts made from igneous rocks, Rolingson and Howard (1997:42) challenge this interpretation and suggest that "people living at the Toltec Mounds site neither controlled access to resources nor processed tools at Toltec that were then distributed to the outlying sites." Ceramic data from Toltec reveal that this site shared a considerable number of traits with Coles Creek groups to the south and east, but that Toltec was a distinct cultural entity (Rolingson 1982). Beyond the Toltec site there were only a couple of mound centers, with only one supporting more than one mound (Nassaney 1991, 1994, 1996). The rest of the Plum Bayou culture peoples in the Arkansas River lowlands lived in small, single-family, or perhaps extended-family, hamlets or house sites (Nassaney 1991; Nassaney and Hoffman 1992). Unlike contemporary communities in the Lower Mississippi Valley proper, Plum Bayou peoples undertook a more intensive subsistence practice, involving the cultivation of corn and the use of domesticated native American plants, such as chenopod and amaranth (Fritz 1990; Fritz and Kidder 1993; Nassaney 1994).

After A.D. 1000, there are a number of fundamental changes in the societies living in and around the Lower Mississippi Valley. To the west, in the Arkansas River lowlands, the Plum Bayou culture inexplicably collapses and mound construction ceases at the Toltec site by about A.D. 1100 (Nassaney 1994:49–50). The Arkansas River lowlands do not seem to be reoccupied by any groups (or at least by archaeologically visible groups) until the late Mississippi period (Nassaney 1991, 1994; Rolingson 1990). The collapse of the Plum Bayou culture had a number of ramifications in the western peripheries of the Lower Valley (Kidder 1994a; Nassaney 1994), but otherwise does not seem to have dramatically affected peoples in the river's main corridor. In the Lower Mississippi Valley proper, we see an acceleration of the trends of increasing size and complexity of mound groups, and by about A.D. 1200 the area witnesses a marked change in the number of mound communities, with some centers clearly emerging as dominant in their respective regions. Marked shifts in community patterns and in mound function accompany these larger trends, and there is an overall shift in regional economies as new subsistence practices are introduced and as economic and political power continues to be increasingly centralized. Interestingly, the populations living in the Yazoo and Tensas basins begin to differ in their behaviors, such that their basic cultural trajectories become markedly different through time.

Although the changes at and through the Mississippi period in the Lower Mississippi Valley are considerable, most cultural changes are incremental and gradual rather than sudden and abrupt. The basic "Mississippian" mound pattern was established in the region at least several hundred years before the arbitrary A.D. 1000 divide between Late Woodland and Mississippian. All of the structural elements that comprise the core of the later Mississippi period manifestations of mound and town community patterning are evident in the Coles Creek period. These include the basic architectural configuration of the mound-plaza arrangements; the use of perishable structures atop flat mound summits; the construction of earthen ramps facing into the plaza; the erection of structures adjacent to large axially situated mounds, sometimes on earthen platforms; and the development of midden deposits flanking plazas that were otherwise kept remarkably clean. Future developments in the next four and a half centuries before European contact would elaborate on these themes, but alter them very little.

Plaquemine differs from Coles Creek in more than ceramics. Settlement patterns change throughout the region. The most notable facet of Mississippi period settlement in the Lower Mississippi Valley is the rapid increase in mound building efforts at a limited number of sites in the Yazoo Basin and Natchez Bluffs regions (Brain 1978). Brain attributes many of the changes in the early part of the Mississippi period to an influx of Mississippian cultural traits and culture bearers in the period around A.D. 1000–1200 (Brain 1989). The initial process is said to be a slow influx of traits, followed by "limited demographic encroachment" (Brain 1989:116). Brain (1989:117) argues that around A.D. 1200 there was a period of "strong, organized contact from the Cahokia climax of the Stirling and/or Moorehead phases which intruded deeply into the Coles Creek world." This contact is said to have had "considerable influence" (Brain 1989:117) and was the "catalyst for, if not the source of" many of the Mississippian elements in the Lower Mississippi Valley, including, but not limited to, new developments in "settlement patterns, site plans, and artifact inventories" (1989:132). Brain's argument that the "hybrid Plaquemine culture was a veritable explosion beyond the previously set [Coles Creek] limits" (1989:132, see also table 11) is questionable on a number of grounds. Although there was a broad-based transformation at some sites in the Yazoo Basin, notably Winterville and Lake George, it may not have been as rapid as suggested (see Brain 1978, 1989; Williams and Brain 1983). In the Tensas Basin the data indicate a far more gradual transformation in the various traits indicated as significant in Brain's hypothesis (Brain 1989:table 11; Hally 1972; Kidder 1993). The traits characteristic of "Mississippianization" never penetrated into the Red River Valley area or farther south toward the coast, yet by all measures Plaquemine culture developed in these regions (Kidder 1994b; Quimby 1951, 1957; Weinstein 1987). These conflicting interpretations of the extent of Mississippian influence and the nature of the Mississippian/Plaquemine transition simply heighten the need for awareness that these behavioral changes are locally conditioned and are not simple, linear, patterned evolutionary events.

During the early Mississippi period there appears to be a process of political centralization and consolidation, at least as reflected in the mound communities. Two seemingly opposite patterns can be detected in the settlement record. On the one hand, large mound sites become larger, albeit fewer in number, and, on the other hand, nonmound settlements seem to become smaller, but more numerous (Brain 1978; Williams and Brain 1983). This pattern is evident in the Yazoo, Tensas, and Natchez Bluffs regions, although to different degrees. Clear evidence of community ranking emerges at this time, and, on the basis of the quantity and size of mounds, at least two, and possibly three, tiers of mound communities can be recognized (Belmont 1985; Brain 1978). These data are generally interpreted to reflect the emergence of strongly ranked, centralized chiefdom-level polities, with subchiefs and/or lesser nobles occupying smaller mound centers and with agricultural hamlets or communities distributed across the landscape.

In the Tensas Basin the number of mound communities with more than one large mound decreases in comparison with that in earlier periods (Kidder 1992b). Three exceptionally large mound centers, Raffman, Routh, and Fitzhugh, emerge to dominate the political landscape (Hally 1972). These sites consist of multiple mounds arranged around a central plaza, which is dominated at one end by the largest mound. The site plans of these three mound groups are remarkably similar (Hally 1972; unpublished data on Raffman from Harvard Lower Mississippi Survey) (Figure 6.3). The next largest possible Tensas Basin contemporary is the Somerset site in Tensas Parish, which consisted of possibly up to four mounds but today only supports one large flat-topped earthen structure (Hally 1972). Most other contemporary mound sites consist of one low mound and associated habitation debris. These sites all appear to have been initially occupied by Coles Creek peoples and subsequently expanded.

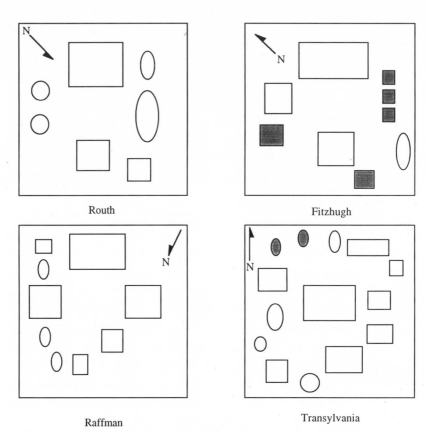

Figure 6.3. Schematic plans of the four major Mississippi period sites in the Tensas Basin. The size of the rectangle is a general indication of the size of the mound it represents. Mounds without definite rectangular shape are shown as ovals; however, this shape may not represent the original mound configuration. *Shaded symbols* represent mounds reported in the literature but that could not be verified at the time of survey. Data for the Routh, Fitzhugh, and Transylvania sites are taken from Hally (1972). The Raffman map is based on a sketch map of the site made by John Belmont and Stephen Williams in 1981.

While the number of large mound communities appears to decrease, small house sites or hamlets emerge as the predominant nonmound Mississippian settlement type. The only excavated site of this kind is the Emerson site in Tensas Parish, which provides us with a glimpse of Mississippi period community life (Fritz, Smith, and Kidder 1992; Kidder, Fritz, and Smith 1993). At Emerson two small (ca. 10- to 15-meter diameter) midden patches are hypothesized to represent two distinct houses, and the midden debris from the two appears to be essentially contemporary (Kidder, Fritz, and Smith 1993). Floral remains from the Emerson site, which is radiocarbon dated to the fifteenth century, demonstrate a relatively dramatic increase in the quantity of maize relative to the volume of soil in flotation samples (Kidder, Fritz, and Smith 1993). Wild plant foods were still exploited at this site, however, indicating that while maize cultivation was of considerable importance it had not completely supplanted the existing native food economy. Emerson represents a small, dispersed farming community, whose occupants grew corn and collected wild plants and animal foods. Emerson appears to have been occupied year-round, but we cannot be certain from the small faunal sample available. Other Mississippi period occupations in the Tensas Basin are very small, often consisting of midden patches of roughly 20 to 30 meters in diameter. Rarely are larger midden scatters noted, although in some instances these later occupations cannot be adequately separated from earlier components. In the Yazoo Basin the settlement data are inconclusive because so few small sites have been investigated. However, as noted by Williams and Brain (1983:fig. 11.20), the number of sites, many of which do not bear mounds, is quite high, suggesting an evenly distributed population across the landscape.

In the Yazoo Basin the process of mound site nucleation is even more dramatic than in the Tensas. The two biggest sites, Winterville and Lake George, continued to grow during the late prehistoric period (Brain 1989; Williams and Brain 1983). Both sites were expanded vertically as well as horizontally. At Lake George the final mound community was surrounded by a ditch and palisade. Lake George also demonstrates a new twist in community planning. There the mound-and-plaza arrangement was expanded in mirror fashion around the main mound. The plan of the community now encompassed two plazas surrounded by mounds. Brain argues that this pattern is also manifest at the Winterville site, although there the symmetry of the double plaza group is not quite so evident (Brain 1978, 1989). The mound arrangement at the Transylvania site can also be interpreted as representing a double plaza plan (Hally 1972:fig. 4), although there too the layout of the mounds is not completely symmetrical around the central mound (Figure 6.3). Examination of the site plan for the Toltec mound group also suggests a double plaza arrangement, although this pattern is undoubtedly earlier (Rolingson 1990). At both Lake George and Winterville, it is clear that the initial site plan consisted of a single plaza and that this unique site form emerges only in the middle part of the Mississippi period.

Although these major sites clearly dominate the landscape, there are a number of large mound groups in the Yazoo that, although not of the size of Lake George or Winterville, are still not inconsiderable. Sites such as Arcola, Jaketown, Mayersville, Grace, Leland, Magee, and Haynes Bluff were all built or added onto during the Mississippi period (Phillips 1970). These communities support one or two large mounds arranged around a plaza. Most commonly the plan includes three prominent mounds forming a triangular plaza. Frequently smaller mounds bound the plaza or lie outside of the axis of the plaza. Across the river in southeastern Arkansas and northeastern Louisiana are contemporary large sites which, although quite large, still rank below the largest mound centers. The Transylvania and Lakeport mounds, for example, supported important late Mississippi period occupations dominated by shell-tempered ceramics (Hally 1972; Rolingson 1971). Farther south in the Natchez Bluffs region, there is a pattern of dominance by one or two major centers through time (Brain 1978). The Anna site appears to represent the largest community during the early part of the Mississippi period, while the locus of occupation shifted to the interior during the later part of the period and was centered on the Emerald mound site (Brown and Brain 1983).

In virtually every regard, the Mississippian mound site plan is highly exclusionary. Historically, Lower Mississippi Valley mound groups had supported one or more major mounds. The trend through time was to add subsidiary mounds along the boundaries of the plaza, effectively increasing the degree of separation between the plaza and the outside world. Mound construction appears to emphasize access only through the plaza, with ramps facing this space and the slope of mounds becoming more pronounced on the outside of the plaza group. Few sites in the Lower Mississippi Valley appear to have supported deliberate structures for the exclusion of peoples from the mound group. Only at the Lake George site do we see the erection of a moat and palisade to bound the site. At Toltec, possibly Winterville, and even perhaps Routh and Fitzhugh, there may have been ditches and/or low walls surrounding parts of the site. While these features may have served to keep people out, they could also have functioned to help drain the sites as well (Kidder and Saucier 1991). Thus it is not possible to assign a single function to the many features that could have served to inhibit access into mound groups.

Although our survey data are patchy, it seems that Mississippi period house sites and hamlets were clustered into what could be broadly termed dispersed communities—that is, small settlements separated from other contemporary groups by as yet unknown amounts of unoccupied space. It is possible that these communities occupied space bounded by certain geographic features. For example, the historic Taensa "community" appears to have been largely confined to the banks and immediate areas around a single oxbow lake (Jones and Kidder 1994; Swanton 1911). Presumably, these "communities" were centered around a small, usually single-mound, ceremonial center, which was in turn integrated into the larger polity by some relation to the occupants of the major mound sites. The relationship between the very largest communities and those of lesser size is unknown, but we can infer that the sociopolitical system was strongly ranked. Such a model is in keeping with ethnographically documented Mississippian chiefdoms elsewhere in the Southeast, but it is still not adequately proven in the Lower Mississippi Valley.

It is worth noting that the nature of Mississippi period communities seems to change as one moves south in the Lower Mississippi Valley. In the northern Yazoo Basin, for example, Mississippi period communities are frequently large and densely occupied and manifest numerous square to rectangular houses. A good example of this pattern is seen at the Wilsford site in Cohoma County, Mississippi (Connaway 1984). Similar examples have been found, especially in the Clarksdale area (Connaway 1984; Phillips, Ford, and Griffin 1951; Starr 1984, 1991). Farther south, however, especially south of the Greenville-Greenwood line, Mississippi period sites appear to be structurally different. Nucleation of communities is less evident, the number of houses appears to decrease (on the basis of surface densities of daub), and the architecture appears to differ in a number of subtle regards (Brown 1985b).

At some point in the later part of the Mississippi period, possibly after the initial European contacts in the early 1540s, the settlement system changed. The historic documents of the post–de Soto European explorers indicate a significantly different settlement system from that noted archaeologically (Brain 1988). In the Yazoo Basin, the historically known native

Americans appear to have migrated toward the lower reaches of the Yazoo River. The Haynes Bluff site witnessed protohistoric or early historic period construction episodes, and the site is likely to have been the principal village of the Yazoo and Koroa (Brain 1988). The Natchez settlement pattern was one of dispersed settlements with one central mound center that served as the home of the chief and his retinue (Brown 1985a; Neitzel 1965, 1983). The Taensa, one group of evident inheritors of the Mississippi period legacy, were concentrated around Lake St. Joseph in the Tensas Basin (Swanton 1911; Williams 1967). The Taensa provide an interesting model for prehistoric settlement, even though this settlement differed somewhat from that of the late prehistoric period.

The early explorers noted in several instances (see Swanton 1911) that the Taensa were living in a very dispersed settlement on an oxbow lake off of the Mississippi River. They had between eight and nine "villages" and a central ceremonial and civic precinct. This central place was evidently the residence of the chief and his immediate retinue, as well as the location of the Taensa temple. In addition, local "nobility" or leaders gathered there for consultation with the chief and to celebrate various festivals. Both the temple and the chief's residence were demarcated from the other communities by a palisade.

Although none of the explorers noted the use of mounds for the temple or chief's house, the pattern observed seems to mirror that seen in the archaeological record, albeit in a spatially reduced fashion. Communities were widely dispersed along the lakeshore, while civic and ceremonial activities were concentrated in one locality. Settlement survey in the Lake St. Joseph area has revealed a number of very small late prehistoric through early historic sites along the banks of the lake (Jones and Kidder 1994; Williams 1967). No central nonmounded community has been identified. The Routh site, a large Mississippi period mound group, is situated within 500 meters of Lake St. Joseph and may be the locus of the Taensa chief's residence. The Taensa pattern thus can be seen as an analogy for Mississippi period settlements and possibly social organization.

Conclusions

If we examine the patterns and variations evident in the development of Mississippian communities, we can identify several broad trends. Mound centers tend to grow larger, both in the number of mounds present and in their vertical extent. Looking just at this type of community, it appears that centralization was a predominant trend. Fewer, but larger, mound centers come to dominate the landscape. However, there is a counter emphasis in the organization and spatial distribution of nonmound communities. Dispersion seems to be the rule at this level of society. Historically, these patterns move in opposite directions. As mound site nucleation increases, nonmound occupations become more dispersed. Furthermore, mound communities do not appear to be the locus of supporting villages. Williams and Brain, for example, argue that beginning as early as the Coles Creek period we see the development of what amount to "vacant" centers "in the sense that they [the mound sites] were not primarily residential units, although they were occupied by a small group who were presumably religious caretakers and/or privileged personae" (Williams and Brain 1983:407). The articulation of these two systems of settlement is unclear. We presume, largely on the basis of ethnohistorical data, that the privileged elite living in the mound centers "ruled" the landscape and commanded the allegiance and presumably the resources of the dispersed rural settlements.

The historical process appears to have had a centripetal effect—power and authority became increasingly concentrated into fewer and increasingly larger communities. The settlement plans of these now dominant mound groups suggest a deliberate process whereby the outside world was excluded and/or limited in its participation in events occurring within the mounded community. Mound construction, site layout, and even the physical placement of sites relative to the topography suggest that there was a growing gulf between those on the inside and those on the outside. Defense and warfare do not appear to have been contributing factors in the organization of the Mississippian community in the Lower Mississippi Valley. Only at the Lake George site is there any evidence of a palisade and moat. No other feature suggestive of defense has been excavated at any community in the region. This pattern of increasing social differentiation marks perhaps one of the most fundamental shifts in southeastern native American social organization through time. Woodland societies seem to have been truly communally oriented. In some, if not many, cases, community participation in ritual may have been mediated by specific individuals or groups of individuals, but the emphasis seems to be decidedly outward and inclusive. The Mississippianization of the Southeast is in some ways less a technological than a sociological phenomenon. If we use mound center organization as a guide it appears that the notion of inclusiveness was discarded, probably at or around A.D. 800–1000; thereafter Mississippian polities were exclusive, limiting, and highly controlling. Access to space, authority, power, and, by extension, presumably knowledge was denied to those outside of the plaza. The inclusive community was displaced by the exclusive elite.

In the Lower Mississippi Valley it is possible to place these developments in a nearly thousand-year-long historical perspective. The development of Mississippian communities was an evolutionary event with very deep historical precedents. Changes through time were marked less by the actual form of the community plan than by the way this form functioned within the community. Mound-and-plaza groups date back to the Archaic and continue up to the protohistoric. A crucial transformation began about A.D. 800–1000, when, in an almost literal fashion, the occupants of these mound centers turned their backs on the larger populace. Integration and inclusion were replaced by segregation and exclusion. The mounds themselves served as tools by which this change was effected. Once the locus of burials and rituals for the larger group, the mounds appear to be appropriated by a small segment of society that, by constructing its edifices atop these earthen platforms, laid claim to authority and social prerogative. The literal and spiritual power of these elites was enforced and emphasized by the exclusion of persons from the once communal spaces. Physical elevation not only of ritual activities but also of elite residences reinforced the status of the mound occupants. Mississippi period mound centers in the Lower Mississippi Valley demonstrate patterns of continuity and change evident throughout the Southeast. Future research will have to explore how these patterns came about and, more fundamentally, why.

7

Mississippian Towns in Kentucky

Charles Stout and R. Barry Lewis

Much has been written about the spatial patterning of Mississippian towns and the chiefdoms that built them. Far less is known about other architectural aspects of these communities. Our purpose is to describe elements of a design grammar of Mississippian towns in Kentucky, to illustrate these observations with examples, and to interpret their cultural implications. We acknowledge a considerable debt to such researchers as Knight (1981, 1985, 1990b) and Hudson (1984), who have explored the interdependent fit of Mississippian symbols and myths across the Southeast. Much of what we have to say about Kentucky Mississippian sites is stimulated by their work.

Throughout this chapter, the term *town* refers to Mississippian communities with associated plazas. This usage includes all sites with mounds as well as many sites that lack mounds and that would usually be called some kind of village. We have no examples of Kentucky Mississippian communities with mounds but no plazas. Our broad definition of the Mississippian town reflects our working hypothesis that the plaza was a key element in the spatial layout or design of such communities. We develop this point in detail in the first section, in which we examine possible cosmological aspects of Kentucky Mississippian town planning. The second and final section looks at the major functional aspects of town design.

Towns as Mirrors of the Mississippian Universe
Town Planning
The layout of towns and cities in many parts of the world reflects the deliberate integration of cosmological principles and myths with functional

considerations (e.g., Fritz 1986; Fritz and Michell 1991; Lawrence and Low 1990; Vatsyayan 1991; Wheatley 1971). Such relationships also appear to exist in the Mississippian case. They are apparent in the redundant design of mound-and-plaza complexes of towns and in the well-documented importance of ancestor shrines as a vehicle for religious, social, and political power. These patterns suggest that, at minimum, the layout and essential features of the central precinct of Mississippian towns were prescribed by principles that transcended linguistic and regional boundaries and restricted the socially meaningful architectural choices.

Although Mississippian town layout was clearly deliberate, why particular town plans were adopted is still problematic, as is the question of why a deliberate rather than an ad hoc community layout was desirable. Rapoport (1977, 1982) notes that each society chooses, via its own history, a small but contextually meaningful set of architectural styles from the infinite variety that exists. Architectural choices such as these are analogous to linguistic, epigraphic, and iconographic choices societies make in developing language, text, and symbolism (Colloredo-Mansfield 1994; cf. Leach 1976). Viewed in this light, Mississippian groups shared an architectural grammar that conveyed, through the design of their central public precincts, their basic cultural affinity to each other.

The spatially prescribed part of a Mississippian town plan was the mound-and-plaza complex, not the entire town. The distribution of houses and other functional areas of the community around these complexes owed more to the individual characteristics of the location and the size of the population than to cultural constraints on town boundaries. For example, the Turk and Wickliffe town sites (Figure 7.1), each of which was constructed on a ridge or point of land that projected outward from the Mississippi Valley bluffs, covered the inhabitable space of their respective ridges out to the bluff edge. Likewise, the Adams site blankets an entire isolated terrace remnant in the Bayou de Chien bottom of Fulton County. Lowland sites, such as Jonathan Creek, Sassafras Ridge, and Twin Mounds (Figure 7.1), had the potential of expanding in any direction, yet apparently chose to cordon or otherwise define regular town boundaries. Canton (Stout and Lewis 1995; Stout, Walz, and Burks 1996) and McLeod Bluff, also known as O'Byam's Fort (Thomas 1894:280–82), although situated on bluff edges, were delimited, like the lowland sites, with walls.

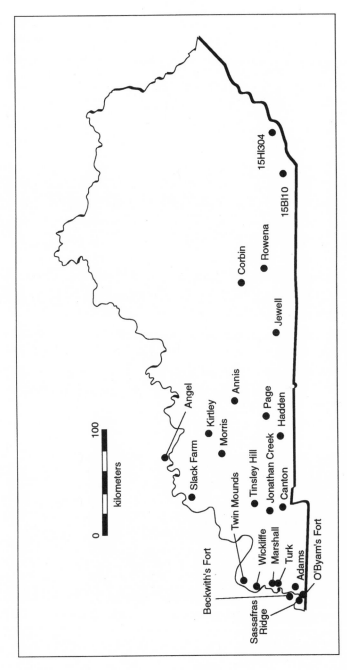

Figure 7.1. Kentucky towns and other Mississippian sites.

Less is known about the planning that went into the residential parts of towns. Reconstructed site plans suggest that, for the most part, village areas were not merely a jumble of houses, gardens, and outbuildings that followed no order of social rank or prestige. At Jonathan Creek (Webb 1952), for example, while the house location pattern appears neither strict nor regular, houses were generally built in a semicircular pattern around an open area, with some houses in small clusters that may have held functional or social meaning. Spaces between houses varied from a couple of meters to more than the width of a house, but provided ample pedestrian access to any other part of the site. A more strictly ordered example of a village plan comes from the Snodgrass site (Price and Griffin 1979) in southeastern Missouri, where houses were built in rows with straight and regular passageways between them (Figure 7.2). Drawings or narrative descriptions of comparable regular town plans exist for historic native American towns elsewhere in the Southeast (e.g., de Bry 1966).

At both the geometrically designed Snodgrass and the more loosely structured Jonathan Creek sites, the patterns of space between buildings clearly provide access to the public area for anyone who wished it, from virtually any portion of the site. There were lanes, but no dedicated streetlike spaces that can be recognized archaeologically. Lanes through the residential areas were clearly planned, but for what—to maximize traffic flow efficiency, to meet the demands of ritual and myth, or to reflect cosmology? The motivation, it seems, may have been a little bit of all of these, but functional considerations alone are sufficient to account for most of the documented patterning. Village lanes appear to have begun with the first plazas, and we tend to view them as one consequence of the development of the Mississippian plaza and not as a deliberate product of true town planning independent of the plaza complex.

In the space between the palisade that often defined the perimeter of a village and the mound-and-plaza complex that was its core, the key feature of a Mississippian town is its fairly loose organization and organic growth. Although households were not scattered helter-skelter, their distribution patterns suggest that each family enjoyed considerable autonomy in deciding where its structures would be placed with respect to existing structures and how these structures would be oriented. House size, however, was subject to tighter constraints, whether by architectural tradition or family wealth or rank. The general impression, however, is of a community in which only

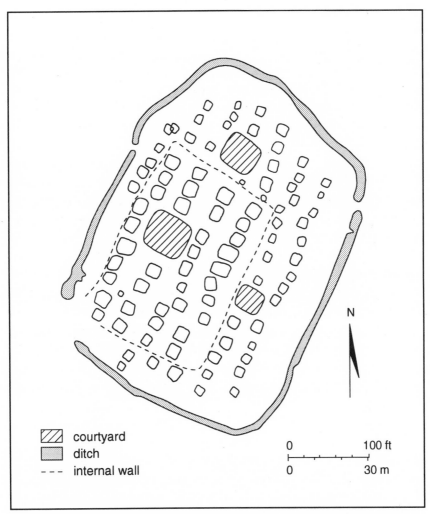

Figure 7.2. The Snodgrass site in southeastern Missouri (adapted from Price and Griffin 1979).

certain key elements, dominated by the plaza, were controlled by the governing body or bodies of the town.

Platform Mounds

Platform mounds are the most visible physical evidence of most Mississippian towns. Their visibility is the key to their existence. Mississippian peoples, like societies around the world, were well aware of the powerful psychological and visual impacts of height relative to the observer, whether in the form of a towering headdress, a platform mound, or a temple roof line. This aspect of Mississippian mounds continues to be exploited. For example, Monks Mound in southwestern Illinois takes its name from the Trappist monastery that once existed there. In St. Louis, several old homes, churches, and public buildings stand atop Mississippian mounds. At the Canton site in Kentucky, a church is built into one of the platform mounds overlooking the Cumberland River bluff edge (Stout and Lewis 1995; Stout, Walz, and Burks 1996).

As elsewhere in the Southeast, platform mounds in Kentucky were constructed in stages by adding new mantles of fill (e.g., Dorwin 1970; Duffield 1967; Edging 1986:16; Edging and Stout 1986:109–10; Fryman 1968; Weinland 1980; Young 1962). The most well-documented Kentucky example is at the Annis site (Figure 7.3) in the Big Bend area of Butler County (Young 1962). The platform mound and most of the town of which it was a part were excavated in the late 1930s by Works Progress Administration crews under the supervision of Ralph Brown and James Greenacre. At the time of the WPA project, the mound, which was being eroded by the Green River, measured roughly 30 meters long, 25 meters wide, and about 4 meters high (Young 1962:6–7). North of the mound was a narrow plaza flanked by at least twelve structures; beyond the buildings were the remains of two stockades.

The first mound construction phase at Annis was capped by a large single-set post structure that had been remodeled and repaired extensively (Young 1962:98–106). This structure contained many hearths, burned areas, and ash pits and was associated with a huge refuse deposit on the mound surface. Each subsequent construction phase added a substructure mantle that increased greatly the mound's height and moved its center slightly to the north, away from the river. The remains of two large structures with hearths and associated burned areas cap the second construction phase mantle. The third mantle contains the remains of a wall trench structure that had been remodeled or repaired several times; burned areas are concentrated in a small space on the western side of the mound near the building. This mantle was capped in turn by the final substructure mantle and any evidence of buildings on this surface was eroded long before the mound was excavated.

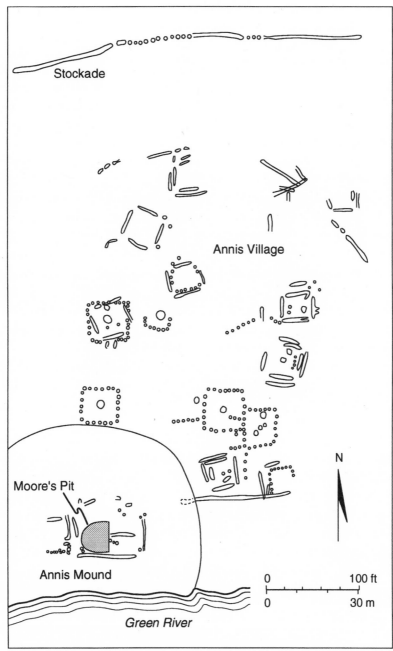

Figure 7.3. Excavation plan of the Annis site, a Mississippian town on the Green River, Butler County (adapted from Young 1962:9).

The basic elements of the Annis mound construction sequence are found in Mississippian towns throughout Kentucky from the Mississippi River (Edging and Stout 1986) to the Eastern Mountains (e.g., Dorwin 1970; Weinland 1980:45–46). On the basis of ethnohistoric names referring to the linear and platform mounds, Knight (1985) has suggested that nineteenth- and twentieth-century linear *tadjos* are descended from earlier Mississippian platform mounds. Like platform mounds, they delineate a plaza, separating the public precinct from the domestic areas and vice versa. In historic through recent times, linear mounds, or *tadjos,* were constructed by accretion of "polluted" dirt swept from the public grounds in an annual plaza purification ceremony (Howard 1981; Knight 1985, 1989; Swanton 1928b). It is plausible that *tadjos,* rather than being descended from Mississippian platform mounds, predated them or developed simultaneously; they may be merely less apparent archaeologically because of their small size relative to mounds and their susceptibility to destruction by recent farming activities.

As elsewhere in the Southeast, the Kentucky platform mounds were constructed in stages using the "compromised earth" of the village midden, and they appear to have often been capped by chief's houses or similar public structures. Each new structure also is markedly different from the preceding ones, a pattern of "anti-historical" change that Knight (1981:80) notes in other Southeastern towns and that Pauketat (1993) documents for Kunnemann Mound at Cahokia in southwestern Illinois.

Ramps, aprons, and multistage construction are also common Mississippian features, but these elaborations tend to be limited to the larger or more important mounds, such as Cahokia's Monks Mound (Fowler 1977). Mound A at Wickliffe (Edging and Stout 1986; Wesler 1989) was aproned on one side. Ramps have been suggested for Mound A at the Adams site (Stout 1989) on the basis of surface appearance; however, no subsurface structural testing has been conducted for confirmation. Also at Adams (Stout 1984, 1989) is a crescent-shaped earthwork with large platform mounds built on each end. This unusual earthwork is similar to two other "saddles" in close proximity to each other, one at the Turk site, 30 kilometers north of the Adams site, and the other at Towosahgy, 20 kilometers to the northwest. These sites also have remarkably similar central precinct plans. The saddle at each of the three sites connects two larger mounds (the Adams saddle differs only in that it is not linear) and forms what looks like an open amphitheater.

Plazas

Although interpretations of Mississippian earth architecture assign considerable symbolic importance to platform mounds (e.g., Phillips, Ford, and Griffin 1951), the plazas, ball grounds, and other public areas that define the liminal spaces around these mounds have received less attention, as have sites that do not have mounds. The size and number of mounds and overall site layout vary between towns, but each location has at least one plaza.

In the American Bottom, which has the most well-defined Mississippian developmental sequence in the Mississippi Valley (Bareis and Porter 1984), the village public space or plaza, which often contained a tall, centrally placed pole, was the first major element of what would become the Mississippian planned community. Platform mounds were not integrated as a common element of village planning for several hundred years after the appearance of the first village. This suggests two important inferences. First, the plaza, not platform mounds, emerges earliest in Mississippian village planning and dominates town space throughout late prehistory. Second, the plaza was an integral element of the symbolic center of the universe in at least part of the Mississippian world. That discussions of the symbolic interpretation of platform mounds have dominated the recent literature is, we believe, yet another interesting artifact of the high visibility of such features. The plaza, not the platform mounds, was the crucial planning element in the design of Mississippian towns.

One pattern, shared by Kentucky Mississippian towns and many comparable southeastern sites, is for the size and dimensions of each plaza to vary proportionally with the footprint of the principal mound that flanks it (Wahls 1986). For most towns with mound-and-plaza complexes, the bigger the main mound, the bigger the plaza (i.e., log–plaza area increases almost linearly with log–mound area) (Figure 7.4). In other words, plazas were scaled to fit the principal mound or mounds, or vice versa. This assertion is supported by Garcilaso de la Vega, who, in describing a Mississippian town, wrote, "On the plain at the foot of the hill, natural or artificial [i.e., the main platform mound], *they make a square plaza corresponding to the size of the pueblo that is to be settled,* surrounding which the nobles and chief men build their houses" (Shelby 1993:186, emphasis added). A similar relationship is seen in European cities, where "the size of plazas . . . is in proportion to the size of the building dominating each plaza; or, to put it otherwise, the height of the building . . . varies in proportion to that dimension of the plaza which

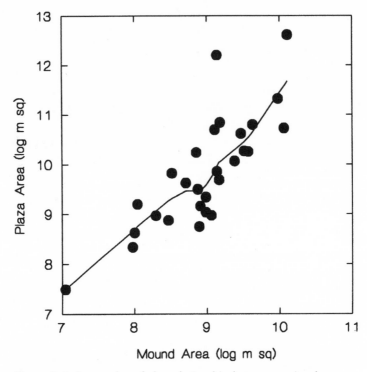

Figure 7.4. Scatterplot of the relationship between main plaza area
(in log square meters) and main mound area (in log square meters)
for twenty-eight Mississippian sites. *Fitted line* is a lowess, or locally
weighted scatterplot smoother line.

is measured perpendicularly to the façade of the building" (Collins and Collins 1986:181–82).

The Mississippian data suggest that the relationship becomes asymptotic for the largest mounds, implying that even Mississippian planners believed a plaza could be too big past a certain point—this point is reached at
plaza lengths greater than roughly 400 to 500 meters. Simply put, this is
why archaeologists do not see huge platform mounds butted against a tiny
main plaza or a pimple of a main mound flanking an immense plaza. Viewed
from the design perspective, these plaza/main mound relationships reinforce
the interdependent nature of Mississippian mounds and plazas.

One set of questions about mound-plaza relationships that cannot yet be answered concerns the design stability of plazas. If, as the data suggest, Mississippian mounds grew gradually or incrementally through the enactment of public rituals, did then the plazas grow along with them? Or, perhaps more interesting given the directions taken in recent studies of Mississippian ritual, were changes to the mounds that flanked a given plaza simply consequences of the ritual use of the plaza (cf. Knight 1985)?

Given the spatial constraints on plazas, it seems inconceivable that plazas could have grown along with the main mounds, although plazas frequently were bounded only on one or two sides for much of the history of many sites, which would have permitted considerable growth (see also Demel and Hall, Chapter 9). The mounds along most plaza edges were a formidable constraint. Together with the main mound or mounds, these secondary mounds defined the space within which the plaza had to fit. In such towns as Adams and Turk (Figure 7.5), which were constructed in locations in which the spatial limits of each town also were fixed by the terrain, an increase in plaza size was simply not an option. Hence, one of the frequent comments heard from visitors to the Turk site is how compact it is. This compactness comes, of course, from the diminutive size of the plaza relative to the surrounding mounds and village area. Even in less circumscribed locations, such as the Jonathan Creek site (Figure 7.6), unless town planners left room in which the plaza could grow, the length-width proportions of plazas and their areas relative to the principal mounds could not have been preserved without radical surgery to the earth architecture of the town.

Our main point is that, viewed architecturally, principal mound–main plaza spatial relationships could not have evolved together. These relationships were fixed by design fairly early in the history of a town and they changed little over time. Barring the discovery of major Mississippian cut-and-fill sections in the towns, the principal mound–main plaza data suggest that big mound-and-plaza complexes started out big, small mound-and-plaza complexes started out small, and they all pretty much stayed that way. Where they did change, we may find evidence of major cut-and-fill type Mississippian engineering projects designed to redefine the spatial relationships of the mound-and-plaza complex (e.g., Dalan 1993; Demel and Hall, Chapter 9).

Secondary plazas were the most common means by which Mississippian towns accommodated the principal mound–plaza relationships discussed above. At the Adams site, for example, existing earth architecture and the

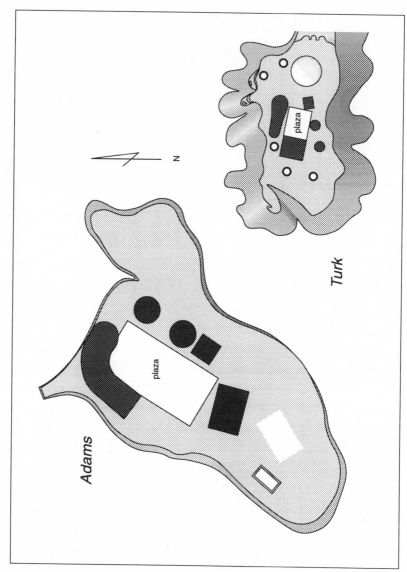

Figure 7.5. Comparison of the mound-and-plaza complexes at the Adams and Turk sites.

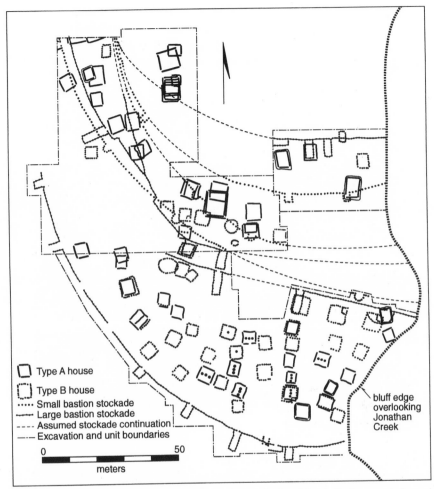

Figure 7.6. Excavation plan of the Jonathan Creek site, Marshall County (adapted from Webb 1952:16–17).

physical limits of the terrace remnant upon which the town was built precluded any increase in the dimensions of the main plaza. However, a secondary plaza was created on the west side of Mound A after Adams was already an old town (Figure 7.7). The construction of the west plaza required the removal of many tons of village midden, which may, in turn, have provided the fill for a Mound A or Mound G mantle, the latter of which contains Late Woodland fill.

To move beyond questions of physical dimensions, Mississippian plazas

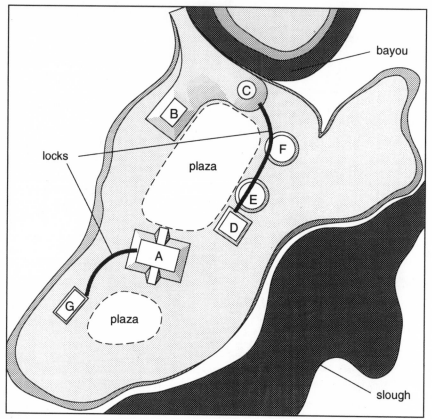

Figure 7.7. The secondary plaza and intrasite locks at the Adams site.

also were constructed with shared symbolic locks or barriers between public, private, and ceremonial spaces (Stout 1989). At many Mississippian sites, the locks between plazas and the rest of the site were arguably physical and symbolic; however, the physical boundaries between major functional areas appear to have provided mainly a reminder of the symbolic ones (cf. Knight 1981, 1985).

Using the Adams site as an example of primarily symbolic boundaries, the lock between the central plaza and the eastern village area is the line formed by Mounds D, E, and F and north to Mound C; the lock between the central plaza and the West Village is Mound A and an apparently natural ridge between Mounds A and G (Figure 7.7). The plaza's lower topographic elevation relative to the eastern village area and much of the western village may also have served as a lock. The topographic disparity between the plaza and habitation areas may have resulted from a long history of cleaning the former and living in the latter. The slough and stream channel that surrounded the site physically separated the Adams town from outsiders. The saddle mound and ramp at the north end of the site may have been the symbolic "gateway" that separated the Adams community from its main communication link to the Mississippi Valley and the world beyond.

Principal Alignments

Cardinal relationships in the planning of archaeological sites have been suggested by many researchers (Aveni 1975; Thom and Thom 1978) and have been considered in the search for Mesoamerican influence on the southeastern United States (Daniel-Hartung 1981; Sherrod and Rolingson 1987). Mississippian peoples could have established cardinal alignments by using celestial body rise and set landmarks at a time of the year other than an equinox (e.g., a solstice). The presence of cardinal alignments in Mississippian site plans would suggest, at the least, a shared desire for order, but it also might well reflect a particular importance of the directions.

The strongest case, by a number of accounts, for Mississippian cardinal alignments is the four-corner arrangement of Cahokia (Daniel-Hartung 1981; Fowler 1977, 1978; Sherrod and Rolingson 1987). Claims for such alignments at other sites are certainly open to question. In their Lower Mississippi Valley site classification scheme, Phillips, Ford, and Griffin (1951) described many site perimeters, plaza axes, and intermound alignments as oriented toward the cardinal directions. Their published maps, however, show that many of the sites' orientations are angled as much as 45 degrees from true cardinal directions (Stout 1991). Daniel-Hartung (1981) concluded that four of five major Mississippian centers she investigated—Angel, Cahokia, Etowah, and Moundville—exhibit strong cardinal direction orientation. She judged the data for Kincaid, the fifth site she investigated, to be inconclusive. Daniel-Hartung considered orientations as much as 20 degrees east of north to be cardinal alignments, noting an orientation of 17 degrees east of north at Teotihuácan, where cardinal alignment has not been challenged (but perhaps should be). Wahls's (1986) investigation of the five sites in Daniel-Hartung's study and several of those illustrated by Phillips, Ford, and Griffin (1951) demonstrated much closer alignment with surrounding topography than with cardinal directions in most cases.

The importance of cardinal directions to indigenous southeastern peoples has an ethnographic basis in the Cherokee cosmos as reported by Mooney and Olbrechts (1932). It is also one element of Hudson's (1984) southeastern Indian religion. It is not clear, however, that Cherokee "cardinal" directions were true north, south, east, and west. Nevertheless, the axes of these directions were perpendicular to each other, with each direction emanating from the Cherokee at the center.

Data presented by researchers proposing cardinal alignments point more to a use of parallel and perpendicular arrangements within site plans than to alignments with true north-south and east-west. Nevertheless, based on the maps of Phillips, Ford, and Griffin (1951), fewer parallel site boundaries exist in the Lower Mississippi Valley than those authors claimed (Stout 1991). Perpendicular intrasite arrangements might well reflect a cosmological order as viewed by Mississippian peoples, a view that may also have been symbolized by the circle and cross motif of the Southeastern Ceremonial Complex (Hudson 1984). If such concepts existed in prehistoric times, and it seems likely at least for Cherokee ancestors that they did (the circle and cross clearly predate Christian influence), do they explain the architectural layout of sites in regions for which we lack ethnographic and ethnohistoric data?

One western Kentucky Mississippian site, Adams (Figure 7.8), does exhibit mound alignments with cardinal directions; whether these alignments are intentional is unclear. A line drawn from the eastern end of Mound A, at the head of a probable ramp to the site's main plaza, to the center of Mound B aligns with the axis of true north-south, as does a line drawn between the probable centers of Mounds C and E (Figure 7.8). Most of the intermound axes at Adams diverge from the cardinal directions by 30 to 45 degrees and are not perpendicular to each other.

Other western Kentucky Mississippian sites, because of mound number, site condition, or map detail, exhibit no unequivocal cardinal alignments. At Turk, a north-south line may have run through Mound A and smaller mounds directly north and south of it, but the northern mound recorded by Loughridge (1888) no longer exists and the southern mound was small and has become too severely deflated to find a center from which to check alignments. Similarly, the eastern conical end of Turk's saddle-shaped Mound B appears to align in Loughridge's map with a small mound south of the plaza, but, again, the smaller mound (shown as a diffusely raised area on Edging's [1985] topographic map) is deflated beyond testing. Two small mounds at

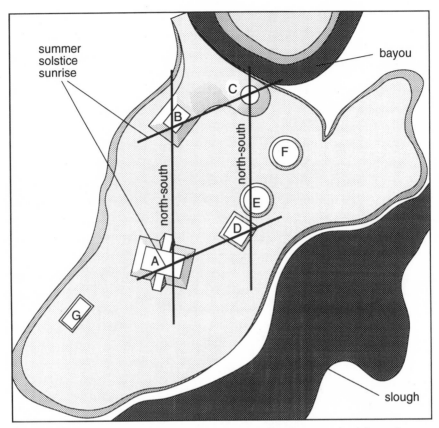

Figure 7.8. Cardinal and summer solstice sunrise alignments at the Adams site.

Jonathan Creek, recorded by Loughridge (1888:193), may also align with true north-south, but they are virtually impossible to locate on Webb's (1952:11) topographic map. None of the examined sites reveals any east-west alignments, suggesting that equinox alignments were not attempted or important. The positioning of mounds that clearly align with a north-south axis makes no suggestion as to whether the alignment is intentional; the north-south–aligned mounds at Adams each also fall along another alignment, approximately the summer solstice sunrise.

Especially in the past decade, archaeologists have expressed interest in the potential Mississippian understanding and use of celestial alignments in the design and location of site structures. Use of structures as celestial observatories or landmarks for calendrical purposes (e.g., O'Brien and McHugh

1987; Wittry 1977) comparable to that suggested for some Mesoamerican structures (e.g., Aveni 1975) is the primary reason offered for proposed celestially oriented plan prescriptions. In other words, practical seasonal concerns have most often been suggested as the basis for possible celestial alignments of Mississippian structures and site plans. Smith (1992) departs somewhat from interpreting Cahokia's "sun-circle" as a ritual calendar to suggest, following Giddens's (1984) notion of cultural development, that the circular arrangement of posts was a "storage container for an authoritative resource" (Smith 1992:28) whose contents were used by Cahokian elites to control scheduling of ceremonies and distribution of goods (cf. Krupp 1992). Despite this departure, there has been little expression that Mississippian towns might reflect a shared concept of "proper" world order, the cosmos, esthetics, or other aspects of culture not directly or predominantly practical (cf. Lawrence and Low 1990). Following Knight's (1990b) point regarding calendrical use of the Cahokia "sun circle," the greatest weakness of arguments that Mississippian structures were designed to observe and predict the seasons is that many, at least, are far more elaborate than necessary for that purpose alone. Each alignment, and presumed alignment, is duplicated in each of two hemispheres of the complete circle. Further, there is no reason to believe that the inhabitants of Cahokia would have ignored other prominent celestial bodies, whose movements would also have provided useful calendrical information. There remains incomplete understanding of the precise dating of the circle and the structures adjacent to it and overlapping it in the Cahokia plan view, which casts a shadow on any interpretation of this feature.

So far, across the Midwest and Southeast, the celestial patterns that seem to be recognizable are only marginally testable, partly because so many potential celestial structure and site alignments exist and partly because locations of landmarks such as structures or posts on mounds usually cannot be certain (Daniel-Hartung 1981; Sherrod and Rolingson 1987; Stout 1989). Site destruction by farming, construction, and archaeological testing has made it difficult to test celestial alignments. The Adams site may appear to have two sets of mound alignments with the summer solstice sunrise through the eastern end of Mound A and the center of Mound C and through Mounds D, E, and F, but the latter mounds are all plow deflated (Stout 1989), so their potential alignments are problematic. Because of the way Adams's mounds delimit the central plaza, this large public area also aligns with the summer solstice sunrise. Another possible alignment with the summer solstice sunset lies along the line from the eastern end of Mound A and the current center of Mound G, but Mound G is so deflated by plowing that its contours are virtually indiscernible. Moreover, Wahls (1986) used the same alignments at Adams as examples of site plan relationships to the topography of sites' natural setting, leaving both the exact alignments and their interpretation equivocal. Plowing at Turk and Jonathan Creek has deflated mounds beyond testing. Plowing, excavation, and construction have eliminated any possibility of testing McLeod Bluff, Wickliffe, Sassafras Ridge, Jonathan Creek, Canton, and others; the locations of block excavations and public buildings at Wickliffe are suggestive of solstice sunrise-sunset alignments, but the 1930s excavations preclude determinations of celestial landmarks. Other sites have earthworks that are too few or too small to ascertain their alignments.

Phillips, Ford, and Griffin (1951) observed a preponderance of Lower Mississippi Valley mound centers with the main mound to the west or southwest of the plaza. Reed (1977) suggested a Mississippian preference for this positioning, possibly changing throughout the Mississippi period, and tacitly interpreted mounds and plazas as primarily socioreligious elements of Mississippian communities and made his interpretations about their location also socioreligious. Williams and Brain's (1983) interpretations of the pattern of mound construction at Lake George in Mississippi follow Reed (1977) and suggest a dynamic socioreligious mound-plaza orientation with possible influences from Cahokia. Stout (1989) offered alternative influences arising from increasing information exchange between Mississippian peoples as regionally distinct groups developed along similar Mississippian trajectories. The pattern of mound-plaza orientation observed by Phillips, Ford, and Griffin (1951) and Reed (1977) is consistent with that at Wickliffe, Turk, Adams, and probably Jonathan Creek in western Kentucky. It is also possible that at Turk and Adams there had been a shift in the location of the primary mound, depending on how the unusual saddle structures are interpreted, that is, whether the saddles found at Adams, Turk, and nearby Beckwith's Fort are special structures in their own right or multistage mounds. To expand, the elaboration of the architecture of the saddle earthworks, transforming them into composite multistage mounds, may reflect a shift in each of these communities' focus from the largest, centrally located mound, which never received such special architectural attention.

In search of simple explanations for Mississippian town spatial patterning, Wahls (1986) measured the alignments of mounds, plazas, and site perimeters at thirty-nine towns in the Midwest and Southeast. Many of the
alignments were those ascribed by other researchers to cardinal or other directional alignments. In all but two of these towns, however, Wahls found
alignment with surrounding topography and water bodies a better fit.
Clearly, many of the mound alignments and orientations at Wickliffe, Turk,
Adams, and Jonathan Creek nearly mirror the surrounding landscape. Central plazas at Adams and Turk appear to align with natural topography.

Units of Measurement

Sherrod and Rolingson (1987) have produced the most extensive research into indigenous North American units of measure. They concluded
that at Toltec Mounds near Little Rock, especially, and at other late prehistoric mound sites generally, a distance of 47.5 meters was a standard unit
found between architectural elements. They determined that distances of
47.5 meters and multiples of this "Toltec Module" (Sherrod and Rolingson
1987) are found throughout the Toltec Mounds site, but representation of
this unit at other sites is unclear. No rigorous test of this module has been
made at western Kentucky Mississippian sites, and no other module has been
detected. At Adams, however, the results of an extensive surface collection–
based spatial analysis (Stout 1989) revealed a consistent average distance of
20 to 30 meters between household clusters along three test axes.

Defense Architecture

Settlement choices clearly involved a trade-off among convenient access
to cropland, the proximity of important communication lines, and defense
considerations. Among these considerations, defense has received far less attention in the literature than other factors of settlement patterning, presumably because there is less direct archaeological evidence by which to study it.
Defense also was probably less a factor in site selection than rich agricultural
lands and waterborne transportation because it was the factor most easily
compensated for technologically, as we describe below.

Just as in modern industrialized societies, Mississippian conflicts and
raids were caused by many factors—territorial expansion, subjugation, re-
venge, fear of the Other, and so on. Steinen (1992:135) comments that
Mississippian defensive works "should not be thought of as architectural fea-

tures constructed at great expense or on a whim." Although this statement is probably accurate, cost and whimsy are relative and were undoubtedly peculiar to the polity deciding whether or not to build defensive structures. In Kentucky, stockades were clearly not substantial. Nevertheless, defensive structures are indeed architectural features and as such reveal interactions between desired function and culturally prescribed norms of design.

In Kentucky towns, evidence of the anticipation of episodic conflicts is found in the siting of towns in locations with good natural defensive characteristics, the general spatial layout of towns, and the stockades that encircled some of these communities.

The basic element of Kentucky Mississippian town defense was the advantage of height. Glacis-like slopes and stockades intimidated an attacking force, handicapped the potential success of surprise raids, and gave defenders a large degree of control of the killing ground immediately outside the stockade. Mississippian planners achieved the advantage of height through good town site choices and, at least in the bottomland towns, an occasional feverish week or so of stockade construction. After the risk of conflict had passed, the stockade could serve as a reserve of firewood and construction material, which allowed recovery of much of the stockade's cost.

The usual course was to build towns in locations that offered topographical advantages for defense. For example, the Turk, Wickliffe, and Adams towns (Figure 7.9) are each on an isolated ridge or island of high

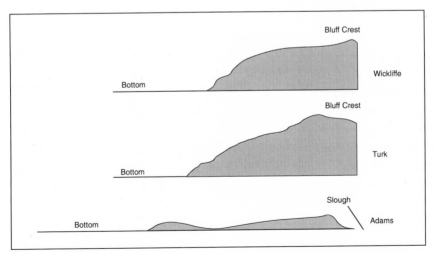

Figure 7.9. Topographical cross sections of the Adams, Turk, and Wickliffe sites.

ground, most approaches to which form a natural glacis. The Turk and Wick-liffe towns cover ridge tops that differ from neighboring bluff crest ridges mostly in the broad expanse of flat area they offered for the construction of a town. The Adams town, on the other hand, exploited the defensive advan-tages of an island of high ground in the middle of a seasonally flooded cy-press swamp. In each place, however, the general pattern is the same—ex-ploitation, when possible, of the defensive characteristics of the terrain.

What about prospective town locations that offered close proximity to important communication lines or rich agricultural land, but lacked natural defensive features? Most town sites in the big river bottoms and on other relatively flat terrain were vulnerable to attack from all quarters. It was at such locations as these, found at Jonathan Creek, Morris, Annis, Corbin, and other sites, that the remains of defensive stockades are found. A stockade confers many of the advantages of elevation on the defenders. Other flat-terrain defensive features, such as ditches or moats, are reported elsewhere in the Mississippi Valley, but are rare or unconfirmed in Kentucky. The island location of the Adams site provided a natural moat during much of the year, which may or may not have been enhanced by the town's occupants (Stout, Tucker, and Kayse 1995). Thomas (1894:280–82) identified a ditch running parallel to the embankment of the McLeod Bluff site. Stout (1984:177) sug-gests that a semicircular depression at the Sassafras Ridge site might be a silt-filled ditch or natural meander, and a similar suggestion is made by Burks and Stout (1995) for the depression partially encircling the Twin Mounds site. However, neither of the latter suggestions has been confirmed by exca-vation. On the Malden Plain in southeastern Missouri, Teltser (1992) de-scribes remote sensing data for a ditch around three sides of the County Line site. Given the natural defensive characteristics of ridge-top Mississippian sites, stockades were not necessarily constructed except where the ridge merged with the bluff crest, as depicted by Loughridge (1888:185) at the Wickliffe site (Figure 7.10).

Like most Mississippian fortifications in the Southeast, Kentucky Mississippian town stockades were insubstantial, and their archaeological re-mains appear almost trivial in comparison with the fortifications of primitive cities and towns in other parts of the world. Mississippian towns were clearly not designed to withstand sieges: all of the necessary elements, such as permanent water supply, warehouses, and granaries, are missing. The most elaborate defensive feature documented to date is the apron gate or bent

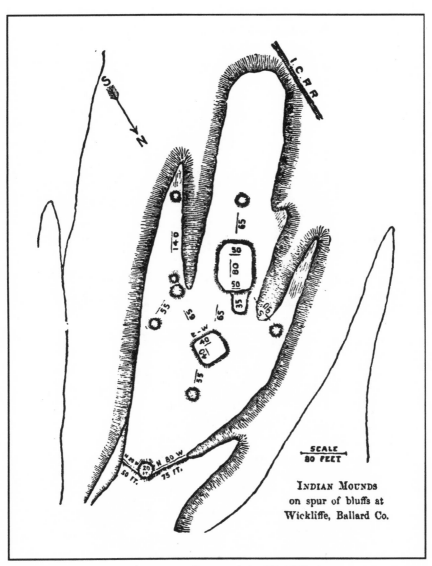

Figure 7.10. Loughridge's (1888:185) map of the Wickliffe site.

entrance at Jonathan Creek (Figure 7.11). Stockades also appear to have been episodic features, constructed in a hurry when the inhabitants of a town felt the threat of a possible attack. No archaeological evidence suggests that defensive stockades or palisade walls were a fixed town feature. Excavations of palisade lines have not revealed, for example, any evidence of structures or

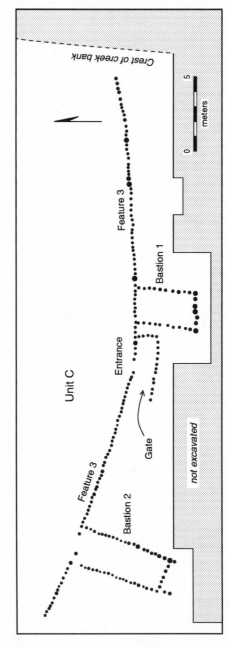

Figure 7.11. The bent entrance and bastions at Jonathan Creek (adapted from Webb 1952:23).

other features that were built against a stockade, as if to use part of it for a fourth wall or additional structural support. Such features are commonly seen elsewhere in the world when defensive works are a permanent feature of the architecture of a town.

What were the military capabilities of Mississippian townspeople? In evaluating defensive works, a good rule of thumb is that the strength of the works will be roughly equal to or greater than the anticipated strength and technological capabilities of an attacking force. Defensive works, therefore, provide good indirect measures of the military capabilities of both attackers and defenders. Applying this reasoning in Kentucky, we infer that the warfare that threatened Mississippian towns was episodic, of brief duration, of essentially constant magnitude across space and through time, and technologically stagnant. In so far as these inferences are correct, the objective of Mississippian town defense planning was to reduce the impacts of surprise attacks and raiding parties. War leaders were not equal to the task of such ambitious undertakings as siege operations or the concentration of forces to breach stockade walls.

Towns as Communities and Homes
Intensity of Occupations

Mississippian towns along the Mississippi and Lower Ohio rivers appear to have been occupied more intensively and longer than sites in the Green, Cumberland, and other Kentucky drainages. The largest excavated communities in the latter regions do not show the intense midden accumulation, mound construction, and evidence of house basin recycling that have been found at Mississippi Valley sites such as Adams (Lewis 1996).

We hesitate to push this inference too strongly since our fieldwork centers on the Ohio and Mississippi valley sites and since the town excavations in other parts of Kentucky were completed twenty-five to fifty-five years ago. Obviously, therein lies the possibility for bias on our part. In the absence of conflicting data, however, there is no choice but to note the patterns as they appear to exist and to go on with our research.

Soil exhaustion was probably not as great a factor in the extinction of towns along the Mississippi and Lower Ohio rivers as it was in the interior regions, given the beneficial impacts of the seasonal overflows in the major river valleys. On the other hand, firewood depletion, insect infestations, deep or protracted floods, epidemic diseases, and earthquakes would have had comparable impacts on all communities.

Inhabitants

We would very much like to know who lived in the towns and whether they were the same as people who lived in the hinterland around these communities. Solving this problem with any measurable probability of being right or wrong continues to elude us. At Adams the village areas were crowded with the houses of hundreds of inhabitants (Stout 1989), but whether a substantial portion of the community had temporary residences elsewhere is unknown. Our working hypothesis is that Kentucky Mississippian towns contained the residences of many of the people who attended rituals on its plaza; it is likely that these people also maintained temporary quarters close to their fields and that other people preferred to live apart in smaller neighborhoods and households.

One archaeological thread of evidence—intertown differences in the fabric of utility vessels—suggests strong continuity among town inhabitants. If one works with a large collection of, say, 10,000 or more potsherds from one town, and then moves on within a few days or weeks to the analysis of a comparable collection from a contemporaneous nearby town, one is struck immediately by subtle but noticeably consistent differences between those sites in the fabric of utility vessels of the same type. At present, this is a subjective impression that we only can describe rather than quantify. What it suggests, of course, is that the people who made and used the pots in each town tended to remain there. The level and pattern of intertown interaction was sufficient to promote a certain congruence of decorative and procedural attributes, but was insufficient to dampen the basic distinctiveness of each town's utility wares.

Conclusions

We really feel the lack of ethnohistorical data in Kentucky when we attempt to understand the symbolic content of Mississippian towns. To construct even the barest of testable interpretations, we must assume that a significant portion of Mississippian culture, especially symbols and myths, was pan-southeastern. In Kentucky and throughout the Southeast, plazas were key features of Mississippian town design—functionally, symbolically, and spatially. Although platform mounds were clearly important elements of town design, the plazas may have been even more so. Town design also employed physical and symbolic locks to separate distinct areas of the site. We have only begun to explore the possible patterning and meanings of these locks and culturally significant alignments between key architectural features, a closely related aspect of town design.

Town site choices and general layout were strongly influenced by local terrain characteristics and the proximity of communication routes. Defense was probably a bigger factor in town design in some parts of the Southeast than its absence from the literature might suggest. Mississippian towns planned for episodic defenses of brief duration against raids that were technologically stagnant and poorly organized.

We close with a brief review of some of the interesting (to us) questions that lie before us in Kentucky. Many issues they raise are generalizable to the study of towns in other parts of the Mississippian world.

Craft Specialization

After having investigated bits and pieces of several Kentucky Mississippian towns, we are impressed by the lack of evidence of craft specialization. These societies were apparently large enough and complex enough to support specialized production, but direct material evidence of it has not been forthcoming. We have already remarked, for example, about how the domestic ware of each town looks: same vessels, motifs, and general paste characteristics, but with obviously different clay sources and local tempering and surface finish conventions. Sites such as Adams, Sassafras Ridge, and Wickliffe contain tons of utility vessel sherds and no demonstrable evidence that production was organized on anything other than the household level.

Town Economy

We also do not yet have sufficient data to reconstruct the extent to which the economies of towns changed over time, both generally throughout the Mississippi period and specifically during the life span of a given town. This information is crucial to the accurate reconstruction of the late prehistory of the region and to the understanding of the final days of the Mississippian world in this part of the midcontinent. Did it end with the chimera of the Vacant Quarter or as part of the indirect effects of pan-Eastern contacts with the Old World and the lack of a sustained European presence in the

Confluence region until relatively late? At least part of the answer will be an economic one.

Towns in Temporal Perspective

Limited excavations at many western Kentucky Mississippian towns have demonstrated that they were built on the remains of Late Woodland villages. Why? Were these towns the result of the evolution of particularly important Late Woodland communities at the same locations, or were these locations simply the ones that offered suitable spaces for a town? Do we see this pattern because there were few potential town locations that had not already been used by the ancestors of the Mississippian peoples? Does it mean that some communities were assigned special meaning even during Late Woodland times? We may never have definite answers to these questions because we would have to remove a Mississippian town in the hope that enough remains of the Late Woodland community for study.

Next, the Ohio-Mississippi Confluence region and western Kentucky contain the remains of many towns. Is it possible to identify spatial patterns in the development and abandonment of towns in the Confluence region? For example, can we identify which towns, if any, replaced Turk and Jonathan Creek when they died? This question motivates another: how long did towns last? Why were they abandoned? What happened to town sites after abandonment? For example, excavation of the outer ditch fill at Beckwith's Fort in the Cairo Lowland of Missouri (Price and Fox 1990) suggests that this town either lasted longer than most archaeologists in the region believe or, at least, that some people continued to live there even after the town was abandoned.

Finally, is there any spatial patterning to the growth of towns? We do not know, for example, of a Mississippian town that can be described as linear in plan. If towns are just clumps of farmsteads, as Muller (1986a:280–82) suggests, there should be no reason linear towns (mound-and-plaza and houses strung along a levee) would not exist. Do they exist and we just have not identified them correctly? Or is it that a "beads on a string" community layout was not a part of the Mississippian architectural grammar?

8

Towns along the Lower Ohio

Jon Muller

The issue of continuity or discontinuity between historical and prehistoric societies has been a key question in eastern archaeology. Some facts about the early historical period are widely accepted: (1) population declined as a result of Old World disease, (2) European-sponsored trade, especially for pelts, had considerable economic impact on many groups, and (3) alliances with European powers became politically and militarily important to native easterners. However, inferences are sometimes drawn that do not logically follow from these facts, and so different levels of interpretation are confused. What happened in some cases is confused with what happened in general. The overall population of the Southeast declined and so did the population of many groups, but southeastern polities did not all have the same population history. A documented general decline, regardless of its scale, does not justify the conclusion that all societies responded to stresses in the same fashion. Some societies became extinct, but others survived periods of cultural and biological hardship and maintained their size and scale. Moreover, population size has been confused with organizational complexity. The overall decline in numbers did not necessarily mean a decline in political and economic complexity, especially among those particular groups that managed to maintain their town and group sizes.

Data on a mix of historical "eastern" societies have often been used to hypothesize about the structures of earlier Mississippian societies in the Southeast (e.g., Hudson's [1976] excellent area-wide survey and such works as that by Howard [1968]). More recently a few seem to deny any useful use of data on historical peoples in the investigation of their Mississippian ancestors. I do not understand this attitude except in that it is true that abuses formerly occurred in too-direct impositions of historical forms on prehistoric data. However, the pendulum has swung too far the other way, and I believe that historical cases provide useful models for Mississippian societies for both scale and character. Whether these were the kinds of organizations really created by Mississippian peoples is another question, but testing of models of organization based on historically descended peoples seems a reasonable beginning. As I will discuss below and have also argued in other places (including Muller 1993a, 1994, 1997a, 1997b), I feel that an artificial gap has been created by underestimation of the complexity of historical societies and overestimation of the scale of prehistoric societies. This chapter warrants an argument for similarity between historical native American societies and those of the prehistoric Mississippi period, especially as the latter are represented in the Lower Ohio Valley.

I will first briefly discuss some aspects of historical southeastern demography to see what kinds of impact historical depopulation had on such variables as town size and the size of these societies. I will ask whether there is justification for the often-expressed opinion that historical populations were so disturbed by early historical population losses that their settlement and other social structures were fundamentally disrupted (e.g., M. Smith 1987). Finally, I will compare historical southeastern data on settlement with data on prehistoric settlement in the Lower Ohio Valley to see whether prehistoric settlement patterns may be similar to those seen in the historical data.[1]

Population and Dispersion

Before proceeding, it is important to understand some of the dimensions of what population reports really mean in the historical record. It should be understood that a report of, say, 158 warriors for a historical group was a matter of real-world concern in military and political terms. Such estimates were usually not casual, although this does not mean that they were always truthful. In addition, as with all census data, such numbers are of "visible" persons, and therefore certain classes of persons will usually be excluded. One key factor in such estimates is the difference in visibility between aggregated and dispersed populations.

Historic descriptions of native eastern populations often drew attention to aggregation and dispersal as a dynamic of those populations. Typically, "barrier" towns were described as having defensive roles, while dispersal was seen as facilitating access to agricultural land. The models for these distinctions were probably drawn from classical "ethnographic" descriptions such as those of the Germans and Celts by Caesar in 51 B.C. He emphasized the roles of buffer zones (*Gallic Wars* sec. 4:3, 6:23, 30, pass.) and the part that land played in internal social distinctions (sec. 6:21). These distinctions were echoed and amplified by Tacitus in *Germania* (sec. 16 [1942:716–17]), and both sources were surely familiar to most literate narrators in our historical record.

Of course, defensive aggregation ("Hey, rube!") and peacetime dispersal do not exhaust the possibilities. While dispersed communities may be vulnerable to raids, dispersal can also be a defensive tactic—especially if the enemy possesses strong local superiority ("Head for the hills!"). We see an example of the latter kind of dispersal in the case of the Grand Village when the Illini were threatened by Iroquois with firearms. Dispersal can occur in any emergencies in which the individual household is thrown on its own resources. In this sense, aggregation and dispersal are dialectically joined in the phenomena that many geographers subsume under the general term *dispersion*. Both are reflections of labor-power requirements in specific historical circumstances.

The reporting of town settlement in the Southeast reflects the historical processes of the formation of the historical record. Military concerns predominated in many cases, but there were many reasons to count (or not to count) aboriginal population.

Historical Town Size and Character

Historical Accounts

A multitude of accounts provide us with a picture of larger communities with outlying smaller settlements in the form of individual farmsteads and hamlets of varying size, as the following paraphrases and quotations indicate.

[Apalachee]

Apalachen was the "largest town in all the region" and "the people beyond were less numerous and poorer, the land little occupied, and the inhabitants much scattered" (Nuñez Cabeça de Vaca 1966:37–38 [1542]).

Sometimes dispersal was done under the influence of European factors or agents.

[Creek]

"Oc-fus-kee with its villages, is the largest town in the nation. They estimate the number of gun men of the old town, at one hundred and eighty; and two hundred and seventy in the villages or small towns" (Hawkins 1971:45 [1799]).

"The Indians have lately moved out and settled in villages, and the town will soon be an old field; the settling out in villages, has been repeatedly stressed by the agent for Indian affairs, and with considerable success; they have seven villages belonging to this town" (Hawkins 1971:45 [1799]).

In other cases, conflict led to abandonment of localities.

[Choctaw]

"They have deserted their eastern frontier towns since their present war with the Creeks" (Romans 1962:73 [1775]).

Other settlement patterns were determined by local conditions.

[Cherokee]

Settlement was located in an E-W territory extending 140 miles in two parts: *Ayrate*—low; *Otare*—mountainous. In the 1730s, there were 6000 fighting men in 64 towns and villages; but in 1760–61 there were only 2300 warriors. "Their towns are still scattered wide of each other, because the land will not admit any other settlement; it is a rare thing to see a level tract of four hundred acres" (Adair 1986:237–39 [1775]).

Settlements were often very close together and it is often difficult to determine what a "town" was by spatial criteria alone.

[Houma to Natchez]

From Ouma to Nadchés the distance on river was 18½ leagues, but in a straight line only 11 leagues " . . . and the distance from the cleared land of one village to the other, by way of the hills, about 5 or 6 leagues" (d'Iberville 1981:126–27 [1699–1702]).

[Arkansas]

On the 29th of the month, Arkansas periguas were encountered. On the 30th Gravier went near to an old Arkansas settlement " . . . half a league from the old village of the Akansea, where they formerly received the late Father Marquette, and which is discernible now only by the old outworks [*dehours*], there being no cabins left." On the 31st, the party arrived at the village of the "Kappa Akansea," half a league from the water's edge (Gravier 1861:126 [1701]).

Such settlements would be difficult to resolve into separate communities in archaeological analysis.

Each larger settlement, including some that were quite dispersed, had a high degree of autonomy. Typically, there would be a "town king" or *mico* who might—or might not—recognize higher authority in the form of what we describe as a paramount chief.

[Virginia Indians]

"The method of the *Indian* settlements is altogether by Cohabitation, in Townships, from fifty to five hundred Families in a Town, and each of these Towns is commonly a Kingdom. Sometimes one King has the command of several of these Towns, when they happen to be united in his Hands by Descent or Conquest; but in such cases there is always a Viceregent appointed in the dependent Town, who is at once Governor, Judge, Chancellor, and has the same Power and Authority which the King himself has in the Town where he resides. This Viceroy is obliged to pay to his Principal some small Tribute, as an acknowledgment of his submission, as likewise to follow him to his Wars whenever he is requir'd" (Beverley 1968:174 [1705]).

"Nature and their own convenience [have] taught them to obey one Chief, who is Arbiter of all things among them. They claim no property in Lands, but they are in common to a whole Nation. Every one Hunts and Fishes, and gathers Fruits in all

places. Their labor in tending Corn, Pompions, Melons, &c. is not
so great, that they need quarrel for room, where the Land is so
fertile, and where so much lyes uncultivated" (Beverley 1968:225
[1705]).

[Chickasaw]

"They live nearly in the center of a very large somewhat uneven
savannah, of a diameter of above three miles; this savannah at all
times has but a barren look" (Romans 1962:62 [1775]).

"They have in this field what might be called one town, or
rather an assemblage of hutts, of the length of about one mile
and a half, and very narrow and irregular; this however they divide
into seven, by the names of Metattaw (i.e.) hat and feather,
Chatelaw (i.e.) copper town, Chukafalaya (i.e.) long town, Hiki-
haw (i.e.) stand still, Chucalissa (i.e.) great town, Tuckahaw (i.e.)
a certain weed, and Ashuck hooma (i.e.) red grass; this was formerly inclosed in palisadoes, and thus well fortified against the attacks of small arms, but it now lays open; a second Artaguette, a
little more prudent than the first, would now find them an easy
prey" (Romans 1962:62–63 [1775]).

"The Chikkasah in the year 1720, had four large contiguous
settlements, which lay nearly in the form of three parts of a square,
only that the eastern side was five miles shorter than the western, with the open part toward the Choktah" (Adair 1986:377–78
[1775]).

Settlement form could also follow from normal seasonal activities.

"I shall therefore only tell you, that when they go a Hunting
into the Out-lands, they commonly go out for the whole Season
with their Wives and Family. At the Place where they find the most
Game they build up a convenient Number of small Cabbins,
wherein they live during that Season. These Cabbins are both begun, and finished in Two or Three Days, and after the Season is
over they make no further Account of them" (Beverley 1968:156
[1705]).

It is also clear from analysis of the context of political decisions (see Muller 1997a:63–68) that even the most "autocratic" chiefs exercised relatively little power to command, notwithstanding their great dignity. Indeed, there were often a substantial number of "chiefs" and "principal persons" even in small societies (of 4500 persons or so) like the Natchez.

[Natchez]

"The Natchez, who lived here formerly, were a very important people. They had several villages ruled by individual chiefs, who in turn were governed by the great chief of the nation. All of these chiefs were called 'Suns,' and all five hundred of them were related to the Great Sun, their sovereign, who wore on his chest a picture of the sun from whom he claimed descent" (Le Page du Pratz 1972:31 [1758]).

Each local authority had potential for asserting claims to hegemony over other groups, and we see indications of substantially different local policies being pursued. For example, in the wars of the late eighteenth century, not all Creek Confederacy town-polities went to war with the enemies of other towns.

The potential for conflict between local and regional authorities in societies in which land and production are household based is, I think, quite clear. Thus we should expect the instability that is so often remarked upon in these kinds of social formations. We should also expect that societies with such notoriously unstable political forms might well evolve mechanisms for accommodating instability of leadership while maintaining necessary production for biological and social reproduction.

[Alabama]

"Each village chief considers himself a sovereign responsible only to the Master of Life, or the Great Spirit.

The Alabamas call their country the white land, or the land of peace, and they rest on their mats, which means that they attack no one. This is an allegorical way of announcing to all the earth's nations that the war hatchet is buried and that trade can be carried on safely in Alabama territory" (Bossu 1962:144 [1768]).

All of this, and a myriad of other data in the historical record, should make it clear that southeastern towns were complex settlement phenomena that cannot be simply resolved into the types of settlement hierarchies often constructed by archaeologists (see also Muller 1993b).

Size of Historic Groups

Some archaeologists seem to have the idea that prehistoric Mississippian societies were very large, while their historical descendants lived in what they suppose to be scattered and unorganized refugee camps. The simple fact is that there were many historical population estimates that exceeded 10,000 persons. As with all census and population data, exact sizes of these populations are sometimes indeterminable, but many historical groups were at least as large as even the exaggerated estimates often given for Mississippian communities.

Table 8.1 shows a summary of these reports of large, historical eastern societies by fifty-year periods.[2] It will be noted that the variation from one period to the next is not very large. There is also a tendency for the rate of change of larger groups to "stabilize" ($\Delta p/\Delta t \to 0$) at population sizes over 10,000 (as I have argued at greater length elsewhere, e.g., Muller 1993a, 1997a, 1997b). These figures are not consistent with the displaced-persons models too many people implicitly impose on the historical Southeast. Many of these historical southeastern peoples endured as long as the American Republic has managed so far. Their long-run "failure" to maintain their independence is not a proof of their organizational "degeneracy"—and that is what is really being said with the politer term *devolution*. To be sure, that the historical roots of the devolution argument lie in the political claims for a manifest destiny and in the rationalization of appropriation of native American territories does not mean that the idea is wrong, but it should flag this debate as being one that requires something more than blithe assumptions and citation of nineteenth-century sources on the part of those who accept the devolution idea. When the "cant of conquest" is disallowed, these historical political entities can be seen as functioning effectively, if not ultimately successfully, against the invading European powers (e.g., Hunt 1940; Jennings 1975).

The data on which the figures in Table 8.1 are based also show that disappearance of many smaller groups is related to the persistence of the larger societies. Larger groups are not necessarily much better at reproduc-

50-Year Period Beginning	Total Population Estimates	No. of Population Estimates >10,000	No. of Population Estimates >15,000	Mean Population Estimates >15,000	Standard Deviation	Maximum Estimate
1500	7	1	1	30,000		30,000
1550	12	0	0			
1600	170	17	15	25,887	6769	35,000
1650	227	16	8	29,888	7572	70,000
1700	476	23	10	31,520	23767	90,000
1750	713	50	18	19,331	4943	36,000
1800	680	69	43	20,946	3142	27,500

Table 8.1. Estimates of Historical Population Size in the Southeast and Adjacent Regions

tion, but they are capable of providing shelter and succor to refugees from smaller and more threatened groups. The Historic period certainly made things worse, but it is worth exploring how much of the phenomena of cycling and instabilities in prehistoric records may reflect similar strategies in prehistoric times.

Town Size in General

Another means of assessing both local and regional social integration is town size. Towns were the core of historical, and probably prehistoric, political economy. Hudson (1976:202–3) was recognizing this when he essentially equated *town* as usually translated (e.g., from *talwa* or *okla*) with *chiefdom*. Most towns in the historical Southeast were fairly small, between 350 and 1000 people, although the usual problem of aggregation and dispersal complicates the definition of towns, which might be recognized as social entities, but still be widely scattered, especially in circumstances in which dispersed settlement presented no security problems.

Of the more than 2200 recorded estimates of population for eastern groups, just over 470 cases have indications of the number of recognized "villages."[3] Town size estimates varied from ten persons in a settlement to a certainly exaggerated estimate of 7500 or more persons in a single town (i.e., the Kaskaskia/Illinois). In fact, out of the "towns" sample, fewer than 5 percent had populations larger than 1000 and only 2 percent were listed as

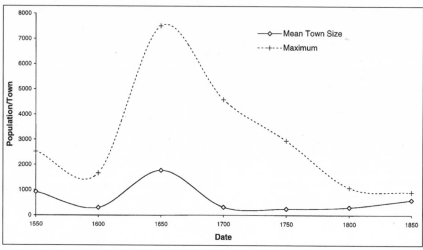

Figure 8.1. Variability in town size.

larger than 2000 persons. In most cases, even these larger estimates were probably not single towns as viewed by their inhabitants. Most individual, self-defined communities in the historical record were small, although they were often situated close to other communities. Taking the entire record and data set, the average town size between A.D. 1500 and 1900 was approximately 369 persons with a standard deviation of 709.

Figure 8.1 graphically presents the shifts in average reported size of towns, showing the mean value by fifty-year periods beginning in 1550 and also showing the maximum given town size for that period.[4] These recorded historical data on town size in the greater Southeast show average size per century may have decreased from some 923 persons per town in the late sixteenth century to 304 persons in the early seventeenth century, but the data prior to 1600 do not seem a very reliable basis for postulating dramatic population changes.[5] The decrease up to A.D. 1600 and the increase in the next fifty years could be real, but there is a large standard deviation of reported town size for this period and the average is clearly affected by the extraordinary Grand Village among the Illinois. The differences among the means for the fifty-year periods do not appear to be significant.[6] Aside from the "blip" caused by the Illinois case the data are fairly consistent. The conventional wisdom is that the populations were transformed over time as a consequence of depopulation. In a kind of "quantitative into qualitative

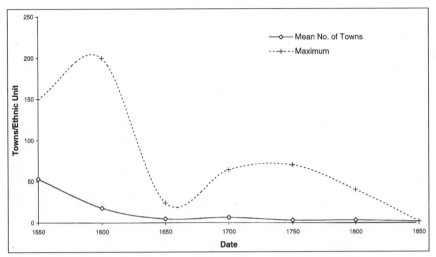

Figure 8.2. Variability in reported numbers of towns per ethnic unit.

change" argument, population decline is often taken to indicate political decline. However, this may not be justified, given the lack of evidence so far for significant declines in the sizes of towns.

A picture of relative stability of town size is very much at odds with interpretations that the decline in total population in the Southeast in historical times implied a drastic reduction in town size. Does this mean that polity size did not decline? Not at all: Figure 8.2 shows the reduction, not in the size of towns, but in the number of towns reported per polity (using the same conventions as Figure 8.1).

Total population decreased through historical times, but people were still congregating into towns of about the same size as in earlier times. Town size was relatively stable, but the number of towns per polity went down. The great diversity within reported estimates at any time indicates the need for caution, however. Despite overall population declines, stability of town size may reflect continuity in political organization. When looked at on a finer scale, as in the case of the Creek Confederacy, it is clear that there are persisting political economic structures through the centuries-long historical record. Some societies did "collapse," but their people did not all die—many of them disappeared by becoming members of surviving, larger groups. The same kind of process was occurring *within* polities. Outlying settlements collapsed into the surviving larger towns that were visible to European visitors and were enumerated in the records being discussed here. Even during overall depopulation, many local groups were able not only to survive, but also to actually increase in size. Threats from other native American groups and from their European allies certainly increased, not decreased, the need for effective defense in the Historic period.

The records also show many population fluctuations associated with historical events such as warfare (often echoing distant European wars). The rapidity of both the declines and recoveries associated with these events, however, makes it clear that these are often events of dispersal and aggregation rather than purely biological declines (see also Muller 1997a, 1997b).

The stability of town population size reflected the political and economic importance of the town. Social, economic, and political needs existed that could be served only if population was at certain minimum levels. Defense alone would favor having enough military force available for protection from probable enemies. At the same time, the data on historical peoples suggest that size was by no means the only measure of importance. Sometimes small settlements might have great political significance: the "capital" town of a confederacy was not always its largest settlement. Finally, I want to reiterate that the aboriginal definition of a "town" might be quite different from "towns" recognized as such by Europeans. We also need to remember how small contemporary settlements were in Europe when we assess early European views of the communities they visited in the Southeast. As European towns grew in the early modern period, it is not surprising that later describers were less impressed with the aboriginal towns they visited.

In addition, it should be noted that the number of men in each town was relatively stable even though there might be overall fluctuations in the number of men (warriors) in a polity (Figure 8.3). The number of towns seems to have been maintained at a level that allowed a relatively constant number of defenders per residential unit, especially during the war-torn eighteenth century.

The historical literature is full of evidence of population aggregation, if we care to look for it. Many towns, even as early as the time of the de Soto accounts, contained persons from other, sometimes recently abandoned, towns and from different ethnic groups. I suggest that this indicates a conservative tendency to try to maintain social life within its former parameters even in the face of dramatic population decline. In the Historic period, these mechanisms of aggregation or dispersal allowed flexible responses in unstable

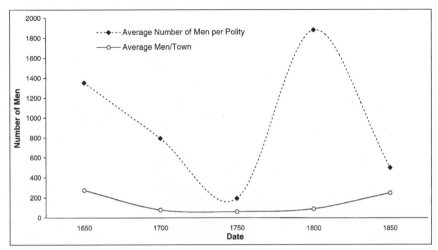

Figure 8.3. Average number of men overall and average number of men per town (for southeastern groups only).

times. There are fewer, but not smaller, towns through time. Indeed, there are fewer, not necessarily smaller, polities. I suggest that these mechanisms for maintenance of social formations in the historical Southeast are of long-standing character and that they initially evolved in the prehistoric context of shifting, unstable, and constantly dynamic "chiefdoms."

Creek Towns and Patterns

The pattern of certain kinds of stability in the midst of chaos becomes even clearer when we examine historic polities such as the Creek Confederacy. Although the core of the confederacy (read *paramount chiefdom?*) was Muskogee speaking, the Confederacy was not a homogeneous ethnic group but was made up of people of widely different origins. Many of these groups had their own towns within the confederacy (such as the Refugee Shawnee and Natchez). I have elsewhere discussed the specifics of Creek towns in more detail (Muller 1997a, 1997b), and a summary will suffice here, I hope, to make the point that what we can see in the historical settlements is not so different from our archaeological views of Mississippian society proper.

Frontier aggregation for defense and dispersal in the interior territories of these polities have often been noted. However, close examination of the records makes it clear that there is a much more complex relation between

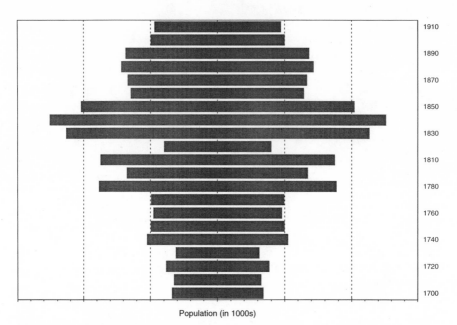

Population (in 1000s)

Figure 8.4. Creek Confederacy population by decade.

aggregation and dispersal than is usually recognized, as discussed earlier. There is no question that recorded populations often dropped in times of conflict. Sometimes this has been interpreted as the result of large numbers of deaths (as among the Cherokee by Thornton [1990]). Nonetheless, as noted in general above, the data shown in Figure 8.4 make it clear that neither the wholesale incorporation of smaller groups nor internal population growth could have accounted for such rapid fluctuations. The overall trend of population for the Creek is upward through the eighteenth century with declines after the Civil War.

When the Creek data are examined for the census years (Figure 8.5), a fair degree of consistency is apparent. Town size remained surprisingly stable, as in other larger historical groups, notwithstanding fluctuations in reported population. The consistency of town size again reflects the political and economic importance of the "normal" historical town. Inspection of the values of the averages of Creek town size indicates overall continuity and even a degree of stability.[7]

Okfuskee and Kasihta were usually the largest individual Creek towns,

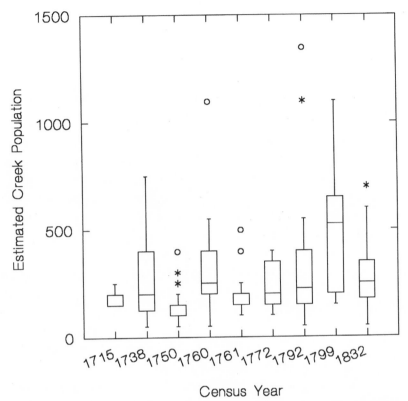

Figure 8.5. Box plot of Creek census data for the years 1715–1832. The plot shows that Creek population figures were relatively stable. The upper and lower ends of each *rectangular box* mark the middle half of the data; the *horizontal line* contained within the box shows the median value; *lines* that extend beyond the boxes include data points that are within one and a half times the range of the middle half of the data; *asterisks* and *circles* drawn beyond these lines are outliers and extreme outliers respectively.

ranging from some 500 to 1400 people, but even these were divided into a series of smaller towns. Hawkins, in 1799, noted that Okfuskee's abandonment for more dispersed settlement was under way (Hawkins 1971:45, quoted above in the discussion of historical accounts).

Similar kinds of analysis for other southeastern peoples such as the Cherokee produce essentially the same kinds of situations as found among the Creek. The historical town was as stable in size, at least, as its inhabitants could make it. Easterners seem to have gone to considerable lengths to maintain as stable a community as they could manage in the midst of war and other disruptions.

Mississippian Settlement in the Lower Ohio
Towns and Other Settlements

The Lower Ohio Valley presents a good place to look at settlement pattern because of the extensive survey and reconnaissance information available from the region. There has been nearly complete survey of the Black Bottom surrounding the Kincaid site, and many other localities in the region have been covered for the entire valley between the Wabash and the Mississippi. The two major centers in the region are at the Kincaid and Angel sites. These sites each rank among the top ten Mississippian sites in total volume of mound construction (see Muller 1997a for comparisons of Mississippian site sizes in this regard). The typical claims for site hierarchy and concentrations of people and economic activities have been made for the Kincaid area as are still made for many other Mississippian sites. I think data from the American Bottom and other regions are showing that the character of Lower Ohio Valley Mississippian is not as different from that of other Mississippian complexes as some have asserted.[8] In addition to the two larger sites, there are a number of smaller mound centers that very probably reveal episodes of mound construction in periods when "control" by Kincaid or Angel was weak.[9] There were also aggregated, palisaded towns with little mound construction such as those at Southwind (Munson n.d.) and Tinsley Hill and Jonathan Creek (Clay 1976, 1997). There were also a few limited-activity sites such as salt and chert extraction sites. These sites should not be confused with *specialized production* sites, which would be a very strong claim for a kind of economic organization that should not be made only on the basis of localization of some production (e.g., Cobb 1988, 1989, 1991; Muller 1984, 1986b, 1997a; Muller et al. 1992).

In most cases, however, the majority of Mississippian peoples in the Lower Ohio lived not in large aggregated communities, but rather in dispersed farmsteads (see Green and Munson 1978; Muller 1978, 1986b, 1993b). In fact, the farmsteads and homesteads were themselves often divided into clusters by the very nature of bottomland ridges and swales. Table 8.2 presents a summary of data on Lower Ohio Valley settlement developed in more detail elsewhere (Muller 1986a, 1997a). I reiterate that the settlement clusters defined here are divided by natural features and are not an arbitrary attempt to define social groups.

As shown in Table 8.2, the size and population of such clusters have a haunting resemblance to the size data on southeastern and Creek towns that were discussed earlier. It would be incorrect to claim that the Lower Ohio Valley clusters were necessarily self-recognized communities, but it is useful to see that the physical traces of historical and prehistoric Mississippian settlement share a similar form and structure. Figure 8.6 shows the comparison of the Creek data presented earlier with the size distributions of the Kincaid

Zone	No. of Sites	Site Area (ha)	Estimated No. of Structures	Estimated Population [a]
Black Bottom I	24	8.8	59	294
Black Bottom II	11	4.1	28	138
Kincaid (BB III)	44	10.8	73	363
Black Bottom IV	4	1.9	13	64
Black Bottom V	6	1	7	35
Black Bottom VI	4	1.5	10	49
Black Bottom VII	11	2.8	19	95
Black Bottom VIII	3	0.3	2	11
Black Bottom IX	4	0.9	6	30
Black Bottom other	16	3.8	26	128
Black Bottom I–IX	*111*	*32.1*	*217*	*1079*
Black Bottom total	*127*	*35.9*	*243*	*1207*
Upper Bottom I	14	6.2	41	207
Upper Bottom II	11	1.4	9	47
Upper Bottom III	3	1.2	8	40
Upper Bottom IV[b]	5	0.5	0	
Upper Bottom total	*33*	*9.3*	*58*	*294*
BB & UB total	*160*	*45.2*	*301*	*1501*
Angel site total	*—*	*4.6*	*31*	*209*

Table 8.2. Black Bottom, Upper Bottom, and Angel Site Organization
[a]Based on the assumptions of 5 persons per structure and 6.7 structures per occupied hectare; all structures assumed to be contemporaneous residences.
[b]Probably refuse disposal areas.

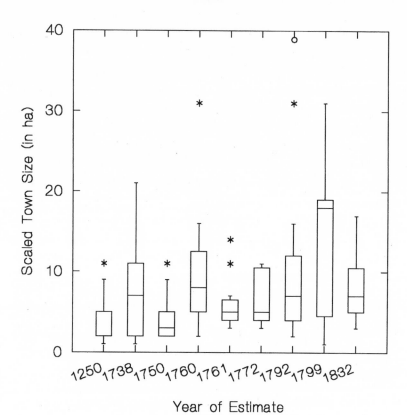

Figure 8.6. Creek town sizes between 1738 and 1832 compared with Lower Ohio Valley archaeological site size estimates at roughly A.D. 1250. See Figure 8.5 for an explanation of the main components of the box plots. The Ohio Valley data are summarized in the box plot marked *1250;* the median bar does not show because its value and that of the first quartile (i.e., the bottom of the box plot) are identical.

clusters (those labeled as 1250 in the box plot). The data in the box plots are a scaled town area based on population in the historical case. In the archaeological cases, the area is that defined in intensive survey, but the population estimates are derived from external support area and structure numbers as well as from site areas (see Muller 1986a for a detailed account of how these were originally defined and cross-checked against different estimation techniques).

The critical issue here is not the details of the scaling, but merely that these settlement data from the Black Bottom and other Lower Ohio Valley localities are structurally similar to the kinds of patterns seen in the historical data. Recent studies of the American Bottom (e.g., Mehrer 1995; Milner 1986) show very similar kinds of site organization, and the Tombigbee data (Blitz 1993) and Choctaw historical data (Voss and Blitz 1988) are other examples of many that could extend the argument outlined here. As more such data—based on modern reconnaissance data, not old catch-as-catch-can surveys from the thirties and forties—become available, I suggest that we will see fewer and fewer qualitative differences between historical and prehistoric settlement organization. Both periods were characterized by fluctuations in size and use of areas, and both also were aggregated or dispersed according to conditions at the time of use of the locations.

Conclusions

In short, the rumors of the death of large-scale chiefdoms in the East in early historical times are much exaggerated. Confederacies like the Choctaw and the Cherokee were larger than most prehistoric groups, with populations in excess of 20,000. The lack of disjunction between historical and prehistoric Mississippian settlement, as briefly outlined above, suggests that historical eastern populations tended to maintain town size even as the number of polities and the number of towns decreased. This also suggests that the supposed disconformities between social practice in historical and prehistoric times are also exaggerated, at the very least.

Two contradictory motives seem to have been at work here. The first was a reprehensible misrepresentation by historians such as Parkman (who seems to have known better; see Jennings 1963, 1975) of historic societies as a justification for European expansion. These misinterpretations are still embedded in interpretations of historic easterners. The second has been a natural desire of modern scholars to show the complexity of prehistoric eastern populations in response to the popular misconception that they were simple hunters and warriors. Unfortunately, overly grandiose pre-European social formations are thus compared with over-simplified views of historical groups. The differences do not seem so great when examined anew. This does not mean that we should interpret prehistoric societies using historical terms and structures. It does mean that it is reasonable to look to the historic East for testable models of prehistoric eastern social, political, and economic formations. Historical decline in population was not insignificant, but general decline has to be taken alongside some cases of local maintenance of population through aggregation and coalescence. Political degeneration has often been avoided in such circumstances, as in the case of late Medieval to early Renaissance Europe. Eastern political structures did change under such pressures, of course, but at least a few societies actually became more complex through the formation of states as a result of pressures from European invaders and their allies. Ironically, then, there is a good case for the attainment by some historical groups of the state levels that are absent in the prehistoric record—but when they did so, it is notable that those states were more "republican" in form than monarchical. What is lacking from both the historical and Mississippian examples is the exaggerated centralization of repressive force that has too often been proposed without any local historical or archaeological evidence requiring such political forms.

Notes

1. This chapter is part of a larger project on Mississippian political economy involving a series of works addressing specific topics as noted. Other works presented and published by me have discussed related aspects of political economy in general and specific issues discussed in this paper (e.g., Muller 1993a, 1994, 1997a, 1997b).

2. These data are drawn from a database of more than 2285 reported population data points on the East, mostly from the Southeast. Almost all sources are historical, but some estimates from twentieth-century ethnographers such as Mooney (1928), Ubelaker (1976), and Swanton (1922, 1946) are also included.

3. In this case, the data are those for historical cases in which there are figures given for population *and* for the number of towns. Because some of these are bound to be grouped multiple villages, these figures err in the direction of overestimating, not underestimating, town size. Data not included are a 1660 estimate for the Illinois (Jesuit Relations as cited in Hodge 1907:597) of 70,000 persons in sixty towns and a 1711 estimate for the Tuscarora of 4680 persons in "more than 3 villages" (see Swanton 1952:88).

4. Similar charts in Muller 1997a and 1997b have slightly different criteria for inclusion and are shown with plus or minus the standard deviation rather than range.

5. While these population figures vary greatly, their authors' main concern remained the number of effective soldiers that could either be allies or opponents. For estimates by politically responsible parties, there were dangers in incorrect estimation. Propagandists, on the other hand, sometimes had reason to exaggerate.

6. The data were analyzed with the Kruskal-Wallis test (Siegel 1956:184–93) using the Statview 4.0 program. If the means by fifty-year periods are compared, the differences from one fifty-year period to the others are not significant at $a = .01$ ($p = .42$). For all cases, there *were* significant ($p = .0004$, $a = .01$) differences between centuries (partly reflecting the predominance of eighteenth-century data that create problems for the statistical analysis, e.g., Kintigh 1989).

7. Despite historical connections, the estimates are largely, though by no means completely, independent. A Kruskal-Wallis analysis of all cases by fifty-year intervals (over half of these were from the late eighteenth century) at $a = .01$ just rejects significance for the variations. If the means for different "censuses" are compared, the statistic suggests strong probability that they are from the same statistical population. Also see comparisons to model rates of growth in Muller (1997a:175–77).

8. I have argued the case for a less exaggerated Mississippian at great length in my *Mississippian Political Economy* (1997a), while by no means denying that there are many regional and local differences among "Mississippian" complexes in general.

9. Increasingly, Mississippian archaeologists like B. Clay (e.g., 1997), B. Lewis, and G. Milner have argued that mound construction is more likely related to autonomy than subservience within rank hierarchies, as I have also done (Muller 1993b).

9

The Mississippian
Town Plan and Cultural
Landscape of Cahokia, Illinois

Scott J. Demel and Robert L. Hall

Located in the American Bottom of the Mississippi River Valley (Figure 9.1), Cahokia was a unique and monumental manifestation of a culture and community that existed from A.D. 800 to 1350 (Emergent Mississippi and Early Mississippi periods). The physical elements of the site, comprised of earthworks and landscape architecture, are human constructs that exemplify the social complexity and cohesion needed to plan such a community.

Cahokia was a dynamic system of structures, surfaces, and spaces purposefully designed with distinct functions in mind. The site grew into a planned community designed to imbue a memorable visual, social, psychological, and emotional impact on its inhabitants and visitors. The town plan and its reconstructed elements reflect a desire for harmony achieved through arrangement and continuous rearrangement of the natural and created physical environment in response to human needs. The community, the constructed site, and the natural environment were adapted to one another.

Accurate interpretations of this urban landscape must also address the social and ideological contexts that generated it. To give a sense of place and community, it is necessary not only to describe the Cahokia town plan and its primary elements, but also to touch on how social, economic, religious, and political factors may have been influenced by Mississippian town planning.

Our objective is to describe the complexity of Cahokia's town plan and the spatial distribution of its monuments and to assess the archaeological

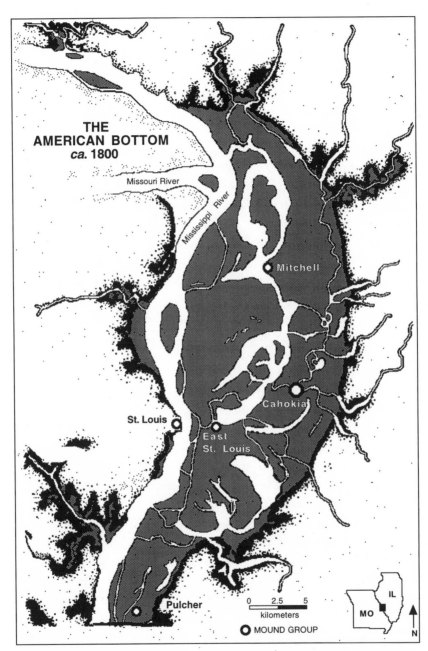

Figure 9.1. Reconstruction of the American Bottom ca. 1800 showing the Cahokia site and other mound group sites (adapted from Fowler 1989:fig. 1.2; source: Mikels Skele, Archaeology Laboratory, Southern Illinois University at Edwardsville).

evidence of urban renewal and multiple land uses at this Mississippian community. Although we examine much the same physical evidence as Fowler (1989) and Dalan (1993), our focus is more on the construction of artificial monuments across the whole site, on site layout and organization, and on urban renewal and landscape modification. We are less concerned with the restructuring of social organization that accompanied the intensification of maize agriculture.

As Cahokia evolved into the major ceremonial center in the American Bottom during the first 200 years of the Mississippi period (the Lohmann, Stirling, and early Moorehead phases), several ecological, economic, technological, and ideational changes occurred. As maize agriculture developed, a well-established hierarchical "complex chiefdom" evolved, building on existing trade networks, monumental architecture and earthworks, and an increasing population, beginning around A.D. 900 and lasting through A.D. 1200 (Bareis and Porter 1984:244; Smith 1978a:494; Stoltman 1991:vii).

By the Lohmann phase (A.D. 1000–1050), a "Cahokia settlement system" had been established, complete with a hierarchy of villages, single mound centers, outlying villages, and farming hamlets (Milner 1991:30). These contributed to and supported Cahokia as a first-line community, in the sense of Fowler (1978:468), and contributed to and supported its arena of social, religious, economic, and political growth (Smith 1978a:495).

Population estimates for Cahokia during this time of growth range between 10,000 and 25,000 persons (Denevan 1992:377; Fowler 1978:467; Gregg 1977:134). Population growth at Cahokia had cumulative effects on the town center and surrounding landscape. These effects may have been ephemeral at first but were quite dramatic over the long run (Butzer 1981:154–55; Denevan 1992:369).

The increasing population and social complexity put pressure on the landscape to accommodate the space needs of the people and spurred the expansion and reorganization of the Cahokian community and town center. Multiple cut-and-fill cycles present at Cahokia demonstrate that homeostatic equilibrium with the environment was never maintained for very long (Butzer 1981:155). Not only did Cahokians alter the landscape with their monumental earthworks and other architecture, but they also went below the natural surface, borrowing, leveling, and reclaiming earth (Dalan 1993:ix). Cahokia's local environment changed through modification of the topography, the creation of grasslands and agricultural fields, and related changes in forest composition, soils, microclimate, hydrology, and wildlife. The dramatic imprint of these activities created a "humanized landscape" (Denevan 1992:369; Stoltman 1991:351).

Downtown Cahokia

The core area of Cahokia was continuously modified by the "prolonged interplay" between the prehistoric inhabitants and their cultural landscape (Lynch 1962:5). During the Stirling phase (A.D. 1050–1150), downtown Cahokia was surrounded by a palisade constructed through an active residential zone. This town center consisted of a large plaza surrounded by eighteen earthen mounds (Figure 9.2). Both the Grand Plaza and some of the mound bases were created by filling and leveling sand ridges and borrow pits in the core area (Dalan 1993:42; Pauketat 1994:91). Most of Monks Mound, the largest and apparently the earliest mound in the town center, was constructed during this phase. Several archaeological excavations have revealed the ever-changing use of the land, particularly near and in the central core area of Cahokia (Figure 9.2).

Downtown Cahokia, also referred to as the "central precinct," was a palisaded central place planned and established at the heart of the site. Included within its fortified walls were elite residential neighborhoods, elite burials, and ritual and ceremonial precincts (Fowler 1989:201). According to Fowler (1989:198, 206), it was the "hub" of economic exchange, of craft production, and of the political domination of a large region. Around this central place grew a town, complete with subcommunities, plazas (Figure 9.3), mound clusters, grandiose architecture, community refuse pits, borrow pits and artificial ponds, woodhenges, and other features. Although only a small fraction of the central precinct has been excavated, the physical contours of the site suggest the cultural contours of a large and complex society.

Anthropogenic changes to the natural landscape at Cahokia were probably far more widespread than can be demonstrated from the existing excavations. Major changes include borrow pits, which were filled with refuse and the location occasionally reclaimed for mound construction; the leveling of vast areas for plazas; and the construction of mounds and mound groups, causeways, palisades, woodhenges, and other public works.

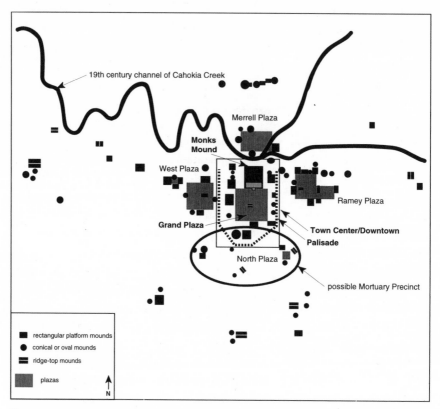

Figure 9.2. A map of the Cahokia site showing the town center or downtown area with the palisade, Monks Mound, and the Grand Plaza; also shown are sub-plazas and the possible Mortuary Precinct (adapted from Fowler 1989:fig. 10.1; source: University of Wisconsin-Milwaukee Archaeological Research Laboratory, 1966 Cahokia site map).

Palisade

Late in the Stirling phase, the first palisade around the central precinct was built with some 20,000 logs (Iseminger 1990:35 cited in Pauketat 1994:91). Surrounding the Grand Plaza and eighteen mounds, the log walls of the palisade probably enclosed a core area of some 82 hectares (Fowler 1989:196) (Figure 9.3). Contained within and protected by these walls were downtown Cahokia's public buildings, elite burial grounds, Grand Plaza, elite residences along the east and west walls, and the seat of Cahokia power (Fowler 1989:198). The log palisade included square bastions that were

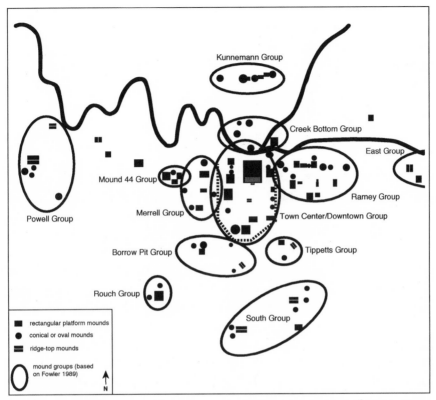

Figure 9.3. A map of the Cahokia site showing possible mound groups (adapted from Fowler 1989:fig. 10.1; source: University of Wisconsin-Milwaukee Archaeological Research Laboratory, 1966 Cahokia site map).

evenly spaced at 20-meter intervals, screened entrances, and perhaps even elevated walkways, all suggesting a defensive purpose for the wall (Anderson 1969:92–94, 98; Fowler 1978:465–66; Pauketat 1994:91).

The palisade, an upright wall of tree trunks, plastered with clay daub and painted, was a visual screen from the outside and a physical reminder of the elite and sacred places that lay hidden behind its walls. The palisade trenches, some sections of which are visible on early aerial photographs, show several episodes of rebuilding and relocation.

The palisade to the east of Monks Mound was built right through an active residential area (Fowler 1978:467; 1989:195–97). Remains of the north wall of the palisade, which would have faced Cahokia Creek, have not been discovered, and floodplain deposits have probably buried any evidence of them. Excavations indicate that the palisade wall was rebuilt at least three times, and the presence of extraction ramps for posts suggests the posts were likely reused during rebuilding efforts (Anderson 1969:98). Before the palisade's construction, the southern portion appears to have been filled with silty clay to raise the surface 1 meter or more above the natural terrain (Dalan 1993:152; Fowler 1989:230).

Plazas

A central plaza surrounded by mounds was a common characteristic of many of the larger Mississippian sites in the Southeast. Plazas were part of the town plan in that they were designed to focus community activity. They became the locale of special-purpose ceremonies and structures around which communities grew. Plazas probably also held public events, feasts, markets, and public games (e.g., chunky). The central Grand Plaza at Cahokia appears to have been constructed over a natural sand ridge that was in part augmented by nearly a meter of fill (Fowler 1989:200, 230), most likely during the Lohmann phase. Besides the Grand Plaza, which covered about 12 hectares, four smaller plazas have been identified around the core of Cahokia (Fowler 1989:199–204) (Figure 9.2). All of these lesser plazas are associated with mound clusters and range in size up to about 4 hectares. The Merrell Plaza is associated with the Creek Bottom Mound Group, the Ramey Plaza with the Ramey Mound Group, the North Plaza with the Tippetts Mound Group, and the West Plaza with the Mound 44 Group. Six other mound clusters have been identified that do not appear to be associated with plazas (Figure 9.3).

Mounds

More than 100 mounds of varying shapes, sizes, and orientations were constructed throughout Cahokia as permanent monuments associated with the ancestors buried within them or with their functions in life.[1] Mounds were used as locales for temples and charnel houses, foundations for residential and public buildings, burial chambers, and marker monuments at critical locations within the community.

The site contains the typical round conical tumuli and flat-topped platform mounds found in other Mississippian towns in the Southeast, but

Cahokia's "ridge-top" mounds are unique to this site (Fowler 1989:13). Mound 72 and the other seven ridge-top mounds may contain mortuary facilities of the elite, charnel houses, large posts, and perhaps sacrificial victims and sumptuous grave offerings (Fowler 1989:192). These ridge-top mounds occur at key locations around the central part of Cahokia and probably served as what Fowler calls "marker mounds" (Figure 9.3).

Flat-topped mounds and conical mounds appear throughout Cahokia, often in pairs. Flat-topped or platform mounds supported religious or residential superstructures that were thus elevated above the common ground surface, as well as above the seasonal flooding waters. Few of these platform mounds had more than one terrace; Monks Mound had an unprecedented four terraces (Figure 9.4). Harriet Smith (1969:86–87) identified two terraces at the Murdock Mound (Mound 55).

Conical mounds may have been mortuary facilities. They are often paired with platform mounds; the largest pair (Mounds 59 and 60) at Cahokia are situated in what has been called the "mortuary precinct" (Fowler

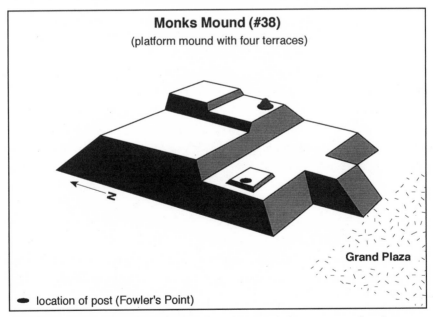

Figure 9.4. A view of Monks Mound (Mound 38) with four terraces; also shown are the small platform mound on the first terrace with location of post (Fowler's Point) and the small conical mound on the third terrace (adapted from Fowler 1989:fig. 5.2; source: 1938 illustration by Byron W. Knoblock).

1989:201) of the core area (Figure 9.2). Most of these mound types were built by incremental construction or in sequential stages (i.e., mounds constructed over submounds or over existing mounds) (Fowler 1989:195; 1991:10). A thorough understanding of the contemporaneity of mound construction and variations in mound content and form is unfortunately lacking because of the limited amount of mound investigations and the great amount of recent agricultural activity.

The functions of mounds at Cahokia appear to have changed over time. According to Smith (1969:62–66), Mound 55 (Murdock Mound) was originally a residential platform mound, but, during the course of eight occupational episodes, it became the substructure for a public building. Altogether, Murdock Mound had twelve building episodes. Although this seems like a lot, Kunnemann Mound had forty-four mantles (Pauketat 1994:87). The above-ground portion of Powell Mound (Mound 86) was constructed with at least six stages, showing continued use. In another example, Mound 72 (constructed during the early Lohmann phase) was at first three smaller mounds, which were then reshaped and covered over (Fowler 1991:10). The smaller mounds included two rectangular platform mounds (Mound 72 Sub 1 and Sub 2), an extended platform mound or modified ridge-top mound (Mound 72 Sub 3), and a series of substages, one of which was a small conical mound that was placed over the buried remains of four headless and handless individuals (Fowler, personal communication, 1996).

Urban renewal is also evidenced at Cahokia by the construction of mounds over preexisting features so that the land was reclaimed for a new use. For example, Mound 55 was built over a circular trench in which there was a central burnt basin or altar containing bone and tobacco (Fowler 1989:86–88; Moorehead 1929:45–47; Smith 1969:58, 60–61). Mounds 44 and 72 were placed over portions of woodhenges (Fowler 1989:114; Wittry 1996:fig. 3.1B) and submounds; others, such as Mounds 20 and 72, were built over submound burials. Several other mounds (e.g., Mounds 84 and 86) were constructed over habitation sites, and in at least one case a mound (Mound 51) was built over a culturally filled-in borrow pit (Chmurny 1973; Titterington 1938:159, 165). The potential for finding out more about the Emergent Mississippi phase lies beneath the mounds at Cahokia, which Gregg (1977:132) estimates to cover 30 hectares of the site.

Village or residential debris has also been found beneath several mounds and in mound fill. Village debris extended to the bottom of Mounds 10, 32, and 33 and was also found beneath Mounds 34 and 84, Murdock Mound (Mound 55), and Powell Mound (Mound 86). Mounds may also be thought of as above-ground refuse heaps, often filled with village or habitation debris (Cahokia examples include Mounds 30, 32, 33, and 50). Moorehead (1929:49) suggests the type of mound fill depends on its location within the site; however, others suggest that choices of mound fill, including that with habitation refuse, are deliberate (Dalan 1993:201–3).

Monks Mound

The largest and most extraordinary example of a unique Mississippian monumental and artificial earthwork is Monks Mound. This mound is an exaggerated example of the physical expression of a religious and political system common to Mississippian peoples (Reed 1977:33). Consisting of four terraces, this mound is more than 30 meters high and has a base covering approximately 5.5 hectares (Fowler 1989) (Figures 9.2 and 9.4). Adding to the height of this earthen monument was a 30- by 12-meter structure situated on the highest terrace. Perhaps an elite residence or public building, this structure is the largest, and perhaps the most important, so far discovered at Cahokia.

Monks Mound was once visible from 8 to 20 kilometers away (Brackenridge 1962). With the additional height provided by the building on top of the mound, it may have been visible from even farther away. Monks Mound was thus a cultural beacon to the many Cahokians within its visual and influential range. Its height attests to the intensity of organized labor and community cooperation involved in such an endeavor (Dalan 1993:181). Built in fourteen to eighteen stages between A.D. 1000 and 1300 (Fowler 1989:104, 214; Reed, Bennett, and Porter 1968:146), it dominated the central precinct, allowing its occupants to view all others from above.

Seventeen other mounds surrounded Monks Mound and the Grand Plaza (roughly 12 hectares); Red Mound (Mound 49) and Jesse Ramey Mound (Mound 56) were between the east and west walls of the palisade and were important in defining the main plaza of Cahokia (Fowler 1989:198). In turn, these downtown mounds were surrounded by a palisade encompassing 82 hectares (Fowler 1989:196). The central core of Cahokia, within the fortified area, is further subdivided by Fowler (1989:201) into three precincts: the Monks Mound Precinct, the Grand Plaza Precinct, and the Mortuary Precinct.

According to Fowler (1989:201), the Monks Mound Precinct takes up the northern one-third of the central core and is centered on Monks Mound; the east side contains a platform mound and a conical mound; the west side has a row of two platform mounds and two conical mounds. The Grand Plaza Precinct covers the central one-third and includes a ridge-top mound near the plaza center; the west side has a large platform mound; the east side has a group of two platform mounds and two conical mounds. The Mortuary Precinct is located in the southern portion of the central core and includes a platform mound and a conical mound (Figure 9.2). Although there are other paired mounds within the palisade that may or may not include burials, Fowler (1989:201) proposes that, on the basis of the size and location of these mounds, the Mortuary Precinct is where the elite persons of Cahokia were buried. Mounds 72 and 96, along with several others located around Borrow Pit 5-1A, are considered part of a "ceremonial complex" or "special-use area" complete with elaborate burials (Fowler 1989:204).[2]

Mound Clusters

Besides the Grand Plaza and the precincts of the central core or "downtown" Cahokia, Fowler (1989) has identified eleven mound clusters,[3] most of which fall within 1 kilometer of Monks Mound; the rest are within 13 kilometers. Five of these groups are situated around open areas or plazas (Figure 9.3), including the Merrell Group, the Ramey Group (about 4 hectares), the Tippetts Group, the Mound 44 Group, and the Creek Bottom Group. Fowler (1989) suggests that these clusters are "subcommunities, satellites, or barrios," all of which seem to surround downtown Cahokia. These mound clusters may represent individual sociopolitical segments of Cahokia, perhaps ruled and occupied by elite members of society related to the rulers of Cahokia and who, in turn, perhaps represented distant subcommunities that had mound centers (Fowler 1989:202). These distant villages may have had a satellite mound center at Cahokia, occupied during certain times of the year for prescribed ceremonies; perhaps their populations periodically aggregated at Cahokia in times of warfare or famine.[4]

Tri-Mound Groups

Another type of mound arrangement found outside the core area at Cahokia is "tri-mound" groups, such as those in the Tippetts Group. Tri-mound groups appear to be located along secondary site axes, or azimuths,

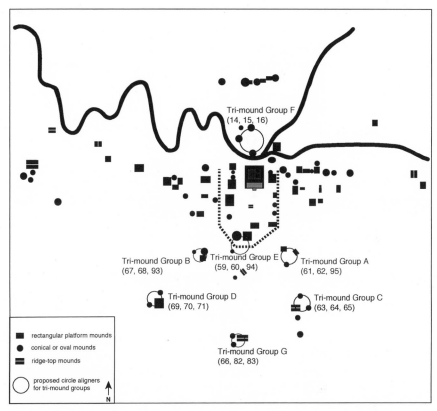

Figure 9.5. A map of the Cahokia site showing possible tri-mound groups (adapted from Fowler 1989:fig. 10.1; source: University of Wisconsin-Milwaukee Archaeological Research Laboratory, 1966 Cahokia site map).

out from the proposed north-south center axis of the Cahokia site (Fowler 1989:151) (Figures 9.5 and 9.6). Most tri-mound groups appear to be associated with artificially created water features.

Within the central section of the Cahokia site, principal axes of site orientation have been proposed by Fowler (1989:151). These cross at a post in the southwest corner of Monks Mound (known as Fowler's Point) and on Post V of Mound 72. Others suggest the center line utilizes an "elevated sighting platform" and a huge post on the fourth terrace of Monks Mound (Reed, Bennett, and Porter 1968:146–47). Adjusting Fowler's north-south axis (1 degree 16 minutes east of true north) to connect to either the center of Mound 96 or to the proposed center post of Woodhenge 72, instead of

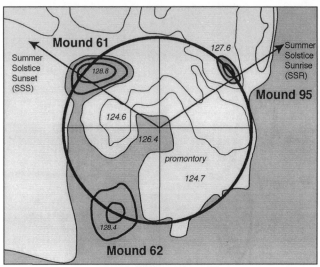

Tippetts Tri-Mound Group (A).

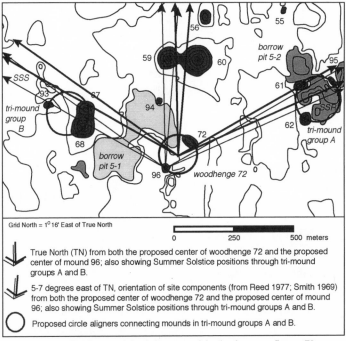

Tri-mound groups, circle aligners, revised site axes; originating from woodhenge 72 components.

Figure 9.6. Detail of the possible Mortuary Precinct area of the Cahokia site showing axes of site orientation (true north and adjusted) and summer solstice axes from the center of Woodhenge 72 and Mound 96; also shown is a detail of tri-mound group A with summer solstice axes and circle aligner (adapted from Fowler 1989:figs. 6.17 and 6.31; source: University of Wisconsin-Milwaukee Archaeological Research Laboratory, 1966 Cahokia site map).

Post V in Mound 72, causes the central axis to move slightly to the west (Figure 9.7). The north-south axis goes through Mound 49 in the central plaza, between the paired mounds (Mounds 59 and 60) at the southern end of the plaza, and exits the central precinct through the opening in the palisade wall. The axis continues southward through Mound 72 and connects to Mound 66. Connecting the four identified ridge-top marker mounds (Fowler 1989:195) and the four possible ridge-top mounds (Mounds 16, 31, 75, and 95) (Figure 9.7) creates a recognizable site organization and mound placement strategy.

Mounds 49, 64, 66, and 72 have all been identified as ridge-top mounds (Fowler 1989:appendix 3; Pauketat 1994:81) and appear to be equidistant from one another. Ridge-top Mounds 64 and 95 also appear to be the same distance apart, 550 to 600 meters, as Mounds 49, 66, and 72. These mounds appear to be station points along the site's main axis. Diagonal distances between these mounds also appear to be nearly equidistant. When a line is drawn between them, it reveals a triangular pattern, perhaps utilized in the layout of the site (Figure 9.7).

Using a realignment of the north-south axis as described above, and taking into account the 5- to 7.5-degree difference between Monks Mound alignment and true north (Reed 1977:33; Reed, Bennett, and Porter 1968:137, 146; Smith 1969:66), new secondary axes from the Mound 72 woodhenge to the summer solstice positions bisect two tri-mound groups (Group A: Mounds 61, 62, and 95; Group B: Mounds 67, 68, and 93) (Figures 9.6 and 9.7). The northeast summer solstice sunrise (SSR) axis, about 30 degrees north of east, bisects tri-mound Group A and leads to a possible ridge-top mound, Mound 95. The northwest summer solstice sunset (SSS) axis, about 30 degrees north of west, bisects tri-mound Group B and leads to the recently discovered Mound 93, another possible ridge-top mound (Figures 9.6 and 9.7).

From ridge-top Mound 66 (part of tri-mound Group G [66, 82, 83]), another SSR axis aligns roughly with ridge-top Mound 64 to the northeast (Figure 9.7), which is also part of a tri-mound group (Group C: Mounds 63, 64, and 65; Figure 9.5). The SSS axis lines up roughly with tri-mound Group D (Mounds 69, 70, and 71) farther to the west. This tri-mound group is situated farther west than expected, but this may be because of the linear swamp just to the east (Fowler 1989:56, fig. 3.10). An SSR axis out from Mound 49 goes through Mounds 31, 32, 33 (James Ramey Mound[5]),

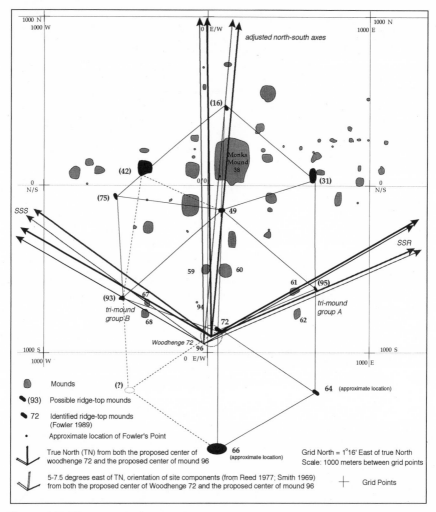

Figure 9.7. The central portion of the Cahokia site showing possible relationships of site components. Shown are connections of identified ridge-top mounds and possible ridge-top mounds indicating a triangle pattern. Also shown are the true north site axis and summer solstice axes (sunrise [*SSR*] and sunset [*SSS*]) originating from the center of Woodhenge 72 (*thick black line*) or from the center of Mound 96 (*thin black line*). In addition, an adjusted (5 to 7.5 degrees) north site axis and summer solstice axes are shown, originating from the center of Woodhenge 72 (*thick gray line*) or from Mound 96 (*thin gray line*). Axes show possible relationships of tri-mound groups A and B, ridge-top mounds, Mounds 59 and 60, Mound 49, and Fowler's Point (adapted from Fowler 1989:figs. 3.10 and 6.31; source: University of Wisconsin-Milwaukee Archaeological Research Laboratory, 1966 Cahokia site map, USGS survey field notes for 1930 and 1931, and Fowler 1996:fig. 4.3).

and 34 (Mound 31 may be a ridge-top mound). An SSS axis from Mound 49 goes through the southwest corner of Mound 42, where an "oval platform mound is built" (Fowler 1989:111), which may have been another ridge-top mound that is now deflated by modern plowing. Although obscured by the number of mounds and fill episodes, it does not appear the axes from Mound 49 are associated with tri-mound groups. A line connecting Mounds 49 and 75 (which may be a ridge-top mound) is seemingly equidistant to those connecting Mound 72 to other possible ridge-top mounds (Figure 9.7), although the angle of the line from Mound 49 to Mound 75 is less than 30 degrees (SSS). Similar lines connect possible ridge-top mounds 16, 31, and 75.

Tri-mound Group A (Mounds 61, 62, and 95) is nearly bisected by the SSR axis (to the northeast). In Figure 9.6, not only does the axis appear to bisect the two closest mounds (Mounds 61 and 62), but it also goes through a portion of Mound 95. If there is a post in Mound 95 along this axis, the positioning would be similar to that of the easternmost summer solstice sunrise post in Mound 72 (Post V). A circle with a diameter of about 95 to 100 meters can be drawn through all three mounds that centers on a promontory that extends into the center of the small borrow pit near Mound 62 (Figure 9.6). The peninsula or promontory that juts out in the middle of this small tri-mound group is itself symmetrical (Fowler 1989:204), and the SSR axis cuts across this approximately 35-square-meter land projection. The arrangement of the circle roughly corresponds to the same circularity of the causeway shown on the Patrick map (Fowler 1989:9, fig. 1.4).

Perhaps this causeway followed the outline of the circular arrangement of the three mounds. A circular arrangement of posts may have been used to align critical points in the landscape. A circle connecting each of the three mounds in tri-mound Group A corresponds roughly to the size of the Mound 72 woodhenge and was possibly laid out in the same manner. A reflection of this arrangement with the SSS axis to the west appears in tri-mound Group B (Mounds 67, 68, and 93) (Figure 9.7). Other tri-mound groups include Group E (Mounds 59, 60, and 94) and Group F (Mounds 14, 15, and 16) (Figure 9.5).

The apparent alignment of these tri-mound groups with strategic solstice positions, seemingly mirrored on either side of the north-south axis line, may have been a recurring theme in the site organization at Cahokia. Although it is unlikely that the tri-mound groups belonged to any woodhenges, they probably contained posts that were important markers in the landscape. Use of these axes and arrangement of mounds around a circle appear to comprise a method of site alignment and structuring. In all cases, the tri-mound groups seem to be arranged in a circular configuration, with the mounds on the perimeter of a circle that connects at least a portion of each mound. Some of the tri-mound groups are also associated with water features, either inside the circle or adjacent to it; some of these appear incidentally shaped and others purposefully dug as borrow pits.

Woodhenges

To the west of downtown Cahokia, in an area known as Tract 15A, several woodhenges have been discovered (Fowler 1989:32). These woodhenges, also known as sun-circles (Wittry 1977:47) or post-circle monuments (Pauketat 1994:88), were built over habitation sites that had been used for several generations (Fowler 1993; Smith 1992). To the south of the downtown area, or central core, another woodhenge has been identified by Fowler (1991:6) near Mound 72.

Many interpretations have been offered for the function of these woodhenges. Most fall into one of five categories, but there is some overlap. The first set of interpretations suggests these woodhenges were used for tracking astronomical events (primarily solar), for celestial orientation, and for monitoring the annual or calendrically determined ceremonial cycles of planting and harvesting (Fowler 1991:6; Helms 1992:187; Knight 1990a; Peebles and Kus 1977; Reed 1977:33; Smith 1992:11). The second suggests they were locations of extreme importance in the community, that is, controlled ceremonial spaces reserved for sacred and secular activities and other public events, such as dances, games, and contests (Fowler 1991:9; Wittry 1980:14, 1996:30, 32). The third idea proposes that these post-circle monuments were structures of domination, containers of esoteric knowledge (Fowler 1991:24), levers of social inequality (Smith 1992:15, 23, 28), or architectural representations of the Mississippian world view (Fowler 1991:9)—all attempts to organize, integrate, and control subcommunities and to legitimize leadership and political domination (Helms 1992:190).

A fourth interpretation suggests the woodhenges were in-the-ground surveying instruments, alidades, or aligners and a way to implement the town plan into the landscape along prescribed axes (Fowler 1991:8; Sherrod and Rolingson 1987). As surveying instruments they could have been utilized for determining the placement of important features across the site, using both angular alignments (such as solstice or equinox positions) from observation points within the woodhenges and fixed distance measurements (Fowler 1991:8–10) between mounds, posts, and other features. These aligners could have been a way of recording the complexity of the site organization and a way of guiding its realization as "technical outputs of site planning" (Lynch 1962:7). To be used as aligners, these woodhenges would have had to have existed before and during the layout and subsequent restructuring of the community layout. According to Smith (1992:15), their initial construction and use occurred during the latter part of the Lohmann phase and the first half of the Stirling phase, precisely when the town of Cahokia reached its florescence and greatest political control over the subcommunities of the American Bottom (Smith 1992:23). Other nonresidential monumental structures included huge rectangular and circular wall-trench buildings in Tracts 15A and 15B and atop larger mounds such as Monks, Murdock, and Kunnemann (Pauketat 1994:87).

The idea of woodhenges as aligners is supported by the placement of posts in certain astronomical positions around the proposed Mound 72 woodhenge. The woodhenge posts were in place early, in submounds beneath the final ridge-top cap of Mound 72. For example, Post PP1 was in place at the summer solstice sunrise position (from the center of the woodhenge) prior to the interment of the elaborate beaded burial (Fowler 1991:10, 24). Another woodhenge is predicted east of Monks Mound, in the vicinity of Mounds 27, 28, 29, and 53 (Fowler, personal communication, 1996). In other areas of the site, additional posts have also been predicted (e.g., in Mound 49) in key locations (the center of the Tippetts Group), some of these along Fowler's proposed site axes. Other prominent posts have been found beneath mounds, placed there before mound construction; some mounds were even constructed around existing posts. For example, during the demolition of a cone-shaped mound at East St. Louis, just west of Cahokia (Figure 9.1), several upright eastern red cedar posts were found near its base (Snyder 1962:249).

Fowler (1989, 1991:14) sees the woodhenges as cognitive maps of the community, useful in the planning and layout of Cahokia. The woodhenges vary in diameter from 72 to 138 meters and vary greatly in the number of actual and predicted posts. The five woodhenges in Tract 15A apparently represent a temporal sequence (late Lohmann and Stirling phases) of increasing diameter, from twenty-four, thirty-six, forty-eight, and sixty to seventy-two posts, increasing by twelve posts each time. If one accepts an "aligner" function for the woodhenges, then the variations necessarily reflect the ever-changing town plan, whereupon these post-circles had to be rebuilt, enlarged, relocated, or even duplicated. The variations among the woodhenges would then reflect a site planner's attempts at conforming to an overall site plan, accumulating experience through trial and error, checking the built environment and performance (Lynch 1962:6–7) of the original site plan and woodhenge, and making necessary corrections.

A fifth interpretation, and the one favored here, views the woodhenges as a cosmogram and the equivalent, on a grand scale, of the world center representations that were part of so many ritual areas in the Plains and Southwest and that served both community functions and personal spiritual quests. As such, their purpose would not have been simply as places for passive solar observations, but as active devices for receiving and focusing the energy of nature within a community or ritual area (Hall 1985, 1996:125) or, in the case of mourning ritual, for facilitating the ascent of the spirit of the deceased into the Spirit World via the center pole (Hall 1997:162; Lame Deer and Erdoes 1972:111–12, 220).

Woodhenges are thus considered to be public monuments or architecture, but only "public" in the sense that they were probably constructed through communal labor and were certainly on public display. The role of the elite in the construction and use of such woodhenges (Fowler 1978:467; Smith 1992:15) is evidenced by the urban renewal of the Tract 15A area, wherein the land's use changed from residential, to woodhenge monuments and public architecture, back to residential use (Fowler 1989:114), and finally to earthen monuments (i.e., Mound 44). These circles of upright wooden posts were privileged intellectual property, and ownership and knowledge of their use was likely limited to a select few, probably members of a particular social class (Lynch 1962:6).

Taken together, these woodhenges would then represent an elaborate special-use area reserved for the use of an elite class, an area that incorporated many social and sacred values into its form (Fowler 1991:9–10). Elite burials in such corporate facilities were often accompanied by elaborate processions through the "life space of the wider community" (Binford 1971:23). Greater amounts of this kind of corporate energy and community involvement correspond to the elevated social rank of the deceased in most if not all societies (Tainter 1978:127), as do the complexity of burial treatment and place of interment (Chapman and Randsborg 1981) and the placement of important or significant grave goods with the interred (Goldstein, personal communication, 1994).

The presence of a woodhenge, like Fowler's Woodhenge 72, in a mortuary area would not be at all anomalous. Around 1692, Father Francisco de Jesus Maria Casanas described the construction of a circle of posts as part of a mortuary ritual among the Caddoan-speaking Hasinai of east Texas (Bolton 1987:156). These posts were said to represent "moons" (read "months") and so were probably twelve in number or some multiple thereof—perhaps a monumental expression of the symbolism represented by certain wooden hoops made by the Caddoan-speaking Pawnee, which contained twenty-four divisions said to symbolize the seasons and the moons or months (Weltfish 1965:400–401). It is clear from the description of the Pawnee hoop that it was meant to correspond to the path through the sky of the sun, moon, and planets, so that a forty-eight-post woodhenge consisting of a full circle and not just a set of sunrise and sunset arcs can be seen as a conflation of the ecliptic and the horizon.

The camp circles of the Omaha and Osage provide other examples of the conflation of a three-dimensional celestial universe into a two-dimensional earthly plane (Hall 1997:84–85, 165, 170, 182). Centermost in the half of the Osage and Omaha camp circles representing the sky were the tipis of the Deer Head clan (Fletcher and La Flesche 1972:60, 177, figs. 10, 20). Because *Deer Head* is the translation of the name of the Pleiades constellation in the Omaha and Osage languages, the central location of the clan in the sky arc could represent a moment during the night when the Pleiades transited the meridian. How this association figured in the ritual activities of the Omaha and Osage, we do not know. For the Caddoan Hasinai the appearance of the Pleiades at the zenith was used to time the beginning of one phase of a fall harvest festival for which a circle of small poles had been constructed, a cultural memory, perhaps, of the former use of a more monumental, woodhenge-like structure (Hall 1996:124).

Causeways

Certain linear areas of land elevated by human hands, situated between mounds and connecting high points of land between water features, have been labeled or described as "causeways." As described above, one such semi-circular bridge of land was identified by Patrick in 1876 between Mounds 61 and 62 (Fowler 1989:132). Another elevated, graded path, flanked by swampy areas, once ran from Fox Mound (Mound 60) in a southerly direction toward Rattlesnake Mound (Mound 66) (Fowler 1989:142; Moorehead 1929:105). Although it is possible that this causeway was aboriginal in origin, it may have been fill added for a railroad spur, given that a railroad track did once bisect the site in an east-west direction (Hall 1991:fig. 1.2) and another still runs along the southern edge of the site. No early maps show a railway in a north-south direction. A steel railroad spike was found within the causeway running south from Mound 60 (J. Anderson, personal communication, 1972), but the preexistence of an aboriginal causeway could have determined the route of any such railroad spur.

Causeways or avenues were noted by early explorers (e.g., Bartram 1996) and often led to bodies of water, which at Cahokia were sometimes water-filled borrow pits. Bartram (1996:100–101), for example, noted high pyramidal mounds with spacious and extensive avenues or highways that linked them to artificial lakes or ponds that could be seen in Florida from the St. Johns River south to the Keys (Figure 9.8). Bartram interpreted these avenues as "for ornament or monuments of magnificence, to perpetuate the power and grandeur of the nation" (Bartram 1996:413). Causeways were no doubt built throughout low areas of Cahokia as routes of overland travel, planned to facilitate trade, administration, warfare, and social interaction (Denevan 1992:377), as well as religious and mortuary rituals.

Borrow Pits

Although artificial bodies of water were a common feature of Mississippian sites throughout the Southeast, they are typically ignored in the discussion of Mississippian community layout and town planning practices. Very little archaeological investigation has been directed toward determining the importance of borrow pits as features or toward finding well-preserved materials for better understanding Cahokia subsistence (Chmurny 1973)

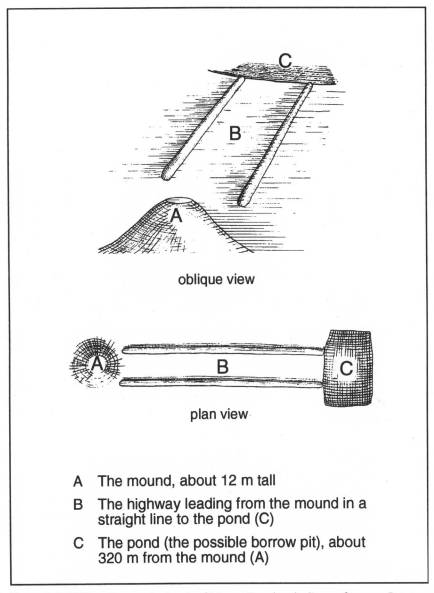

oblique view

plan view

A   The mound, about 12 m tall

B   The highway leading from the mound in a
     straight line to the pond (C)

C   The pond (the possible borrow pit), about
     320 m from the mound (A)

Figure 9.8. William Bartram's sketch of Mount Royal and adjacent features, Putnam County, Florida (adapted from Bartram 1853).

and Mississippian material culture. Artificial bodies of water at Cahokia and most Mississippian ceremonial centers (e.g., the Arcola, Cramer, and Barton Ranch sites) are by-products of the construction of earthen architecture and earthen mounds. The process of obtaining fill, dug by hand in the village and low-lying areas, left gaping holes in the landscape.

Some of these newly created borrow pits were left to fill in naturally.[6] On the basis of the limited archaeological investigation conducted so far at Cahokia's borrow pits, other pits were intentionally filled in with refuse, including human bone[7] (Bareis 1975); these were leveled and reused as new foundations for mound construction. These depressions, often water-filled, may have been purposefully sculpted into the landscape and placed inside ritual and ceremonial areas. For example, the Natchez and Cherokee had a ceremonial means of overcoming pollution, purifying themselves, and increasing longevity that involved going to water or bathing by plunging into water four times a day (Hudson 1976:324, 414).

The water-filled borrow pits probably served as features themselves in the cultural landscape and appear to have been associated with several tri-mound groups (Figure 9.6). They may have also served as aquatic medicinal gardens; as containers of esoteric healing knowledge. Having both utilitarian and medicinal purposes, they likely also served as sources of food (i.e., waterfowl, fish, reptiles) and construction material (bullrushes and reeds) and as sources of drinking water.

Early accounts from travelers and writers such as William Bartram (1996) reported that the Creeks on the Tallapoosa River in Georgia and the Missouri Valley native Americans cultivated one of their favorite floral remedies, the blue flag (*Iris versicolor*), for medicinal (cathartic or laxative) purposes. According to Bartram, "They hold this root in high estimation, every town cultivates a little plantation of it, having a large artificial pond, just without the town, planted and almost overgrown with it, where they dig clay for pottery, and mortar and plaster for their buildings, and I observed where they had lately been digging up this root" (Bartram 1996:366–67; Vogel 1973:104–5).

Other aquatic plants such as ground nut (*Apios americana*), lotus (*Nelumbo lutea*), arrowhead (*Sagitaria sagittifolia*), and duck potato (*Saggitaria latifolia*) were often cultivated and harvested in wet environments (Densmore 1974:292; Foster and Duke 1990:16, 158), possibly formed by water-filled borrow pits that may have acted as aquatic gardens.

At least twenty borrow pits have been identified at Cahokia (Dalan 1993:42, 135; Fowler 1989:230). Borrow pits at Cahokia were probably located in wet and swampy areas rather than in productive agricultural land, and they were likely flooded on a seasonal basis (Smith 1978a:484). Many of these borrow pits were later filled in with refuse and soil and reclaimed for mound construction or habitation (Fowler 1989:188) as part of the expansion and reorganization of the site.

In an example of land reclamation or urban renewal, Mound 51 was constructed over part of a borrow pit that had been filled in quickly with refuse (Chmurny 1973; Fowler 1989:124). A pit beneath Mound 34 was filled in much the same way (Reed, Bennett, and Porter 1968:145). By contrast, a portion of the central part of Borrow Pit 5-1A was filled in by natural sedimentation.[8] The remainder of the pit contained artificial fill and midden,[9] primarily at what appears to be the water edge (about the 38-meter contour) or margin of the pit (Demel 1992).

The typological consistency of most potsherds found in Borrow Pit 5-1A is typical of those found in the Lohmann phase. A small percentage of Stirling phase ceramics were also recovered (Hall 1972), consisting of Powell Plain and Hickory Fine Engraved (Bareis and Porter 1984:168; Fowler and Hall 1975:6). Among the nonceramic artifacts were Mill Creek hoe fragments with visible sickle gloss (Demel 1992), placing the borrow pit within a time when maize was cultivated (also found in the Lohmann phase). Some badly decomposed human skeletal fragments were also recovered from the borrow pit fill (Demel 1992).

The filling of borrow pits and the leveling of areas throughout Cahokia appear to have been more common than once thought. Fowler (1989:179) suggests and Dalan (1993:42, 135) demonstrates that some of the central portion of Cahokia had originally contained several borrow pits. As the population expanded during the Emergent Mississippi period, that portion of the site was filled in with up to 2.8 meters of fill and put to different uses (Woods and Holley 1989:230). These major filling and leveling episodes can also be seen at other Mississippian sites, including, for example, Chucalissa, Ocmulgee, Snodgrass, Angel, and Etowah (Dalan 1993:161). In the vicinity of Monks Mound and Cahokia Creek, existing borrow pits were filled, reexcavated, and sometimes refilled and covered by mounds (Reed, Bennett, and Porter 1968:145). Refuse dumping in areas other than borrow pits has been reported by Vander Leest (1980) in the

Cahokia Creek floodplain to the north of the residential zone in the Ramey field.

Site Linkages

As Lynch (1962) discusses, sites are made up of both tangible and intangible linkages. Intangible linkages are defined as the meanings attached to spaces—their importance; their connection with the past; how they evoke memories, expectations, and fears; the sacredness of an area; and more. These intangible linkages may be fleshed out after further investigation of the tangible linkages, but we need to vastly improve the way we look for and recognize tangible evidence of linkages at Cahokia, both above and below ground. These linkages were both physical and visual. They consisted of pedestrian circulation pathways that physically connected spaces and elements of the town plan. They were the locus of points in the landscape from which the site was seen and experienced.

Site planning efforts at Cahokia should be seen as a continuous stream of modifications applied to a changing symbolic landscape, rather than as the impromptu creation of elements imposed on a static world (Lynch 1962:23). Artificial monuments, whether made of earth, wood, or water, need also to be considered as obstacles (Lynch 1962:133) that may have been methodically placed into the landscape to guide the experience of the user— to channel, enhance, or even purposely block a user's view. Because all segments of the site are in some way linked, tangibly or not, changes in one part of the site would likely have propagated response changes throughout the entire system (Lynch 1962:13). Evidence of such rearrangements at Cahokia are clues to preferred activity and use patterns. These modifications reflect ways of trying to create a new balance, one that better suited the inhabitants' purposes (Lynch 1962:11, 32). If we can continue to identify these anthropogenic modifications and episodes of urban renewal at Cahokia we may begin to form a comprehensive town plan and determine whether site planning objectives were fulfilled.

Summary

Cahokia is far from being a "typical" Mississippian site. It represents the dominant community and seat of cultural influence in a vast regional settlement system. The planned alignment of the town and civic center of Cahokia began to take place during Emergent Mississippi and Early Mississippi period times. During the Lohmann phase, Monks Mound began to rise, the first palisade was erected around the Grand Plaza, and woodhenges were constructed. Nowhere else in the Mississippian world does one find a mound as big as Monks Mound or a plaza as large as the Grand Plaza. Woodhenges have yet to be found archaeologically outside of Cahokia. Certainly the overwhelming evidence of prehistoric urban renewal and changing land use, primarily oriented around the central core area and special use areas, suggests a seat of power that directed the destiny of the Cahokian community (Fowler 1989:198, 206; Smith 1992:25, 27–28). Understanding the town plan of Cahokia and its subcommunities is only a start toward understanding the complexity of this paramount village. The investigation of this purposeful organization of public monuments, plazas, structures, and activities indicates that the site of Cahokia and the central core area were designed to meet the ever-changing needs of its prehistoric human inhabitants.

Our descriptions of the Cahokia town plan and explanation of the archaeological evidence of urban renewal and multiple land use show the complexity of the Cahokia site layout and organization. The physical elements of the town plan were not dispersed at random, but were purposefully linked. We need to consider these links within the town plan and how various earthen monuments, public architecture, activities, and use areas were connected in time and space. The cultural landscape of Cahokia was not merely incidental background to the lives of its inhabitants and visitors, but its "sense of place" somehow defined and shaped their experience, a feat it continues to accomplish today.

Notes

1. Most mounds are oriented approximately to the cardinal directions, but vary between 5 and 7.5 degrees east of true north (Reed 1977; Smith 1969).

2. At Aztalan, the platform mound and plaza are considered part of the specialized-mortuary precinct (Stoltman 1991).

3. Fowler (1989:198–205) lists these eleven groups as follows: the Kunne-

mann or North Group, the East Group, the Rattlesnake or South Group, the Rouch Group, the Powell or West Group, the Creek Bottom Group, the Ramey Group, the Tippetts Group, the Borrow Pit Group or Mound 72 Group, the Mound 44 Group, and the Merrell Group.

4. Ten pairs of mounds at the Moundville site in west-central Alabama may represent satellite mound centers for the ten minor ceremonial centers associated with major villages (Steponaitis 1978:437) located along the Black Warrior River Valley.

5. This alignment of Mounds 32, 33, and 34 with the SSR may indicate that the posts in Mound 33 and the associated offertory-like pottery sherd commemorate the summer solstice sunrise position. It is not clear, however, whether the pottery sherd (Moorehead 1929:plate 21, fig. 5), similar in appearance to the sherd found in an offertory pit adjacent to the winter solstice sunrise location in Woodhenge 3, Tract 15B, is from the Ramey Mound or the Ramey Field (Fowler 1989:87; Moorehead 1929).

6. Gregg (1977:132) estimates that some 600 hectares of land located below the 37-meter contour were periodically flooded.

7. A borrow pit in the Ramey Field east of Monks Mound was filled in with cultural refuse and "dismembered and certain skeletal parts were included in the fill placed in the pit (Zone G-G1)" (Bareis 1975). In addition, "subsequent to this event, Zone G-G1 was covered with thatch that was burned intermittently which sealed off the underlying garbage and finalized the preceding mortuary event. Zone F was then capped with Zone E, and the filling of the pit was completed by the construction of a platform or foundation (Zone D) which actually represents the final phase of land reclamation" (Bareis 1975).

8. Borrow Pit 5-1A was tested by the University of Illinois-Chicago under the direction of Robert L. Hall.

9. Shell-tempered ware dominates the pottery assemblage throughout the entire depth of the test pit. According to project notes (Hall 1972), pottery types included Powell Plain, Cahokia Red Filmed, Merrell Filmed, Holly Fine Engraved, Powell-Ramey, Ramey, Cahokia Red, Monks Mound Red, and Ramey Incised. Few sherds were smooth; most were cross-hatched and cord-marked. A duck effigy adorno was also recovered. Potsherds found at the lowest levels of excavation in the borrow pit were of the same type as those found at the uppermost levels of some of the mounds in the area (Mound 72), providing a chronological relationship between the two phenomena. Cahokia Red Filmed and Powell Plain were the only types to be found below 60 centimeters. The radiocarbon date from the charcoal found in Borrow Pit 5-1A is A.D. 1030 ± 50 (WIS-635) and also relates to the dates at Monks Mound (Stage A) (Fowler 1989:214; Hall 1972). This corresponds to the earliest stages of Mound 51, the construction of the palisade, and the later stages of Mound 72.

10

The Town as Metaphor

R. Barry Lewis and Charles Stout

If there can be said to be any physical representation of Mississippian views of the cosmos, it is the town. At the macro level, it reflects the political organization, economy, and religious beliefs of Mississippian peoples. At the micro level, its archaeology is the primary means by which we reconstruct Mississippian household organization, kinship, gender relations, technology, and subsistence. Its deliberately planned elements are as close to a direct mapping of the Mississippian world as we are likely to get. It is the critical mass of what it was to be Mississippian. It is the ultimate metaphor for these extinct societies.

The preceding chapters examine the archaeological representation of this metaphor across the Southeast and up the Mississippi River as far as Cahokia. These case studies place Mississippian towns in physical, temporal, and situational contexts to illuminate the reasons for their existence and for the specific ways in which they were constructed. Taken together, they define the major dimensions of an architectural grammar, centered on the design of the mound-and-plaza complex, that was shared by different societies across the Mississippian world.

Do, however, the designed portions of Mississippian towns reflect myth-based architectural rites, as implied in Chapter 1 by our reference to Kramisch's Hindu temple? The general similarities of Mississippian towns from the Atlantic to the Mississippi River and from the Gulf Coast to the Ohio Valley suggest strongly that this or something like it, which was sufficient to cross linguistic lines, was indeed at work. As seen in other preliterate societies, one effective means of storing and communicating coherent systems of information is to wrap it in myth. As the research of Knight,

Hudson, and others demonstrates, not only are the elements of such bodies of myth interpretable from existing Mississippian evidence, but also much more remains to be learned in this domain of southeastern archaeology.

Here we consider some of the patterns revealed by these analyses and discuss the important contributions they make to our overall understanding of the societies that created the towns and mound centers considered in this book. The main threads we follow are, first, the course of town development; second, spatial patterns—about which there is much to say; and third, temporal patterns—about which archaeologists have less to say than one might imagine at first glance.

Town Development

Kidder's (Chapter 6) examination of the roots of the Lower Mississippi Valley towns and mound centers is broadly applicable to the rest of the Southeast. Fresh interpretations and new research on the antiquity of mound building (e.g., Russo 1994; Saunders, Allen, and Saucier 1994) and the undeniable evidence of complex site planning evident at Poverty Point, Louisiana, suggest that researchers must first demonstrate that Mississippian towns and central places cannot be explained as indigenous phenomena before they attribute their origins to diffusion from other parts of the Americas. The town appears to have been a largely indigenous phenomenon and one should not feel compelled to raise the specter of *pochteca,* Mexican migrants, or the psychic unity of mankind to account for the development of Mississippian culture or its settlements.

If the roots of the town rest in the Archaic and Woodland cultures of the East, then archaeologists must explain why towns (viewed for the moment simply as settlements larger and more complex than villages) did not emerge until Mississippian times. To construct this explanation, we must isolate the elements of the Mississippian town that distinguish it from a Middle Woodland village or a Late Archaic base camp. The single most distinctive element (and the key planned part) was the mound-and-plaza complex. Subtract that from the picture and you have a community that does not differ much from older villages and base camps. Maybe the town was bigger and maybe it was occupied for more generations, but the design "distance" between the Mississippian town and the Woodland village is small.

Given that the mound and plaza is the thing that most distinguishes the Mississippian town from older settlements, the next problem is to explain *why* the mound-and-plaza complex developed as an integral part of these communities. Much of past research on Mississippian chiefdoms has grappled, both directly and indirectly, with the relative importance of economic, political, social, and unique historical factors at work in their creation. Of these factors, the social ones have received the least attention, but these may yet prove to contain the most compelling explanations for the emergence of the Mississippian town.

Among the social factors of possible significance in the development of the Mississippian town are (1) changes in the concept of personhood, or individual identity, in Late Woodland times and (2) the changing relationships of status, legitimacy, and sacredness that were part of the development of social ranking. We will consider each of these factors, beginning with the concept of personhood.

Charles and Buikstra (1983) argue that, beginning in Archaic times in the Illinois Valley, mortuary ritual was linked to community identity. Cemeteries were placed in prominent bluffcrest locations that were easily seen from the valley. Each cemetery was an icon for the community that buried its dead there. It was the symbol of identity, of territorial legitimacy, of belonging. It was also a system that subsumed individual identity to that of the community as a whole.

Charles and Buikstra (1983) describe one example of social context that we believe can be generalized, at least in broad terms, across much of the prehistoric East. The distinguishing feature of this system is that personhood was primarily corporate. Individual identity meant little and most of one's self-identity was defined in relation to a particular community. To get just a taste of this, consider the analogy to western European conventions of naming. If your self-identity was community centered, your name might be location-based ("John Chicago[+]son") rather than father's family–based ("John Robert['s +]son") or occupation/guild-based ("John [the] Tanner"), both of the latter of which are probably the most common name forms in modern American society. But what's in a name? Quite a lot, as can be quickly seen if you take these examples and consider what implications they might have for, say, the selection of spouses or regional dialects of American English.

The point of this digression is not to assert anything about prehistoric names, but to emphasize that a corporate concept of personhood can differ

greatly from modern western European notions of self-identity. A corporate
identity also is in keeping not only with the apparent egalitarian nature of
pre-Mississippian societies across much of the interior Southeast and Midwest but also with mortuary rituals that emphasize the mortuary facility and
the social group more than the individual. To return to the Illinois Valley,
full-fledged members of a community are buried in the cemetery (Charles
and Buikstra 1983), are processed through the village's log-lined "tomb"
(Brown 1979), or are cremated in the stone cist crematorium (Buikstra and
Goldstein 1973). Other individuals, of which infants and small children are
a near-universal example, may not be treated in the same manner in death
because they are not socially defined as members of the community until
they survive past a certain age. These socially defined "nonpersons" are the
ones who end up being buried separately, perhaps in the village midden, a
house floor, or a special cemetery of their own or, if they are buried in the
community cemetery, accompanied by an adult.

This is where the second factor, social ranking and its effects, can also
be profitably considered. Increased social differentiation is one of the features
that set Mississippian culture apart from the Woodland and Archaic cultures
of the East. The man on the beaded blanket and the mass graves found beneath Mound 72 (Fowler 1991) are unequivocal evidence that there existed
individuals in Cahokia society who viewed themselves and who were viewed
by others as being socially distinct from the masses. Such individuals can only
exist if personhood among the members of the highest social ranks is individual-centered rather than community-centered. This, we argue, is a correlate of increased social differentiation in the Mississippi period: the individual emerges as a distinct social entity for the first time across much of the
East.

In the Archaic and Woodland worlds, individual identity was unimportant and social differentiation was meaningless. It was the corporate identity,
the claim on membership in a given village, that meant something. In the
Mississippian world, on the other hand, some individuals, and probably some
lineages, emerge as the primary actors of social differences that are framed
in reference to particular individuals. If nowhere else, the changed focus of
identity in Mississippian times can be seen in ancestor cults, which venerated
the ancestors of the elites of a community (Brown 1976, 1985); in the increased numbers of wooden or stone ancestor cult figures in the archaeologi-

cal record (Brown 1985:102–8); in such iconographic figures as the falcon impersonator (Brown 1985:113–23); and in a community's architecture.

As Murray Milner (1994:21) explains, the development of ranked status differences "seems to be closely related to the differentiation of the sacred and the profane." This, taken together with the factor just discussed, gives us a context within which the integration of the mound-and-plaza complex into the village can be explained. Viewed from Milner's perspective, if the basic elements of the mound-and-plaza complex had not existed by late Late Woodland times, then the emerging socially differentiated community landscape would have promoted the development of something structurally analogous to it. The mound-and-plaza complex was a mechanism used by some persons or families to signify their status and, most important, the legitimacy of their claim to status, by virtue of their visible, personal link to the sacred on the one hand and the corporate identity of the community on the other. In this way, individual status and the sacred are inseparably intertwined in a form of social power that is implicitly legitimate because it is inalienable. If your house is on a mound that fronts the plaza, you can easily claim status, but only if no one else can build a bigger house on a bigger mound on the same plaza. The *legitimacy* of your presence is forged by your links to the sacred. If it is your ancestors' bones in the charnel house at the other end of the plaza and if you are a primary actor in cyclical rituals that ensure the well-being of the community, then your legitimacy and social power are secure, if for no other reason than your place cannot be usurped. Your status is inalienable.

The addition of earth mantles to platform mounds can also be interpreted, at least in part, as a reaffirmation of individual-centered status and legitimacy. Knight (1981, 1986, 1989) has emphasized that earth mantles can be interpreted as symbolic purifications of mounds. In his view, this and other aspects of platform mound ceremonialism are linked with mortuary ritual in a symbolic complex that is relatively independent of "warrior-chief office rituals" (Knight 1981:136). Although we agree strongly with Knight's interpretation of the symbolic meaning of mounds and mound mantles, we also believe that his delineation of two more or less independent symbolic complexes may be unwarranted.

Many aspects of platform mound ceremonialism can be interpreted as integral parts of "warrior-chief office rituals," as reaffirmations of the status and legitimacy of the individuals and lineages that figure prominently in these rituals, whether as actors or patrons. Viewed in this light, the thickness of a given earth mantle may indeed have met a "community's need for purification" (Knight 1981:52), but it also reaffirmed the wealth or prestige of a high-status individual or lineage or displayed a bid for increased status (in much the same way that wealthy patrons endow temples, universities, and hospitals in other cultures). Rather than marking the final ritual burial of mounds (Knight 1981:51), the clay caps on mound stages may signify yet another kind of donation/reaffirmation by individuals, here again linked to the status and legitimacy of individuals.

In summary, the architectural grammar of the Mississippian town was more the effect of social and economic changes, a kind of cultural weather vane, than it was a causal factor in those changes. Our discussion emphasizes the possible social factors that may underlie its development. Among these factors, a change in the concept of personhood from a community-centered identity to an individual-centered identity during the Mississippi period is hypothesized as one of the main social differences that distinguished higher social rank individuals from lower ranked persons and that set Mississippian polities apart from those of their Woodland predecessors. This social change was a key element in defining the status, legitimacy, and, ultimately, the sacredness of some individuals and roles in Mississippian society and contributed to the development of the mound-and-plaza complex as a characteristic element of the Mississippian town.

Spatial Patterns

Site Setting

Much of Mississippian settlement archaeology since the 1960s (e.g., Smith 1978b) has involved, in one way or another, examinations of the following site selection factors: (1) access to lines of communication, including agricultural fields and friendly neighbors, (2) good drainage and low susceptibility to flooding, (3) ease of defense, and (4) availability of natural resources, including potable water, firewood, and game.

This research has demonstrated that, at least in the East, every landscape contains far more good potential locations for a Mississippian town than it does bad ones. The main implications are, first, that the site distribution patterns reflect more the operation of cultural choices than the effects of geography and nature and, second, that to explain the location of any given town is to necessarily invoke a unique historical explanation. The latter cannot be done with prehistorical data, so we must turn to generalizing at a fairly high level of abstraction about the cultural processes of site selection. This approach, although successful, cannot get us as close to the unique contexts of the archaeological data as we would like to be.

Excavations show that Mississippian towns were built both at locations where there is no evidence of earlier use (i.e., creating a new "node" in a settlement system) and at places that had been previously inhabited (i.e., replacing an existing node in a settlement system). It is common, for example, to see the remains of Late Woodland communities beneath Mississippian towns. We must keep open the possibility that many of these older communities represent earlier components of what were essentially continuous occupations. In other cases, for example at the Adams site in western Kentucky (Stout and Lewis, Chapter 7), there is no apparent direct continuity between the two occupations.

There was a Mississippian settlement hierarchy, but all of the chapters of this book suggest that it was a minimal one: a few big sites in a region, many small ones, and, in the middle, a few sites with a mound or two. Payne and Scarry (Chapter 2) and Fowler (1978) write of four-level hierarchies in the Lake Jackson and Cahokia regions, respectively, and Williams (1995) describes two-level hierarchies in Georgia, but there appears to be more evidence of Mississippian site hierarchies that are of three levels: a clear top, a clear base, and something fuzzy going on in the middle. Archaeologists have developed many hypotheses about how these parts fit together, but the accurate delineation of the middle level is hard to nail down (e.g., Kreisa 1990).

A related concern to that of settlement hierarchies is the meaning that should be ascribed to clumps of sites. Hally and Kelly (Chapter 3), writing about site distributions in the upper Coosa and Tennessee river drainages of northwestern Georgia and eastern Tennessee, identify "town clusters," each of which may represent a separate chiefdom. Schroedl (Chapter 4) challenges this interpretation and the assumption that all of the clumps of sites of the same archaeological culture were contemporaneous. Schroedl argues that the site clumping may, in fact, be more an artifact of site survey biases than a real pattern that requires explanation in terms of Mississippian culture.

Town Layout

The planned part of the Mississippian town was the mound-and-plaza complex. On this point, at least, all of the authors agree (but some would add other bits, such as palisades, that others exclude). Demel and Hall (Chapter 9) show that planning could be complex, with major cut-and-fill sections being undertaken as part of the topographical reshaping of a town site. On the basis of their work at the Lake Jackson site in Florida, Payne and Scarry (Chapter 2) also argue that town planning continued throughout the life of a town and reflected the existence of a strong central authority.

Was the planning evident in the remains of most Mississippian towns a necessary consequence of a strong central authority? Yes, if we are to accept many of the claims made about the social and political complexity of Mississippian polities and Mississippian "urbanism" (e.g., Fowler 1975; O'Brien 1989). No, if we reach beyond the East and weigh cross-cultural evidence of the relationship between site planning and central authority. Consider, for example, the Ifugao of the Philippines. They construct incredibly complex rice terraces in the narrow river valleys of northern Luzon, but these terraces were built and are maintained by egalitarian "Big Man" systems (Conklin 1980). Surely it was more difficult to construct, use, and maintain these terraces over many generations than it was to build and maintain a Mississippian town. The example suggests that, while a strong central authority was clearly a part of Mississippian towns, this authority was not necessarily acted out in the context of true social stratification. What is "strong" and what is "central" are relative.

Another observation about mound-and-plaza complexes comes from Payne's (1994; Payne and Scarry, Chapter 2) analysis of 103 Mississippian towns. Her research shows that roughly three-fourths of main mounds are located on the edges of the mound-and-plaza complex and one-fourth are in the centers of the mound-and-plaza complex. The latter sites also tend to be larger than those that have their main mound on the edge of the plaza. Although we concur with Payne and Scarry (Chapter 2) that the towns with centrally placed main mounds were probably of greater regional significance than the towns with plaza-edge mounds, we suggest that the main mounds got into the center of the mound-and-plaza complexes of these sites by the construction of secondary plazas well after the development of the town. *Why* these plazas were constructed may have had more to do with the relative wealth of a given town and the self-serving ambitions of individuals who wished to redefine themselves in the status web than with deeper symbolism.

Plazas, public buildings, and palisades also were planning anchors that influenced the development of each town (Schroedl, Chapter 4). Such anchors are characteristic of the built environment. Existing buildings and spaces constrain or enable future buildings and spaces around them. What is important to consider in the Mississippian case is whether the plazas, public buildings, and palisades acted together or separately in their effects on town development. The archaeology of Mississippian towns suggests that the mound-and-plaza complex and the buildings associated with it were bound together by design. The locations and forms of palisades also were linked by design to the mound-and-plaza complex, but the association was primarily a strategic one: to defend the mound-and-plaza complex.

Palisade gateways, however, were not linked to the Mississippian mound-and-plaza complex. The horizontal plans of Mississippian towns do not show a consistent pattern of palisade gate placement with respect to any interior feature of towns. The available evidence suggests that, when you entered a Mississippian town through a gateway, you were not presented with a guardroom, a tax collector, a market, or a visual display of the staggering power and sacredness of the ruling elite: you were just inside the town. This needs to be studied more thoroughly. We argued in Chapter 7 that palisades (and, by implication, gateways) were episodic features of Kentucky towns. The absence of any pattern or patterns to gateway spaces lends support to the argument that palisades were episodic generally in the Mississippian world.

Finally, plazas fit into a narrow domain in the Mississippian world. The plaza was an important component of the center of gravity of the town, but its design seems more akin to that of the Forum at Pompeii, which was both architecturally and functionally a diverse space (Sitte 1965:6–8), than to the plazas of medieval European cities. In the latter, there were often multiple plazas, each of which was associated with a different power structure but also served a variety of cross-cutting social functions. The cathedral (sacred power), for example, would be set at the edge or in the middle of one plaza; the central municipal building or city hall (political power) would dominate another plaza; and the main market (economic power) might be associated with yet another plaza (Sitte 1965:13–14).

To move beyond the mound-and-plaza complex to the rest of the community, horizontal excavations at many towns show a jumble of houses, which suggests that the "living" area of towns was not planned, but grew organically (*sensu* Morris 1994:9–10). There are exceptions, of which Snodgrass is our favorite example (Figure 7.2), but the general pattern is evident across the South and up the Mississippi Valley.

In keeping with the organic nature of habitation space within towns, waste removal also was unplanned. Extensive excavations have yet to expose anything that can be interpreted as evidence of Mississippian drainage systems, such as wooden or stone-lined drains, within towns. Mississippian peoples were technologically capable of constructing such systems and there is no reason to doubt that they were needed. Their absence and the solid waste accumulations that form much of each town's archaeological deposit suggest, first, that any "central authority" who controlled the mound-and-plaza complex was too weak to dictate how people used the town's living space and, second, that Mississippian ideas about waste disposal differed from our own. Like the Missouri Valley earthlodge villages described in the 1830s by Karl Bodmer (Wied 1982), one could probably smell a Mississippian town from a kilometer away downwind, and it would not have smelled good.

Town boundaries and gates have already been discussed briefly in relation to the question of whether they were linked by design to the mound-and-plaza complexes. There is, however, more to say about them.

Gates appear to be placed to facilitate the movement of people and goods into the town. They do not, as noted earlier, have any design relationship with the mound-and-plaza complex. Also, they do not appear to have been embellished with architectural features, such as decorated facades, that symbolically "announced" the town. When found archaeologically (e.g., Figure 7.11), gates tend to be no wider than the space needed to permit two persons to pass abreast. Given the defensive works of which Mississippian gates are typically a part and the absence of beasts of burden other than humans, it would be surprising if these gateways were wider than about 2 meters. (If this is true, then we should also expect to see wider town gateways after roughly A.D. 1600 to permit the easy passage of packhorses. As yet, however, there are probably too few data to test this hypothesis.)

The most common, archaeologically identifiable, Mississippian town boundaries are defensive in nature. The presence of defensive works such as palisades, bastions, and ditches could also perhaps be seen as setting Mississippian towns apart from older sites, but there is abundant evidence of pre-Mississippian enclosures in the East (Morgan 1980), some of which may have been intended for defense. We find it significant, however, that insofar as one can accurately infer the objective of Mississippian town defense from the remains of the palisade, the ultimate goal was, as noted earlier, to deny access to the mound-and-plaza complex. This objective can be seen readily at Toqua, Tennessee, for example, where excavations revealed the remains of three palisade construction episodes (Schroedl, Chapter 4). Palisade A defended the entire village, Palisade B defended the outer ring of the mound-and-plaza complex, and Palisade C defended only the core of the mound-and-plaza complex (Figure 4.6). In addition, at the Jonathan Creek site in Kentucky, if one extends the arcs of the excavated portions of its series of seven stockades (Stout and Lewis, Chapter 7, Figure 7.6), all of them enclosed minimally the plaza and the smaller mounds on its edge, but only one of them protected most of the town's houses. Other examples include the bastioned palisade that surrounded "downtown" Cahokia (Demel and Hall, Chapter 9, Figure 9.3).

Defensive features were not a consistent component of Mississippian town design. Schroedl (Chapter 4) argues that palisaded settlements were not the norm in eastern Tennessee. Kidder (Chapter 6) echoes this view and reports that, with the exception of Lake George, there is little evidence of palisades and moats at Lower Mississippi Valley Mississippian towns. Palisaded towns appear to have been more common in western Kentucky, but even there Stout and Lewis (Chapter 7) note that such features were constructed as needed and then uprooted or left to rot.

Some aspects of Mississippian culture are similar across the Southeast and southern Midwest because of what Morris (1994:10–11) would call "natural world determinants" (which should not be read as "environmental determinism"). Construction in stone, for example, is largely absent from the Mississippian world. The most visible exception to this generalization is stone-lined graves, which are found across the middle and upper South. The explanation for the absence of stone as a building material has far more to do with southern geology and geography than it does with Mississippian culture. Similarly, the characteristic riverine focus of Mississippian towns is partly culture, partly geography, and partly stereotype created by archaeologists. As Payne and Scarry's study (Chapter 2) of Lake Jackson shows, Mississippian peoples could live around lakes just as easily as around rivers and the experience did not make them less "Mississippian."

Other aspects, such as house floor plans and wall footings, are similar across much of the Mississippian world, partly because of natural world determinants and partly because of shared notions of gender relations, family composition, aesthetics, and other cultural factors. Were the late prehistoric Southeast and southern Midwest to have been a culturally homogeneous place, these similarities would hardly be worth mentioning. But it was not culturally homogeneous, if the de Soto narratives (Clayton, Knight, and Moore 1993) and other early accounts are to be believed.

Vertical Patterns

The design of the mound-and-plaza complex is patterned vertically as well as horizontally. When you stand in the remains of a Mississippian town plaza, say at Adams, Kentucky, and look around, the spatial patterns that catch your attention are the use of elevation and vertical and horizontal mass to define the plaza boundaries and to identify the main mound as a design focal point.

Arnheim (1977:32) observes that, in the three-dimensional space of our existence, the pull of gravity distinguishes the vertical dimension from the other two dimensions. Since it acts on all creatures the same, it is to be expected therefore that the vertical dimension will assume the same basic meaning cross-culturally. Nowhere is this seen more forcibly than in architecture.

As in our society, elevation was used in Mississippian architecture as a focal point or symbol of social, political, and religious power. The building on the main mound announced visually the locus of this power. It towered above the rest of the mound-and-plaza complex, over the houses that surrounded the complex, and over the boundaries of the town itself. Because our own culture uses elevation in a similar way, the design of Mississippian main mounds and the plaza complexes of which they are a part tends not to provoke comment (or study) by archaeologists.

There is a similar "layering" of vertical spaces in the Mississippian town and the skyline of a small American town. Elevations tend to be low on the periphery of the American town, higher in the central business district, and highest with the clock tower of the city hall and the church spires that dot

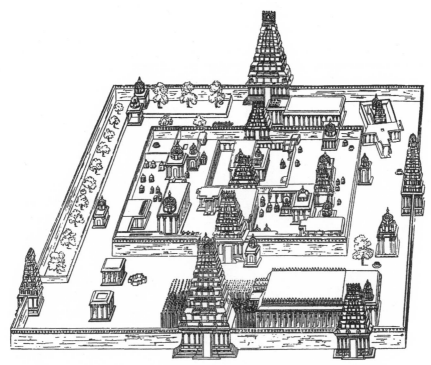

Figure 10.1. The temple at Tiruvallur, Tamil Nadu, India (Fergusson 1891:340).

the landscape. This pattern is not, however, a cultural universal. In many South Indian Hindu temples, for example, elevation patterns are reversed from what would seem "normal" to a Mississippian person and someone from a western European tradition. For example, at Tiruvallur (Figure 10.1) and at Madura (Brown 1965:I:87–90; Malville 1991:138–39), the highest elevations of the temple complex are the outermost gateways or *gopuras,* not the temple. To reach the temple, one passes through a series of *gopuras* nested within the temple complex, each one of which is lower in elevation than the preceding one. The building or buildings enclosed by the temple walls often strike Western observers as relatively insignificant structures. They certainly often violate Western notions about the direct relationship between "power" and elevation, as expressed in architecture. It is probably for this reason that most westerners who have never visited South India tend to misidentify pictures of *gopuras* as temples. Mississippian peoples would make the same mistake.

Temporal Patterns

There is much that we would like to know about stability and change in the Mississippian architectural grammar, but the answers require a detailed understanding of Mississippian towns that does not yet exist. This section explores some of the temporal trends identified by the authors of this book and suggests others that may bear examination in the future.

The immediate roots of the Mississippian town can be seen during Late Woodland times in the Midwest at such sites as Range (Kelly et al. 1987; Kelly, Ozuk, and Williams 1990) in the Central Mississippi Valley and during the Coles Creek period in the Lower Mississippi Valley (Kidder, Chapter 6). There is no "Mississippian Heartland." What archaeologists choose to call Mississippian culture coalesced across the southern Midwest and Southeast around A.D. 900–1000.

There appears to be no consistent temporal or regional pattern to the longevity of Mississippian towns. New towns were founded throughout the Mississippi period and into the nineteenth century. Some were abandoned after less than a generation and a few may have lasted the entire Mississippi period. Muller (Chapter 8) examines in detail the ethnohistorical and archaeological evidence of native American towns in the Southeast. He concludes that after contact with peoples from the Old World, towns did not diminish in average size, but there were fewer of them, an inference further supported by what is known of the historic period demographics for the Southeast.

Conclusions

Mississippian towns rank among the largest and most archaeologically complex prehistoric cultural spaces in the eastern United States. Although surface collected, looted, excavated, and mapped by generations of archaeologists, interested citizens, and pothunters, surprisingly little is known about them beyond excavation reports and spatial assessments of settlement patterns.

From North Carolina to Mississippi and from Illinois to Georgia, Mississippian towns and central places tend to look broadly alike. What makes them similar? First, these towns were built by societies of similar scale and general economic organization. Second, the mound-and-plaza complex, the main and planned part of these communities, is the key feature that sets them apart from older settlements. Third, the community beyond the mound-and-plaza complex tended to grow organically, with few constraints other than topography on its shape and internal order. Finally, there is the inherent simplicity of these towns.

The point about the simplicity of Mississippian towns is worth pursuing. Although they are the most imposing archaeological sites in eastern North America, they pale in comparison with the communities of many chiefdoms and early states in other parts of the world. The tendency of some archaeologists to speak of Mississippian culture and its settlements as though they were comparable in scale, political power, economic production, and social complexity to early Old World civilizations is ambitious, understandable, and unconvincing.

Following the lead of such researchers as Vernon Knight, Jr., and Claudine Payne, this book examines town design patterns and explores their possible cultural meanings. Our focus, which we describe in Chapter 1 as a delineation of an architectural grammar, yields not a trait list of things, but a series of relationships, some of which are summarized in this chapter, and possible explanations, all of which are subject to test. Taken together, these relationships do not form a coherent whole, a fully formed set of rules, in the manner of Mitchell (1990), with which one could diagram the plan of a town. Indeed, we are uncertain what one could do with such a set of rules were it to be constructed. This architectural grammar is a means, not an end. The most important goal is to motivate investigation of these and similar Mississippian town design relationships before the opportunities to do so vanish.

References Cited

Adair, James
   1986 *Adair's History of the American Indians.* Reprint of 1930 edition
      edited by S. C. Williams and published by National Society of the Co-
      lonial Dames of America, Nashville, Tennessee. Originally published in
      1775. Promontory Press, New York.

Aitken, Bill
   1995 *Exploring Indian Railways.* Oxford University Press, Delhi.

Alexander, Michelle
   1984 *Paleoethnobotany of the Fort Walton Indians: High Ridge, Velda, and
      Lake Jackson Sites.* Unpublished master's thesis, Department of Anthro-
      pology, Florida State University, Tallahassee.

Allerton, David, George M. Luer, and Robert S. Carr
   1984 Ceremonial Tablets and Related Objects from Florida. *Florida An-
      thropologist* 37:5–54.

Anderson, David G.
   1994 *The Savannah River Chiefdoms: Political Change in the Late Prehis-
      toric Southeast.* University of Alabama Press, Tuscaloosa.

Anderson, James
   1969 A Cahokia Palisade Sequence. In *Explorations into Cahokia Archae-
      ology,* edited by M. L. Fowler, pp. 89–99. Bulletin 7, Illinois Archae-
      ological Survey, University of Illinois, Urbana.

Arnheim, Rudolf
   1977 *The Dynamics of Architectural Form.* University of California Press,
      Berkeley.

Aspiration Stores
   1995 *Hampi and Its Environs.* Hampi, India.

Autin, Whitney J., Scott F. Burns, Bobby J. Miller, Roger T. Saucier, and
John I. Snead
   1991 Quaternary Geology of the Lower Mississippi Valley. In *The Geol-
      ogy of North America,* vol. K-2, *Quaternary Nonglacial Geology; Coter-
      minous United States,* edited by R. B. Morrison, pp. 547–82. Geological
      Society of America, Boulder.

Aveni, Anthony
   1975 *Archaeoastronomy in Pre-Columbian America.* University of Texas
      Press, Austin.

Bacon, Edmund N.

1976 *Design of Cities.* Penguin, New York.

Baden, William W.

1987 *A Dynamic Model of Stability and Change in Mississippian Agricultural Systems.* Unpublished Ph.D. dissertation, Department of Anthropology, University of Tennessee, Knoxville.

Ball, Donald B., Victor P. Hood, and E. Raymond Evans

1976 The Long Island Mounds, Marion County Tennessee–Jackson County, Alabama. *Tennessee Anthropologist* 1:13–47.

Ballard, W. L.

1978 *The Yuchi Green Corn Ceremonial: Form and Meaning.* American Indian Studies Center, Los Angeles.

Bareis, Charles J.

1975 Report of 1971 University of Illinois-Urbana Excavations at the Cahokia Site. In *Cahokia Archaeology: Field Reports,* edited by M. L. Fowler, pp. 9–11. Papers in Anthropology 3, Illinois State Museum, Springfield.

Bareis, Charles J., and James W. Porter

1984 *American Bottom Archaeology.* University of Illinois Press, Urbana.

Barker, Alex W.

1988 *Coles Creek in the Heartland: Information Stress and Hierarchy Formation in Simple Chiefdoms.* Presented at the forty-fifth annual meeting of the Southeastern Archaeological Conference, New Orleans.

1993 *Settled on Complexity: Defining and Debating Social Complexity in the Lower Mississippi Valley.* Presented at the fifty-eighth annual meeting of the Society for American Archaeology, St. Louis.

Bartram, William

1853 Observations on the Creek and Cherokee Indians. *Transactions of the American Ethnology Society* 3(1):1–81. New York.

1996 *Travels and Other Writings.* Library of America, New York.

Beaudry, Mary C., Lauren J. Cooke, and Stephen A. Mrozowski

1991 Artifacts and Active Voices: Material Culture as Social Discourse. In *The Archaeology of Inequality,* edited by R. H. McGuire and R. Paynter, pp. 150–91. Blackwell, Cambridge.

Belmont, John S.

1967 The Culture Sequence at the Greenhouse Site, Louisiana. *Southeastern Archaeological Conference Bulletin* 6:27–34.

1980 *Gold Mine (16R I13): Preliminary Report on the 1980 Season.* Report submitted to Jerome Rose, principal investigator, National Science Foundation grant BNS 79-23538. Ms. on file, Department of Anthropology, University of Arkansas, Fayetteville.

1983 Analysis of the Bone and Shell. In *Excavations at the Lake George Site, Yazoo County, Mississippi, 1958–1960,* by S. Williams and J. P. Brain, pp. 453–69. Papers of the Peabody Museum of Archaeology and Ethnology 74, Harvard University, Cambridge, Massachusetts.

1984 The Troyville Concept and the Gold Mine Site. *Louisiana Archaeology* 9:65–98.

1985 A Reconnaissance of the Boeuf Basin, Louisiana. *Louisiana Archaeology* 10:271–84.

Benchley, Elizabeth E.

1974 *Mississippian Secondary Mound Loci: A Comparative Functional Analysis in a Time-Space Perspective.* Unpublished Ph.D. dissertation, University of Wisconsin-Milwaukee.

Bender, Barbara

1993 Introduction: Landscape-Meaning and Action. In *Landscape: Politics and Perspectives,* edited by B. Bender, pp. 1–17. Berg, Providence.

Benson, Elizabeth P.

1985 Architecture as Metaphor. In *Fifth Palenque Roundtable,* edited by M. G. Robertson, pp. 183–88. Pre-Columbian Art Research Institute, San Francisco.

Bentz, Charles Jr., and Lance Greene

1991 *Archaeological Investigations at Site 40Bt47: A Multicomponent Site in the Eastern Ridge and Valley of East Tennessee.* Report submitted to the Tennessee Department of Transportation, Nashville.

Beverley, Robert

1968 *The History and Present State of Virginia,* edited by L. B. Wright. Originally published in 1705. Dominion Books, University Press of Virginia, Charlottesville.

Binford, Lewis

1971 Mortuary Practices: Their Study and Their Potential. In *Approaches to the Social Dimensions of Mortuary Practices,* edited by L. Binford, pp. 6–29. Memoir 25, Society for American Archaeology, Washington, D.C.

Bitgood, M. J.

1989 *The Baytown Period in the Upper Tensas Basin.* Bulletin 12, Lower

Mississippi Survey, Peabody Museum, Harvard University, Cambridge, Massachusetts.

Blakely, Robert L., ed.

    1988 *The King Site: Continuity and Contact in Sixteenth-Century Georgia*. University of Georgia Press, Athens.

Blitz, John H.

    1993 *Ancient Chiefdoms of the Tombigbee*. University of Alabama Press, Tuscaloosa.

Bogan, Arthur, and Richard Polhemus

    1987 Faunal Analysis. In *The Toqua Site: A Late Mississippian Dallas Phase Town*, by R. Polhemus, pp. 971–1111. Report of Investigations 41, Department of Anthropology, University of Tennessee, Knoxville.

Bolton, Herbert Eugene

    1987 *The Hasinais: Southern Caddoans as Seen by the Earliest Americans*. University of Oklahoma Press, Norman.

Bossu, Jean-Bernard

    1962 *Travels in the Interior of North America, 1751–1762,* translated and edited by S. Feiler. Originally published in 1768. University of Oklahoma Press, Norman.

Bourdieu, Pierre

    1977 *Outline of a Theory of Practice*. Cambridge University Press, Cambridge.

Bourne, Edward G., ed.

    1922 *Narratives of the Career of Hernando de Soto*. Allerton Book Co., New York.

Boyd, C. Clifford, Jr., and Donna C. Boyd

    1991 A Multidimensional Investigation of Biocultural Relationships among Three Late Prehistoric Societies in Tennessee. *American Antiquity* 56:75–88.

Boyd, Donna C.

    1984 *A Biological Investigation of Skeletal Remains from the Mouse Creek Phase and a Comparison with Two Late Mississippian Skeletal Populations from Middle and East Tennessee*. Unpublished master's thesis, Department of Anthropology, University of Tennessee, Knoxville.

    1986 A Comparison of Mouse Creek Phase to Dallas and Middle Cumberland Culture Skeletal Remains. In *Skeletal Analysis in Southeastern*

Archaeology, edited by J. E. Levy, pp. 103–26. North Carolina Archaeological Council Publication 24, Raleigh.

Brackenridge, Henry Marie

1962 *Views of Louisiana Together with a Journal of a Voyage up the Missouri River, in 1811.* Quadrangle Books, Chicago.

Bradley, Richard, ed.

1996 Sacred Geography. *World Archaeology* 28(2):161–274.

Brain, Jeffrey P.

1978 Late Prehistoric Settlement Patterning in the Yazoo Basin and Natchez Bluffs Regions of the Lower Mississippi Valley. In *Mississippian Settlement Patterns,* edited by B. D. Smith, pp. 331–68. Academic, New York.

1988 *Tunica Archaeology.* Papers of the Peabody Museum of Archaeology and Ethnology 78, Harvard University, Cambridge.

1989 *Winterville: Late Prehistoric Culture Contact in The Mississippi Valley.* Archaeological Report 23, Mississippi Department of Archives and History, Jackson.

1991 Cahokia from the Southern Periphery. In *New Perspectives on Cahokia: Views from the Periphery,* edited by J. B. Stoltman, pp. 93–100. Monographs in World Archaeology 2. Prehistory Press, Madison, Wisconsin.

Brain, Jeffrey P., and Philip Phillips

1996 *Shell Gorgets: Styles of the Late Prehistoric and Protohistoric Southeast.* Peabody Museum Press, Cambridge.

Brown, Ian W.

1985a Plaquemine Architectural Patterns in the Natchez Bluffs and Surrounding Regions of the Lower Mississippi Valley. *Midcontinental Journal of Archaeology* 10:251–305.

1985b *Natchez Indian Archaeology: Culture Change and Stability in the Lower Mississippi Valley.* Archaeological Report 15, Mississippi Department of Archives and History, Jackson.

Brown, Ian W., and Jeffrey P. Brain

1983 Archaeology of the Natchez Bluffs Region, Mississippi: Hypothesized Cultural and Environmental Factors Influencing Local Population Movements. *Southeastern Archaeological Conference Bulletin* 20:38–49.

Brown, James A.

1976 The Southern Cult Reconsidered. *Midcontinental Journal of Archaeology* 1:115–35.

1979 Charnel Houses and Mortuary Crypts: Disposal of the Dead in the Middle Woodland Period. In *Hopewell Archaeology: The Chillicothe Conference,* edited by D. S. Brose and N. Greber, pp. 211–19. Kent State University Press, Kent, Ohio.

1985 The Mississippian Period. In *Ancient Art of the American Woodland Indians,* by D. S. Brose, J. A. Brown, and D. W. Penney, pp. 93–145. Harry N. Abrams, New York.

Brown, James A., Richard A. Kerber, and Howard D. Winters

1990 Trade and the Evolution of Exchange Relations at the Beginning of the Mississippian Period. In *The Mississippian Emergence,* edited by B. D. Smith, pp. 251–80. Smithsonian Institution, Washington, D.C.

Brown, Percy

1965 *Indian Architecture.* 5th ed., 2 vols. D. B. Taraporevala Sons, Bombay.

Buikstra, Jane E., and Lynne Goldstein

1973 *The Perrins Ledge Crematory.* Illinois State Museum, Reports of Investigations 28, Illinois Valley Archaeological Program, Research Papers 8, Illinois State Museum, Springfield.

Bullen, Ripley P.

1978 Tocobaga Indians and the Safety Harbor Culture. In *Tacachale: Essays on the Indians of Florida and Southeastern Georgia during the Historic Period,* edited by J. T. Milanich and S. Proctor, pp. 50–58. University Presses of Florida, Gainesville.

Burks, Jarrod, and Charles Stout

1995 Continuing Studies at the Twin Mounds site (15Ba2): 1991–92. In *Current Archaeological Research in Kentucky,* vol. 4, edited by T. N. Sanders, S. Sanders, and C. Stout, pp. 234–63. Kentucky Heritage Council, Frankfort.

1999 Controlled Surface Collection and Salvage Data Recovered at the Twin Mounds site (15Ba2). In *Current Archaeological Research in Kentucky,* vol. 5, edited by K. Carstens, C. Stout, S. Mills, and C. Hockensmith. Kentucky Heritage Council, Frankfort.

Butzer, Karl W.

1981 *Site Planning.* MIT Press, Cambridge.

Caesar, Gaius Julius

51 B.C. *Gallia. Roma.* Translation in *The Gallic War and Other Writings,* edited by M. Hadas, 1957. Modern Library, New York.

Caldwell, Joseph R.

1958 *Trend and Tradition in the Prehistory of the Eastern United States.* Scientific Papers 10, Illinois State Museum, Springfield.

Cannon, Kenneth P.

1986 *An Assessment of the Archaeological Resources of the Watts Bar Reservoir, East Tennessee.* Report submitted to the Tennessee Valley Authority, Knoxville.

Carlson, John B.

1981 A Geomantic Model for the Interpretation of Mesoamerican Sites: An Essay in Cross-Cultural Comparison. In *Mesoamerican Sites and Worldviews,* edited by E. P. Benson, pp. 143–211. Dumbarton Oaks, Washington, D.C.

Chapman, Jefferson

1990 *The Kimberly-Clark Site and Site 40Ld207.* Miscellaneous Paper 14, Tennessee Anthropological Association, Knoxville.

Chapman, Robert W., and Klavs Randsborg

1981 Perspectives on the Archaeology of Death. In *The Archaeology of Death,* edited by R. W. Chapman, I. Kinnes, and K. Randsborg, pp. 1–24. Cambridge University Press, Cambridge.

Charles, Douglas K., and Jane E. Buikstra

1983 Archaic Mortuary Sites in the Central Mississippi Drainage: Distribution, Structure, and Behavioral Implications. In *Archaic Hunters and Gatherers in the American Midwest,* edited by J. L. Phillips and J. A. Brown, pp. 117–45. Academic, New York.

Chmurny, William Wayne

1973 *The Ecology of the Middle Mississippian Occupation of the American Bottom.* Unpublished Ph.D. dissertation, Department of Anthropology, University of Illinois, Urbana-Champaign.

Clark, Grahame

1986 *Symbols of Excellence: Precious Materials as Expressions of Status.* Cambridge University Press, New York.

Clay, R. Berle

1976 Tactics, Strategy, and Operations: The Mississippian System Responds to its Environment. *Midcontinental Journal of Archaeology* 1:138–62.

1997 The Mississippian Succession on the Lower Ohio. *Southeastern Archaeology* 16:16–32.

Clayton, Lawrence A., Vernon J. Knight, Jr., and Edward C. Moore, eds.

1993 *The De Soto Chronicles: The Expedition of Hernando de Soto to North America in 1539–1543.* University of Alabama Press, Tuscaloosa.

Cobb, Charles

1988 *Mill Creek Chert Biface Production: Mississippian Political Economy in Illinois.* Unpublished Ph.D. dissertation, Department of Anthropology, Southern Illinois University at Carbondale.

1989 An Appraisal of the Role of Mill Creek Chert Hoes in Mississippian Exchange Systems. *Southeastern Archaeology* 8:79–92.

1991 100 Years of Investigations on the Linn Site in Southern Illinois. *Illinois Archaeology* 3:56–76.

Cole, Patricia E.

1975 *A Synthesis and Interpretation of the Hamilton Mortuary Pattern in East Tennessee.* Unpublished master's thesis, Department of Anthropology, University of Tennessee, Knoxville.

Collins, George R., and Christiane C. Collins

1986 *Camillo Sitte: The Birth of Modern City Planning.* Revised edition. Rizzoli, New York.

Colloredo-Mansfield, Rudolf

1994 Architectural Conspicuous Consumption and Economic Change in the Andes. *American Anthropologist* 96:845–65.

Conklin, Harold C.

1980 *Ethnographic Atlas of Ifugao: A Study of Environment, Culture, and Society in Northern Luzon.* Yale University Press, New Haven.

Connaway, John M.

1984 *The Wilsford Site (22-CO-516), Cohoma County, Mississippi: A Late Mississippi Period Settlement in the Northern Yazoo Basin of Mississippi.* Archaeological Report 14, Mississippi Department of Archives and History, Jackson.

Cooper, Paul L., Jesse D. Jennings, and Charles H. Nash

1995 The Davis Site. In *The Prehistory of the Chickamauga Basin,* 2 vols., by T. M. N. Lewis and M. D. Kneberg Lewis, compiled and edited by L. P. Sullivan, pp. 419–40. University of Tennessee Press, Knoxville.

Cordell, Ann S.

1992 Technological Investigation of Pottery Variability in Southwest Florida. In *Culture and Environment in the Domain of the Calusa*, edited by W. H. Marquardt with the assistance of C. Payne, pp. 105–89. Monograph 1, Institute of Archaeology and Paleoenvironmental Studies, University of Florida, Gainesville.

Corkran, David H.

1967 *The Creek Frontier, 1540–1783.* University of Oklahoma Press, Norman.

Cosgrove, Denis

1993 Landscapes and Myths, Gods and Humans. In *Landscape: Politics and Perspectives,* edited by B. Bender, pp. 281–305. Berg, Providence.

Cunningham, Clark

1972 Order in the Atoni House. In *Reader in Comparative Religion: An Anthropological Approach,* edited by W. A. Lessa and E. Z. Vogt, pp. 116–34. Harper and Row, New York.

Dagens, Bruno

1984 *Architecture in the Ajitagama and the Rauravagama.* Sitaram Bhartia Institute of Scientific Research, New Delhi.

Dalan, Rinita A.

1993 *Landscape Modification at the Cahokia Mounds Site: Geophysical Evidence of Culture Change.* Unpublished Ph.D. dissertation, Department of Anthropology, University of Minnesota, Minneapolis.

Daniel, Ann L.

1980 *An Application of the Techniques of Archaeoastronomy to a Selection of Mississippian Sites in the Southeastern United States.* Ph.D. dissertation, State University of New York. University Microfilms 8019750, Ann Arbor, Michigan.

Daniel-Hartung, Ann L.

1981 Archaeoastronomy at a Selection of Mississippian Sites in the Southeastern United States. In *Archaeoastronomy in the Americas,* edited by R. A. Williamson, pp. 101–10. Ballena, Los Altos, California.

Davis, R. P. Stephen, Jr.

1990 *Aboriginal Settlement Patterns in the Little Tennessee River Valley.* Report of Investigations 50, Department of Anthropology, University of Tennessee, Knoxville.

DeBoer, Warren

   1988 Subterranean Storage and the Organization of Surplus: The View from Eastern North America. *Southeastern Archaeology* 7:1–20.

de Bry, Theodore

   1966 *Thomas Hariot's Virginia.* Readex Microprint, New York.

DeJarnette, David L., and Steve B. Wimberly

   1941 *The Bessemer Site: Excavations of Three Mounds and Surrounding Village Areas near Bessemer, Alabama.* Museum Paper 17, Geological Survey of Alabama, Tuscaloosa.

De Marrias, Elizabeth, Luis Jamie Castillo, and Timothy Earle

   1996 Ideology, Materialization, and Power Strategies. *Current Anthropology* 37:15–31.

Demel, Scott J.

   1992 *Report of Archaeological Investigations into Borrow Pit 5-1A.* Ms. in possession of the author.

Denevan, William M.

   1992 The Pristine Myth: The Landscape of the Americas in 1492. In "The Americas before and after 1492: Current Geographical Research," edited by K. W. Butzer. *Annals of the Association of American Geographers* 82:369–80.

Densmore, Frances

   1974 *How Indians Use Wild Plants for Food, Medicine and Crafts.* Dover Publications, New York.

DePratter, Chester

   1991 *Late Prehistoric and Early Historic Chiefdoms in the Southeastern United States.* Garland, New York.

Derrida, Jacques

   1976 *Of Grammatology.* Johns Hopkins University Press, Baltimore.

d'Iberville, Pierre LeMoyne

   1981 *Iberville's Gulf Journals,* translated and edited by R. G. McWilliams. Original written 1699–1702. University of Alabama Press, University.

Donley-Reid, Linda

   1990 A Structuring Structure: The Swahili House. In *Domestic Architecture and the Use of Space,* edited by S. Kus, pp. 114–26. Cambridge University Press, New York.

Dorwin, John T.

    1970 *Archaeological Survey of the Hodge Mound, Pineville, Kentucky.* Ms. on file, Office of State Archaeology, University of Kentucky, Lexington.

Duffield, Lathel F.

    1967 *Preliminary Excavations at the Mont Corbin Site, Adair County, Kentucky.* Ms. on file, Office of State Archaeology, University of Kentucky, Lexington.

Dunnell, Robert C.

    1989 Aspects of the Application of Evolutionary Theory in Archaeology. In *Archaeological Thought in America,* edited by C. C. Lamberg-Karlovsky, pp. 35–49. Cambridge University Press, Cambridge.

Earle, Timothy

    1990 Style and Iconography in Complex Chiefdoms. In *The Uses of Style in Archaeology,* edited by M. Conkey and C. Hastorf, pp. 73–81. Cambridge University Press, New York.

Eco, Umberto

    1976 *A Theory of Semiotics.* Indiana University Press, Bloomington.

    1984 *Semiotics and the Philosophy of Language.* Indiana University Press, Bloomington.

Eco, Umberto, Marco Santambrogio, and Patrizía Viola, eds.

    1988 *Meaning and Mental Representations: Advances in Semiotics.* Indiana University Press, Bloomington.

Edging, Richard B.

    1985 [Editor] *The Turk Site: A Mississippian Town of the Western Kentucky Border.* Western Kentucky Project Report 3, Department of Anthropology, University of Illinois, Urbana.

    1986 [Adams Site] Core Sampling. In *Mississippian Towns of the Western Kentucky Border: The Adams, Wickliffe, and Sassafras Ridge Sites,* edited by R. B. Lewis, pp. 14–17. Kentucky Heritage Council, Frankfort.

Edging, Richard B., and Charles B. Stout

    1986 The Wickliffe Site (15Ba4): Excavations and Stratigraphy. In *Mississippian Towns of the Western Kentucky Border: The Adams, Wickliffe, and Sassafras Ridge Sites,* edited by R. B. Lewis, pp. 109–11. Kentucky Heritage Council, Frankfort.

Egnatz, Dennis G.

    1983 Appendix A: Analysis of Human Skeletal Materials from Mound

C. In *Excavations at the Lake George Site, Yazoo County, Mississippi, 1958–1960,* edited by S. Williams and J. P. Brain, pp. 421–41. Papers of the Peabody Museum of Archaeology and Ethnology 74, Harvard University, Cambridge, Massachusetts.

Eliade, Mircea

1959 *The Sacred and the Profane.* Harcourt and Brace, New York.

Fairbanks, Charles H.

1952 Creek and Pre-Creek. In *Archeology of Eastern United States,* edited by J. B. Griffin, pp. 285–300. University of Chicago Press.

Fairbanks, Charles H., and Stuart Neitzel

1995 The Rymer Site. In *The Prehistory of the Chickamauga Basin,* 2 vols., by T. M. N. Lewis and M. D. Kneberg Lewis, compiled and edited by L. P. Sullivan, pp. 467–97. University of Tennessee Press, Knoxville.

Faupel, W. John, ed.

1992 *A Foothold in Florida: The Eye-Witness Account of Four Voyages Made by the French in that Region and Their Attempt at Colonisation, 1562–1568.* Antique Atlas, West Sussex, England.

Fergusson, James

1891 *History of Indian and Eastern Architecture.* John Murray, London.

Fisk, Harold N.

1944 *Geological Investigation of the Alluvial Valley of the Lower Mississippi River.* U.S. Army Corps of Engineers, Mississippi River Commission, Vicksburg, Mississippi.

Fletcher, Alice, and Francis La Flesche

1972 *The Omaha Tribe,* 2 vols. University of Nebraska Press, Lincoln.

Fletcher, Banister

1963 *A History of Architecture on the Comparative Method.* 17th ed. Athlone, London.

Fletcher, Roland

1989 The Messages of Material Behavior: A Preliminary Discussion of Non-Verbal Meanings. In *The Meaning of Things: Material Culture and Symbolic Expression,* edited by I. Hodder, pp. 33–40. Unwin Hyman, London.

Ford, James A.

1951 *Greenhouse: A Troyville–Coles Creek Period Site in Avoyelles Parish,*

Louisiana. Anthropological Papers 44(1), American Museum of Natural History, New York.

Ford, James A., Philip Phillips, and William G. Haag

1955 *The Jaketown Site in West-Central Mississippi*. Anthropological Papers 45(1), American Museum of Natural History, New York.

Foster, Steven, and James A. Duke

1990 *A Field Guide to Medicinal Plants: Eastern and Central North America*. Houghton Mifflin, New York.

Foucault, Michele

1977 *Discipline and Punish*. Vintage, New York.

1984 Space, Knowledge, and Power. In *The Foucault Reader*, edited by P. Rabinow, pp. 239–56. Pantheon Books, New York.

Fowler, Melvin L.

1975 A Pre-Columbian Urban Center on the Mississippi. *Scientific American* 233(2):92–101.

1977 The Cahokia Site. In *Explorations into Cahokia Archaeology*, edited by M. L. Fowler, pp. 1–30. Bulletin 7, Illinois Archaeological Survey, University of Illinois, Urbana.

1978 Cahokia and the American Bottom: Settlement Archaeology. In *Mississippian Settlement Patterns*, edited by B. D. Smith, pp. 455–78. Academic, New York.

1989 *The Cahokia Atlas*. Studies in Illinois Archaeology 6, Illinois Historic Preservation Agency, Springfield.

1991 Mound 72 and Early Mississippian at Cahokia. In *New Perspectives on Cahokia: Views from the Periphery*, edited by J. B. Stoltman, pp. 1–28. Monographs in World Archaeology 2. Prehistory Press, Madison, Wisconsin.

1993 *Mound 72, Woodhenge 72, Archaeoastronomy and Public Monuments at Cahokia*. Unpublished ms. on file, Department of Anthropology, University of Wisconsin-Milwaukee.

1996 The Mound 72 and Woodhenge 72 Area of Cahokia. In "The Ancient Skies and Sky Watchers of Cahokia: Woodhenges, Eclipses, and Cahokian Cosmology," edited by M. Fowler. *Wisconsin Archaeologist* 77(3-4):36–59.

Fowler, Melvin L., and Robert L. Hall

1975 Archaeological Phases at Cahokia. In *Perspectives in Cahokia Ar-*

chaeology, edited by J. A. Brown, pp. 1–14. Bulletin 10, Illinois Archaeological Survey, Urbana.

Frankenstein, Susan, and Michael Rowlands

   1978 The Internal Structure and Regional Context of Early Iron Age Society in South-Western Germany. *Bulletin of the Institute of Archaeology of London* 15:73–112.

Fritz, Gayle J.

   1990 Multiple Pathways to Farming in Precontact Eastern North America. *Journal of World Prehistory* 4:387–435.

Fritz, Gayle J., and Tristram R. Kidder

   1993 Recent Investigations into Prehistoric Agriculture in the Lower Mississippi Valley. *Southeastern Archaeology* 12:1–14.

Fritz, Gayle J., Christopher J. Smith, and Tristram R. Kidder

   1992 *Plaquemine Plant Use in Tensas Parish, Louisiana.* Presented at the forty-ninth annual meeting of the Southeastern Archaeological Conference, Little Rock.

Fritz, John M.

   1986 Vijayanagara: Authority and Meaning of a South Indian Imperial Capital. *American Anthropologist* 88:44–55.

Fritz, John M., and George Michell

   1991 *City of Victory: Vijayanagara, The Medieval Hindu Capital of Southern India.* Aperature Foundation, New York.

Fryman, Frank, Jr.

   1968 *The Corbin Site: A Possible Early Component of the Green River Phase of the Mississippian Tradition in Kentucky.* Ms. on file, Office of State Archaeology, University of Kentucky, Lexington.

   1969 *Lake Jackson Site (8LE1).* Unpublished field notes on file, Florida Division of Historical Resources, Tallahassee.

Gano, Laura

   1917 A Study in Physiographic Ecology in Northern Florida. *Botanical Gazette* 63:337–72.

Geiger, Maynard, trans.

   1936 *The Martyrs of Florida (1573–1616),* by Luis Geronimo de Oré. Franciscan Studies 18. Joseph F. Wagner, New York.

Giardino, Marco J.

   1977 *An Osteological Analysis of the Human Population from the Mount*

Nebo Site, Madison Parish, Louisiana. Unpublished master's thesis, Department of Anthropology, Tulane University, New Orleans.

1984 Temporal Frameworks: Archaeological Components and Burial
Styles. The Human Osteology of the Mt. Nebo Site in North Louisiana.
Louisiana Archaeology 9:99–126.

Gibson, Jon L.

1984 The Troyville-Baytown Issue. *Louisiana Archaeology* 9:29–62.

1994 Before Their Time? Early Mounds in the Lower Mississippi Valley.
Southeastern Archaeology 13:162–86.

Gibson, Jon L., and J. Richard Shenkel

1988 Louisiana Earthworks: Middle Woodland and Predecessors. In
*Middle Woodland Settlement and Ceremonialism in the Mid-South and
Lower Mississippi Valley*, edited by R. C. Mainfort, pp. 7–18. Archae-
ological Report 22, Mississippi Department of Archives and History,
Jackson.

Giddens, Anthony

1979 *Central Problems in Social Theory*. Macmillan, London.

1981 *A Contemporary Critique of Historical Materialism*. Macmillan,
London.

1984 *The Constitution of Society*. University of California Press, Berkeley.

Glassie, Henry

1975 *Folk Housing in Middle Virginia: A Structural Study of Folk Artifacts*. University of Tennessee Press, Knoxville.

Goggin, John M.

1947 Manifestations of a South Florida Cult in Northwestern Florida.
American Antiquity 12:273–76.

1949 A Southern Cult Specimen from Florida. *Florida Anthropologist*
2:36–38.

Gramsci, Antonio

1971 *Selections from the Prison Notebooks*, edited by Q. Hoare and G. N.
Smith. International, New York.

Gravier, Jacques

1861 Journal of the Voyage of Father Gravier. In *Early Voyages Up and
Down the Mississippi Valley*, by Cavelier, St. Cosme, Le Sueur, Gravier,
and Guignas, edited by J. D. G. Shea, pp. 115–63. Original written
1701. Joel Munsell, Albany.

Green, Thomas J., and Cheryl A. Munson

1978 Mississippian Settlement Patterns in Southwestern Indiana. In *Mississippian Settlement Patterns*, edited by B. D. Smith, pp. 293–330. Academic, New York.

Greengo, Robert E.

1964 *Issaquena: An Archaeological Phase in the Yazoo Basin of the Lower Mississippi Valley*. Memoirs of the Society for American Archaeology 18, Salt Lake City, Utah.

Gregg, Michael L.

1977 A Population Estimate for Cahokia. In *Explorations into Cahokia Archaeology*, edited by M. L. Fowler, pp. 126–36. Bulletin 7, Illinois Archaeological Survey, University of Illinois, Urbana.

Griffin, John W.

1947 Comments on a Site in the St. Marks National Refuge, Wakulla County, Florida. *American Antiquity* 13:182–83.

1950 Test Excavations at the Lake Jackson Site. *American Antiquity* 16:99–112.

Griffin, John W., and Ripley P. Bullen

1950 *The Safety Harbor Site, Pinellas County, Florida*. Florida Anthropological Society Publications 2, Florida Anthropological Society, Gainesville.

Hall, Robert L.

1972 *1972 Cahokia Borrow Pit 5-1A*. Unpublished excavation notes, University of Illinois-Chicago.

1985 Medicine Wheels, Sun Circles, and the Magic of World Center Shrines. *Plains Anthropologist* 30:181–93.

1991 Cahokia Identity and Interaction Models of Cahokia Mississippian. In *Cahokia and the Hinterlands*, edited by T. E. Emerson and R. B. Lewis, pp. 3–34. University of Illinois Press, Urbana.

1996 American Indian Worlds, World Quarters, World Centers, and Their Shrines. *Wisconsin Archaeologist* 77(3-4):120–27.

1997 *An Archaeology of the Soul: North American Indian Belief and Ritual*. University of Illinois Press, Urbana.

Hally, David J.

1972 *The Plaquemine and Mississippian Occupations of the Upper Tensas Basin, Louisiana*. Unpublished Ph.D. dissertation, Department of Anthropology, Harvard University, Cambridge.

1980 *Archaeological Investigations of the Little Egypt Site (9Mu102), Murray County, Georgia, 1970–72 Seasons.* Report submitted to the National Park Service, Heritage Conservation and Recreation Service, Atlanta.

1981 Plant Preservation and the Content of Paleobotanical Samples: A Case Study. *American Antiquity* 46:723–42.

1983 The Interpretive Potential of Pottery from Domestic Contexts. *Midcontinental Journal of Archaeology* 8:163–96.

1994a The Chiefdom of Coosa. In *The Forgotten Centuries: Indians and Europeans in the American South 1521–1704,* edited by C. Hudson and C. C. Tesser, pp. 227–53. University of Georgia Press, Athens.

1994b An Overview of Lamar Culture. In *Ocmulgee Archaeology 1936–1986,* edited by D. J. Hally, pp. 144–74. University of Georgia Press, Athens.

1996 Platform Mound Construction and the Instability of Mississippian Chiefdoms. In *Political Structure and Change in the Prehistoric Southeastern United States,* edited by J. Scarry, pp. 92–127. University Press of Florida, Gainesville.

Hally, David J., Marvin T. Smith, and James B. Langford, Jr.

1990 The Archaeological Reality of de Soto's Coosa. In *Columbian Consequences: Archaeological and Historical Perspectives on the Spanish Borderlands East,* vol. 2, edited by D. H. Thomas, pp. 121–38. Smithsonian Institution, Washington, D.C.

Hatch, James W.

1976 The Citico Site (40Ha65): A Synthesis. *Tennessee Anthropologist* 1:75–103.

1995 Lamar Period Upland Farmsteads of the Oconee River Valley, Georgia. In *Mississippian Communities and Households,* edited by J. D. Rogers and B. D. Smith, pp. 135–55. University of Alabama Press, Tuscaloosa.

Hawkins, Benjamin

1971 *A Sketch of the Creek Country in the Years 1798 and 1799.* Reprint of the 1848 edition published in the Collections of the Georgia Historical Society 3(1). Originally published in 1799. Kraus Reprint, New York.

Healan, Dan M.

1972 *Surface Delineation of Functional Areas at a Mississippian Ceremonial Center.* Memoir 10, Missouri Archaeological Society, Columbia.

Heidegger, Martin

1972 *Martin Heidegger, Basic Writings,* edited by D. Krell. Routledge, London.

Helms, Mary W.

1979 *Ancient Panama: Chiefs in Search of Power.* University of Texas Press, Austin.

1988 *Ulysses' Sail.* Princeton University Press, Princeton, New Jersey.

1992 Political Lords and Political Ideology in Southeastern Chiefdoms: Comments and Observations. In *Lords of the Southeast: Social Inequality and the Native Elites of Southeastern North America,* edited by A. W. Barker and T. R. Pauketat, pp. 185–94. Archeological Papers 3, American Anthropological Association, Washington, D.C.

Hendry, Charles W., and Charles R. Sproul

1966 *Geology and Ground-water Resources of Leon County, Florida.* Florida Geological Survey Bulletin 47, Florida Geological Survey, Tallahassee.

Heyden, Doris

1975 An Interpretation of the Cave Underneath the Pyramid of the Sun in Teotihuacan, Mexico. *American Antiquity* 40:131–47.

1981 Caves, Gods, and Myths: World-View and Planning in Teotihuacan. In *Mesoamerican Sites and World Views,* edited by E. P. Benson, pp. 1–35. Dumbarton Oaks, Washington, D.C.

Hodder, Ian

1985 Postprocessual Archaeology. In *Advances in Archaeological Method and Theory 8,* edited by M. B. Schiffer, pp. 1–26. Academic, Orlando.

Hodge, Frederick W., ed.

1907 *Handbook of American Indians North of Mexico.* Bulletin 30(1), Bureau of American Ethnology, Smithsonian Institution, Washington, D.C.

Hood, Victor P.

1977 *The Davis-Noe Site (40Re137): A Study of Functional Variability in Early Mississippian Subsistence and Settlement Patterning.* Unpublished master's thesis, Department of Anthropology, University of Tennessee, Knoxville.

House, John H.

1982 *Powell Canal: Baytown Period Occupation on Bayou Macon in South-*

east Arkansas. Research Series 19, Arkansas Archeological Survey, Fayetteville.

1990 Powell Canal: Baytown Period Adaptation on Bayou Macon, Southeast Arkansas. In *The Mississippian Emergence,* edited by B. D. Smith, pp. 9–26. Smithsonian Institution, Washington, D.C.

Howard, James H.

1968 *The Southeastern Ceremonial Complex and Its Interpretation.* Memoir 6, Missouri Archaeological Society, Columbia.

1981 *Shawnee! The Ceremonialism of a Native Indian Tribe and Its Cultural Background.* Ohio University Press, Athens.

Hudson, Charles

1976 *The Southeastern Indians.* University of Tennessee Press, Knoxville.

1984 *Elements of Southeastern Indian Religion.* Iconography of Religions 10(1), Institute of Religious Iconography, State University of Groningen, Leiden, The Netherlands.

Hunt, George T.

1940 *The Wars of the Iroquois: A Study in Intertribal Trade Relations.* University of Wisconsin Press, Madison.

Iseminger, William R.

1990 Features. In *The Archaeology of the Cahokia Palisade: The East Palisade Investigations,* by W. R. Iseminger, T. R. Pauketat, B. Koldehoff, L. S. Kelly, and L. Blake, pp. 18–38. Illinois Cultural Resources Study 14, Illinois Historic Preservation Agency, Springfield.

Jennings, Frances

1963 A Vanishing Indian: Francis Parkman Versus His Sources. *Pennsylvania Magazine of History and Biography* 87:306–23.

1975 *The Invasion of America: Indians, Colonialism, and the Cant of Conquest.* University of North Carolina, Chapel Hill.

Johnson, Kenneth W.

1991 *The Utina and the Potano Peoples of Northern Florida: Changing Settlement Systems in the Spanish Colonial Period.* Unpublished Ph.D. dissertation, Department of Anthropology, University of Florida, Gainesville.

Johnson, Kenneth W., and Bruce C. Nelson

1990 The Utina: Seriation and Chronology. *Florida Anthropologist* 43:48–62.

Jones, B. Calvin

1982 Southern Cult Manifestations at the Lake Jackson Site, Leon County, Florida: Salvage Excavation of Mound 3. *Midcontinental Journal of Archaeology* 7:3–44.

1990 A Late Mississippian Collector? *Soto States Anthropologist* 90:83–86.

1994 The Lake Jackson Mound Complex (8LE1): Stability and Change in Fort Walton Culture. *Florida Anthropologist* 47:120–46.

Jones, B. Calvin, and John T. Penman

1973 Winewood: An Inland Fort Walton Site in Tallahassee, Florida. *Bureau of Historic Sites and Properties Bulletin* 3:65–90.

Jones, Patrick J., and Tristram R. Kidder

1994 *Results of the 1993 Historic Taensa Survey, Tensas Parish, Louisiana.* Archaeological Report 3, Center for Archaeology, Tulane University, New Orleans.

Jones, Reca

1979 Human Effigy Vessels from Gold Mine Plantation. *Louisiana Archaeology* 4:117–21.

Kelly, Hypatia

1988 *The Architecture of the King Site.* Unpublished master's thesis, Department of Anthropology, University of Georgia, Athens.

Kelly, John E., Andrew C. Fortier, Steven J. Ozuk, and Joyce A. Williams

1987 *The Range Site: Archaic through Late Woodland Occupations.* University of Illinois Press, Urbana.

Kelly, John E., Steven J. Ozuk, and Joyce A. Williams

1990 *The Range Site 2: The Emergent Mississippian Dohack and Range Phase Occupations (11-S-47).* University of Illinois Press, Urbana.

Kidder, Tristram R.

1990 *Final Report on the 1989 Archaeological Investigations at the Osceola (16TE2) and Reno Brake (16TE93) Sites, Tensas Parish, Louisiana.* Archaeological Report 1, Center for Archaeology, Tulane University, New Orleans.

1992a Coles Creek Period Social Organization and Evolution in Northeast Louisiana. In *Lords of the Southeast: Social Inequality and the Native Elites of Southeastern North America,* edited by A. W. Barker and T. R. Pauketat, pp. 145–62. Archeological Papers 3, American Anthropological Association, Washington, D.C.

1992b Timing and Consequences of the Introduction of Maize Agriculture in the Lower Mississippi Valley. *North American Archaeologist* 13:15–41.

1993 *1992 Archaeological Test Excavations in Tensas Parish, Louisiana.* Archaeological Report 2, Center for Archaeology, Tulane University, New Orleans.

1994a Matheny: A Multicomponent Site on Bayou Bartholomew, Northeast Louisiana. *Midcontinental Journal of Archaeology* 19:137–69.

1994b Ceramic and Cultural Chronology. In *Cultural Resources Survey and Testing for Davis Pond Freshwater Diversion, St. Charles Parish, Louisiana,* edited by K. R. Jones, H. A. Franks, and T. R. Kidder, pp. 397–432. Submitted to the New Orleans District, U.S. Army Corps of Engineers, New Orleans.

Kidder, Tristram R., and Gayle J. Fritz

1993 Subsistence and Social Change in the Lower Mississippi Valley: Excavations at the Reno Brake and Osceola Sites, Louisiana. *Journal of Field Archaeology* 20:281–97.

Kidder, Tristram R., Gayle J. Fritz, and Christopher J. Smith

1993 Emerson (16TE104). In *1992 Archaeological Test Excavations in Tensas Parish, Louisiana,* by T. R. Kidder, pp. 110–37. Archaeological Report 2, Center for Archaeology, Tulane University, New Orleans.

Kidder, Tristram R., and Roger T. Saucier

1991 Archaeological and Geological Evidence for Protohistoric Water Management in Northeast Louisiana. *Geoarchaeology: An International Journal* 6:307–35.

Kidder, Tristram R., and Douglas C. Wells

1992 *Baytown Period Settlement Organization in the Lower Mississippi Valley.* Paper presented at the forty-ninth annual meeting of the Southeastern Archaeological Conference, Little Rock.

Kimball, Larry R., ed.

1985 *The 1977 Archaeological Survey: An Overall Assessment of the Archaeological Resources of Tellico Reservoir.* Report of Investigations 40, Department of Anthropology, University of Tennessee, Knoxville.

Kimball, Larry R., and William Baden

1985 Quantitative Model of Woodland and Mississippian Ceramic Assemblages for the Identification of Surface Collections. In *The 1977 Archaeological Survey: An Overall Assessment of the Archaeological Resources of Tellico Reservoir,* edited by L. R. Kimball, pp. 121–274. Report of Investigations 40, Department of Anthropology, University of Tennessee, Knoxville.

Kintigh, Keith W.

1989 Sample Size, Significance, and Measures of Diversity. In *Quantifying Diversity in Archaeology,* edited by R. D. Leonard and G. T. Jones, pp. 25–36. Cambridge University Press, Cambridge, United Kingdom.

Kleppe, Else Johansen

1989 Divine Kingship in Northern Africa: Material Manifestations of Social Institutions. In *The Meaning of Things: Material Culture and Symbolic Expression,* edited by I. Hodder, pp. 195–201. Unwin Hyman, London.

Kneberg, Madeline

1952 The Tennessee Area. In *Archaeology of Eastern United States,* edited by J. B. Griffin, pp. 190–98. University of Chicago Press.

Knight, Vernon J.

1981 *Mississippian Ritual.* Ph.D. dissertation, University of Florida, Gainesville. 81-27,439, University Microfilms, Ann Arbor, Michigan.

1985 Theme and Variation in Mississippian Ritual Expression. In *Indians, Colonists, and Slaves: Essays in Memory of Charles H. Fairbanks,* edited by K. W. Johnson, J. M. Leader, and R. C. Wilson, pp. 105–16. Special Publication 4, Florida Journal of Anthropology, Gainesville.

1986 The Institutional Organization of Mississippian Religion. *American Antiquity* 51:675–87.

1989 Symbolism of Mississippian Mounds. In *Powhatan's Mantle,* edited by P. Wood, G. Waselkov, and T. Hatley, pp. 279–91. University of Nebraska Press, Lincoln.

1990a Social Organization and the Evolution of Hierarchy in Southeastern Chiefdoms. *Journal of Anthropological Research* 46:1–23.

1990b [Discussant Comments] *Lords of the Southeast: Elites in Archaeological and Ethnohistorical Perspective.* Symposium presented at the forty-seventh annual meeting of the Southeastern Archaeological Conference, Mobile, Alabama.

1991 *Lake Jackson, and Speculations on a Demographic Paradox.* Paper presented at the forty-eighth annual meeting of the Southeastern Archaeological Conference, Jackson, Mississippi.

1992 *Preliminary Report on Excavations at Mound Q, Moundville.* Paper presented at the forty-ninth annual meeting of the Southeastern Archaeological Conference, Little Rock, Arkansas.

1993 *Moundville as a Diagrammatic Ceremonial Center.* Paper presented at the fifty-eighth annual meeting of the Society for American Archaeology, St. Louis.

1997 Some Developmental Parallels between Cahokia and Moundville. In *Cahokia: Domination and Ideology in the Mississippian World,* edited by T. R. Pauketat and T. E. Emerson, pp. 229–47. University of Nebraska Press, Lincoln.

Knight, Vernon J., and Vincas Steponaitis

1996 *A New History of Moundville.* Paper presented at the sixty-first annual meeting of the Society for American Archaeology, New Orleans, Louisiana.

Kramisch, Stella

1976 *The Hindu Temple,* 2 vols. Motilal Banarsidas, Delhi.

Kreisa, Paul P.

1990 *Organizational Aspects of Mississippian Settlement Systems in Western Kentucky.* Unpublished Ph.D. dissertation, Department of Anthropology, University of Illinois at Urbana-Champaign, Urbana.

Krupp, Edwin C.

1992 Cahokia: Corn, Commerce, and the Cosmos. *Griffin Observer* 4:10–20.

Kubler, George

1948 *Mexican Architecture in the Sixteenth Century,* 2 vols. Yale University Press, New Haven.

Kus, Susan M.

1983 The Social Representation of Space: Dimensioning the Cosmological and the Quotidian. In *Archaeological Hammers and Theories,* edited by J. A. Moore and A. S. Keene, pp. 277–98. Academic, New York.

Lafferty, Robert H.

1973 *An Analysis of Prehistoric Southeastern Fortifications.* Unpublished master's thesis, Department of Anthropology, Southern Illinois University, Carbondale.

Lame Deer, John, and Richard Erdoes

1972 *Lame Deer, Seeker of Visions.* Revised edition. Washington Square, New York.

Larson, Lewis

1993 An Examination of the Significance of a Tortoise-Shell Pin from the Etowah Site. In *Archaeology of Eastern North America: Papers in Honor of Stephen Williams,* edited by J. B. Stoltman, pp. 169–85. Archaeological Report 25, Mississippi Department of Archives and History, Jackson.

Lawrence, Denise L., and Setha M. Low

1990 The Built Environment and Spatial Form. *Annual Review of Anthropology* 19:453–505.

Leach, Edmund

1976 *Culture and Communication: The Logic by Which Symbols Are Communicated.* Cambridge University Press, Cambridge.

Leader, Jonathan M.

1988 *Technological Continuities and Specialization in Prehistoric Metalwork in the Eastern United States.* Unpublished Ph.D. dissertation, Department of Anthropology, University of Florida, Gainesville.

Leone, Mark P.

1984 Interpreting Ideology in Historical Archaeology: Using the Rules of Perspective in the William Paca Garden, Annapolis, Maryland. In *Ideology, Power, and Prehistory,* edited by D. M. and C. Tilley, pp. 25–36. Cambridge University Press, Cambridge.

1986 Symbolic, Structural, and Critical Archaeology. In *American Archaeology Past and Future,* edited by D. J. Meltzer, D. D. Fowler, and J. A. Sabloff, pp. 415–38. Smithsonian Institution, Washington, D.C.

1988 The Georgian Order as the Order of Merchant Capitalism in Annapolis, Maryland. In *The Recovery of Meaning,* edited by M. P. Leone and P. B. Potter, pp. 235–61. Smithsonian Institution, Washington, D.C.

Leone, Mark P., and Parker B. Potter, Jr.

1988 Issues in Historical Archaeology. In *The Recovery of Meaning,* edited by M. P. Leone and P. B. Potter, Jr., pp. 1–22. Smithsonian Institution, Washington, D.C.

Le Page du Pratz, Antoine S.

1972 *The History of Louisiana.* Claitor, Baton Rouge, Louisiana.

Lewis, Madeline D. Kneberg

1995 Burial Customs and Physical Types. In *The Prehistory of the Chickamauga Basin,* 2 vols., by T. M. N. Lewis and M. D. Kneberg

Lewis, compiled and edited by L. P. Sullivan, pp. 177–92. University of Tennessee Press, Knoxville.

Lewis, R. Barry
1986 [Editor] *Mississippian Towns of the Western Kentucky Border: The Adams, Wickliffe, and Sassafras Ridge Sites.* Kentucky Heritage Council, Frankfort.
1996 Mississippian Farmers. In *Kentucky Archaeology,* edited by R. B. Lewis, pp. 127–59. University Press of Kentucky, Lexington.

Lewis, Thomas M. N., and Madeline Kneberg
1946 *Hiwassee Island: An Archaeological Account of Four Tennessee Indian Peoples.* University of Tennessee Press, Knoxville.

Lewis, Thomas M. N., and Madeline D. Kneberg Lewis
1995 *The Prehistory of the Chickamauga Basin,* 2 vols., compiled and edited by L. P. Sullivan. University of Tennessee Press, Knoxville.

Lidberg, George, Charles Fairbanks, Stuart Neitzel, John Alden, and William Beatty
1995 The Ledford Island Site. In *The Prehistory of the Chickamauga Basin,* 2 vols., by T. M. N. Lewis and M. D. Kneberg Lewis, compiled and edited by L. P. Sullivan, pp. 523–61. University of Tennessee Press, Knoxville.

Loughridge, Robert H.
1888 *Report on the Geological and Economic Features of the Jackson Purchase Region.* Kentucky Geological Survey, Lexington.

Luer, George M.
1985 Some Comments on Englewood Incised, Safety Harbor Incised, and Scarry's Proposed Ceramic Changes. *Florida Anthropologist* 38:236–39.

Luer, George M., and Marion M. Almy
1981 Temple Mounds of the Tampa Bay Area. *Florida Anthropologist* 34:127–55.

Lynch, Kevin
1962 *Site Planning.* MIT Press, Cambridge.

McAnany, Patricia A.
1995 *Living with the Ancestors: Kinship and Kingship in Ancient Maya Society.* University of Texas Press, Austin.

McGuire, Randall H.
1991 Building Power in the Cultural Landscape of Broome County,

New York 1880 to 1940. In *The Archaeology of Inequality*, edited by
R. H. McGuire and R. Paynter, pp. 102–24. Blackwell, Providence.

Mainfort, Robert C.

1986 *Pinson Mounds: A Middle Woodland Ceremonial Center*. Research
Series 7, Tennessee Department of Conservation, Division of Archaeology, Nashville.

Malville, J. McKim

1991 Astrophysics, Cosmology, and the Interior Space of Indian Myths
and Temples. In *Concepts of Space: Ancient and Modern*, edited by
K. Varsyayan, pp. 123–47. Indira Gandhi National Centre for the Arts,
New Delhi.

Mariaca, M. T.

1988 *Late Marksville/Early Baytown Period Subsistence Economy: Analysis of Three Faunal Assemblages from Northeastern Louisiana*. Unpublished master's thesis, Department of Archaeology, Boston University,
Boston.

Marquardt, William H.

1989 Return to Battey's Landing. *Calusa News* 3:1–3.

1992a Recent Archaeological and Paleoenvironmental Investigations
in Southwest Florida. In *Culture and Environment in the Domain of
the Calusa*, edited by W. H. Marquardt with the assistance of C. Payne,
pp. 9–57. Monograph 1, Institute of Archaeology and Paleoenvironmental Studies, University of Florida, Gainesville.

1992b Calusa Culture and Environment: What Have We Learned? In
Culture and Environment in the Domain of the Calusa, edited by W. H.
Marquardt with the assistance of C. Payne, pp. 423–36. Monograph 1,
Institute of Archaeology and Paleoenvironmental Studies, University of
Florida, Gainesville.

Marrinan, Rochelle A., John F. Scarry, and Rhonda L. Majors

1990 Prelude to de Soto: The Expedition of Pánfilo de Narváez. In *Columbian Consequences*, vol. 2, *Archaeological and Historical Perspectives
on the Spanish Borderlands East*, edited by D. H. Thomas, pp. 71–82.
Smithsonian Institution, Washington, D.C.

Mason, Carol I.

1963 Eighteenth Century Culture Change among the Lower Creeks.
Florida Anthropologist 16:65–80.

Mehrer, Mark W.

1988 *Settlement Patterns and Social Power of Cahokia's Hinterland Households.* Unpublished Ph.D. dissertation, Department of Anthropology, University of Illinois, Urbana.

1995 *Cahokia's Countryside: Household Archaeology, Settlement Patterns, and Social Power.* Northern Illinois University Press, DeKalb.

Mehrer, Mark W., and James M. Collins

1995 Household Archaeology at Cahokia and in Its Hinterlands. In *Mississippian Communities and Households,* edited by J. D. Rogers and B. D. Smith, pp. 32–57. University of Alabama Press, Tuscaloosa.

Milanich, Jerald T.

1978 The Western Timucua: Patterns of Acculturation and Change. In *Tacachale: Essays on the Indians of Florida and Southeastern Georgia during the Historic Period,* edited by J. T. Milanich and S. Proctor, pp. 59–88. University Presses of Florida, Gainesville.

1994 *Archaeology of Precolumbian Florida.* University Press of Florida, Gainesville.

Milanich, Jerald T., and Charles H. Fairbanks

1980 *Florida Archaeology.* Academic, New York.

Miller, Daniel

1982 Artefacts as Products of Human Categorisation Processes. In *Symbolic and Structural Archaeology,* edited by I. Hodder, pp. 17–25. Cambridge University Press, Cambridge.

Milner, George R.

1986 Mississippian Period Population Density in a Segment of the Central Mississippi River Valley. *American Antiquity* 51:227–38.

1991 American Bottom Mississippian Cultures: Internal Developments and External Relations. In *New Perspectives on Cahokia,* edited by J. B. Stoltman, pp. 29–47. Monographs in World Archaeology 2, Prehistory Press, Madison, Wisconsin.

Milner, Murray, Jr.

1994 *Status and Sacredness: A General Theory of Status Relations and an Analysis of Indian Culture.* Oxford University Press, Oxford.

Mitchell, William J.

1990 *The Logic of Architecture: Design, Computation, and Cognition.* MIT Press, Cambridge.

Mitchem, Jeffrey M.

1989 *Redefining Safety Harbor: Late Prehistoric/Protohistoric Archaeology in West Peninsular Florida.* Unpublished Ph.D. dissertation, Department of Anthropology, University of Florida, Gainesville.

Mooney, James

1928 *The Aboriginal Population of America North of Mexico.* Edited by J. R. Swanton. Smithsonian Miscellaneous Collections 80:1–40, Washington, D.C.

Mooney, James, and Frans Olbrechts

1932 *The Swimmer Manuscript: Cherokee Sacred Formulas and Medicinal Prescriptions,* by J. Mooney, revised, completed, and edited by F. Olbrechts. Bulletin 99, Bureau of American Ethnology, Smithsonian Institution, Washington, D.C.

Moore, Clarence B.

1895 Certain Sand Mounds of the Oklawaha River, Florida. *Journal of the Academy of Natural Sciences of Philadelphia* 10:518–44.

1905 Certain Aboriginal Remains of the Black Warrior River. *Journal of the Academy of Natural Sciences of Philadelphia* 13:125–224.

1907 Moundville Revisited. *Journal of the Academy of Natural Sciences of Philadelphia* 13:337–405.

1915 Aboriginal Sites on Tennessee River. *Journal of the Academy of Natural Sciences of Philadelphia,* 2d ser, 16:169–428.

Moore, John H.

1994 Ethnoarchaeology of the Lamar Peoples. In *Perspectives on the Southeast: Linguistics, Archaeology, and Ethnohistory,* edited by P. B. Kwachka, pp. 126–41. University of Georgia Press, Athens.

Moorehead, Warren K.

1929 *The Cahokia Mounds.* University of Illinois Bulletin 26(4), Urbana.

Morgan, William N.

1980 *Prehistoric Architecture in the Eastern United States.* MIT Press, Cambridge.

Morris, A. E. J.

1994 *History of Urban Form before the Industrial Revolutions.* 3d ed. John Wiley & Sons, New York.

Mrozowski, Stephen A.

1991 Landscapes of Inequality. In *The Archaeology of Inequality,* edited by R. H. McGuire and R. Paynter, pp. 79–101. Blackwell, Providence.

Muller, Jon

1978 The Kincaid System: Mississippian Settlement in the Environs of a Large Site. In *Mississippian Settlement Patterns,* edited by B. D. Smith, pp. 269–92. Academic, New York.

1984 Mississippian Specialization and Salt. *American Antiquity* 49:489–507.

1986a *Archaeology of the Lower Ohio River Valley.* Academic, New York.

1986b Pans and a Grain of Salt: Mississippian Specialization Revisited. *American Antiquity* 51:405–9.

1989 The Southern Cult. In *The Southeastern Ceremonial Complex: Artifacts and Analysis,* edited by P. Galloway, pp. 11–26. University of Nebraska Press, Lincoln.

1993a Eastern North American Population Dynamics. *Illinois Archaeology* 5:84–99.

1993b Lower Ohio Valley Mississippian Revisited: An Autocritique. In *Archaeology of Eastern North America: Papers in Honor of Stephen Williams,* edited by J. B. Stoltman, pp. 127–42. Archaeological Report 25, Mississippi Department of Archives and History, Jackson.

1994 *Southeastern Interaction and Integration.* Paper presented at Great Towns and Regional Polities: Cultural Evolution in the Southwest and the Southeast Symposium, Jill Neitzel, organizer. Amerind Foundation, Dragoon, Arizona.

1997a *Mississippian Political Economy.* Plenum, New York.

1997b Native Eastern American Population Continuity and Stability. In *Integrating Archaeological Demography,* edited by R. R. Paine, pp. 343–64. Occasional Paper 24, Center for Archaeological Investigations, Southern Illinois University at Carbondale.

Muller, Jon, ed., assisted by Lisa Renken, George Avery, and others

1992 *The Great Salt Spring: Mississippian Production and Specialization.* Draft report of March, 1992, on file with the Shawnee National Forest, U.S. Forest Service, Harrisburg, Illinois.

Munson, Cheryl, ed.

n.d. *The Southwind Site.* Ms. prepared for the Indiana Port Authority by the Glenn A. Black Laboratory, Indiana University, Bloomington.

Nash, Charles H., Stuart Neitzel, Jesse D. Jennings, Charles H. Fairbanks, and Wendell Walker

1995 The Dallas Site. In *The Prehistory of the Chickamauga Basin,* 2 vols., by T. M. N. Lewis and M. D. Kneberg Lewis, compiled and edited by L. P. Sullivan, pp. 305–71. University of Tennessee Press, Knoxville.

Nassaney, Michael S. `

1991 Spatial-Temporal Dimensions of Social Integration during the Coles Creek Period in Central Arkansas. In *Stability, Transformation, and Variation: The Late Woodland Southeast,* edited by M. S. Nassaney and C. R. Cobb, pp. 177–220. Plenum, New York.

1992 Communal Societies and the Emergence of Elites in the Prehistoric American Southeast. In *Lords of the Southeast: Social Inequality and the Native Elites of Southeastern North America,* edited by A. W. Barker and T. R. Pauketat, pp. 111–43. Archeological Papers 3, American Anthropological Association, Washington, D.C.

1994 The Historical and Archaeological Context of Plum Bayou Culture in Central Arkansas. *Southeastern Archaeology* 13:36–55.

1996 Aboriginal Earthworks in Central Arkansas. In *Mounds, Embankments, and Ceremonialism in the Midsouth,* edited by R. C. Mainfort and R. Walling, pp. 22–25. Research Series 46, Arkansas Archeological Survey, Fayetteville.

Nassaney, Michael S., and Rob Hoffman

1992 Archaeological Investigations at the Fitzhugh Site (3LN212): A Plum Bayou Culture Household in Central Arkansas. *Midcontinental Journal of Archaeology* 17:139–65.

Neitzel, Robert Stuart

1965 *Archaeology of the Fatherland Site: The Grand Village of the Natchez.* Anthropological Papers 51(1), American Museum of Natural History, New York.

1983 *The Grand Village of the Natchez Revisited.* Archaeological Report 12, Mississippi Department of Archives and History, Jackson.

1995 The Sale Creek Site. In *The Prehistory of the Chickamauga Basin,* 2 vols., by T. M. N. Lewis and M. D. Kneberg Lewis, compiled and edited by L. P. Sullivan, pp. 441–66. University of Tennessee Press, Knoxville.

Neitzel, Stuart, and Charles H. Fairbanks

1995 The Mouse Creeks Site. In *The Prehistory of the Chickamauga Basin,* 2 vols., by T. M. N. Lewis and M. D. Kneberg Lewis, compiled and edited by L. P. Sullivan, pp. 498–522. University of Tennessee Press, Knoxville.

Neitzel, Stuart, and Jesse D. Jennings

    1995 The Hixon Site. In *The Prehistory of the Chickamauga Basin,* 2 vols., by T. M. N. Lewis and M. D. Kneberg Lewis, compiled and edited by L. P. Sullivan, pp. 372–418. University of Tennessee Press, Knoxville.

Norberg-Shulz, Christian

    1971 *Existence, Space & Architecture.* Praeger, New York.

    1980 *Genius Loci: Towards a Phenomenology of Architecture.* Rizzoli, New York.

Nuñez Cabeça de Vaca, Alvar

    1966 *Relation of Alvar Nuñez Cabeça de Vaca,* translated by B. Smith. Reprint of the 1871 New York edition. Original written in 1542. University Microfilms, Ann Arbor, Michigan.

O'Brien, Michael J.

    1977 *Intrasite Variability in a Middle Mississippian Community.* Ph.D. dissertation, University of Texas, Austin. University Microfilms 77-23,006, Ann Arbor, Michigan.

O'Brien, Patricia J.

    1989 Cahokia: The Political Capital of the "Ramey" State? *North American Archaeologist* 10:275–92.

O'Brien, Patricia, and William P. McHugh

    1987 Mississippian Solstice Shrines and a Cahokia Calendar: An Hypothesis Based on Ethnohistory and Archaeology. *North American Archaeologist* 8:227–47.

Orser, Charles E., Jr.

    1991 The Continued Pattern of Dominance: Landlord and Tenant on the Postbellum Cotton Plantation. In *The Archaeology of Inequality,* edited by R. H. McGuire and R. Paynter, pp. 40–54. Blackwell, Providence.

Palkovich, Ann M.

    1988 Asymmetry and Recursive Meanings in the 18th Century: The Morris Pound House. In *The Recovery of Meaning,* edited by M. P. Leone and P. B. Potter, Jr., pp. 293–306. Smithsonian Institution, Washington, D.C.

Pauketat, Timothy R.

    1992 The Reign and Ruin of the Lords of Cahokia: A Dialectical of Dominance. In *Lords of the Southeast: Social Inequality and the Native*

Elites of Southeastern North America, edited by A. W. Barker and T. R. Pauketat, pp. 31–51. Archeological Papers 3, American Anthropological Association, Washington, D.C.

1993 *Temples for Cahokia Lords: Preston Holder's 1955–56 Excavations of Kunnemann Mound.* Memoirs 26, Museum of Anthropology, University of Michigan, Ann Arbor.

1994 *The Ascent of Chiefs: Cahokia and Mississippian Politics in Native North America.* University of Alabama Press, Tuscaloosa.

Payne, Claudine

1982 *Farmsteads and Districts: A Model of Fort Walton Settlement Patterns in the Tallahassee Hills.* Paper presented at the thirty-ninth annual meeting of the Southeastern Archaeological Conference, Memphis.

1989 *Archaeological Investigations at the Lake Jackson Mound Group, Tallahassee, Florida.* Paper presented at the forty-sixth annual meeting of the Southeastern Archaeological Conference, Tampa.

1994 *Mississippian Capitals: An Archaeological Investigation of Precolumbian Political Structure.* Ph.D. dissertation, University of Florida. University Microfilms, Ann Arbor, Michigan.

Payne, Claudine, and John F. Scarry

1990 *Apalachee Prehistory: The Origins and Evolution of the Lake Jackson Phase.* Paper presented at the forty-seventh annual meeting of the Southeastern Archaeological Conference, Mobile.

Pearson, Michael Parker

1984 Social Change, Ideology and the Archaeological Record. In *Marxist Perspectives in Archaeology,* edited by M. Spriggs, pp. 59–71. Cambridge University Press, Cambridge.

Peebles, Christopher

1971 Moundville and Surrounding Sites: Some Structural Considerations of Mortuary Practices II. *Society for American Archaeology, Memoirs* 25:68–91.

1974 *Moundville: The Organization of a Prehistoric Community and Culture.* Unpublished Ph.D. dissertation, Department of Anthropology, University of California, Santa Barbara.

1978 Determinants of Settlement Size and Location in the Moundville Phase. In *Mississippian Settlement Patterns,* edited by B. D. Smith, pp. 369–416. Academic, New York.

1981 Archaeological Research at Moundville, 1840–1980. *Southeastern Archaeological Conference Bulletin* 24:77–81.

1987 The Rise and Fall of the Mississippian in Western Alabama: The Moundville and Summerville Phases, A.D. 1000 to 1600. *Mississippi Archaeology* 22:1–31.

1991 Annalistes, Hermeneutics and Positivists: Squaring Circles or Dissolving Problems. In *The Annales School and Archaeology*, edited by J. Bintliff, pp. 108–24. Leicester University Press, New York.

Peebles, Christopher, and Susan Kus

1977 Some Archaeological Correlates of Ranked Societies. *American Antiquity* 42:421–48.

Pénicaut, André

1988 *Fleur de Lys and Calumet*, translated and edited by R. G. McWilliams. University of Alabama Press, Tuscaloosa.

Penton, Daniel T.

1968 *Lake Jackson Site (8LE1)*. Unpublished field notes on file, Florida Division of Historical Resources, Tallahassee.

Peregrine, Peter N.

1992 *Mississippian Evolution: A World-Systems Perspective*. Prehistory Press, Madison, Wisconsin.

Phillips, Philip

1970 *Archaeological Survey in the Lower Yazoo Basin, Mississippi, 1949–1955*. Papers of the Peabody Museum of Archaeology and Ethnology 60, Peabody Museum, Harvard University, Cambridge.

Phillips, Philip, and James A. Brown

1978 *Pre-Columbian Shell Engravings from the Craig Mound at Spiro, Oklahoma, Part I*. Peabody Museum Press, Cambridge.

Phillips, Philip, James A. Ford, and James B. Griffin

1951 *Archaeological Survey in the Lower Mississippi Alluvial Valley, 1940–1947*. Papers of the Peabody Museum of American Archaeology and Ethnology 25, Harvard University, Cambridge.

Polhemus, Richard R.

1979 *Archaeological Investigations of the Tellico Blockhouse Site (40Mr50): A Federal Military and Trade Complex*. Report of Investigations 26, Department of Anthropology, University of Tennessee, Knoxville.

1985 *Mississippian Architecture: Temporal, Technological, and Spatial Pat-*

terning of Structures at the Toqua Site (40Mr6). Unpublished master's thesis, University of Tennessee, Knoxville.

1987 [Editor] *The Toqua Site: A Late Mississippian Dallas Phase Town,* 2 vols. Report of Investigations 41, Department of Anthropology, University of Tennessee, Knoxville.

1990 Dallas Phase Architecture and Sociopolitical Structure. In *Lamar Archaeology: Mississippian Chiefdoms in the Deep South,* edited by M. Williams and G. Shapiro, pp. 125–38. University of Alabama Press, Tuscaloosa.

Polhemus, Richard R., and Jan F. Simek

1996 *Community Organization at Carden Farm II, Tennessee.* Paper presented at the fifty-third annual meeting of the Southeastern Archaeological Conference, Birmingham, Alabama.

Potter, W. B.

1880 *Archaeological Remains in Southeastern Missouri, Earthworks of Missouri, Part 1: Pottery.* Contributions to the Archaeology of Missouri, pt. 1, pp. 5–30. Archaeological Section of the St. Louis Academy of Science, St. Louis, Missouri.

Powell, Mary Lucas

1988 *Status and Health in Prehistory: A Case Study of the Moundville Chiefdom.* Smithsonian Institution, Washington, D.C.

1992 In the Best of Health? Disease and Trauma among the Mississippian Elite. In *Lords of the Southeast: Social Inequality and the Native Elites of Southeastern North America,* edited by A. W. Barker and T. R. Pauketat, pp. 81–97. Archeological Papers 3, American Anthropological Association, Washington, D.C.

Price, James E.

1978 The Settlement Pattern of the Powers Phase. In *Mississippian Settlement Patterns,* edited by B. D. Smith, pp. 201–32. Academic, New York.

Price, James E., and Gregory L. Fox

1990 Recent Investigations at Towosahgy State Historic Site. *Missouri Archaeologist* 51:1–71.

Price, James E., and James B. Griffin

1979 *The Snodgrass Site of the Powers Phase of Southeast Missouri.* Anthropological Papers 66, Museum of Anthropology, University of Michigan, Ann Arbor.

Priestly, Herbert I.

1928 *The Luna Papers: Documents Relating to the Expedition of Don Tristan de Luna Y Arellano for the Conquest of La Florida in 1559–1661.* Florida State Historical Society, Deland.

Puri, H. S., and R. O. Vernon

1964 *Summary of the Geology of Florida and Guidebook to the Classic Exposures.* Florida Geological Survey Special Publication 5, Florida Geological Survey, Tallahassee.

Quimby, G. I.

1951 *The Medora Site, West Baton Rouge Parish, Louisiana.* Anthropological Series 24(2), Field Museum of Natural History, Chicago.

1957 The Bayou Goula Site, Iberville Parish, Louisiana. *Fieldiana: Anthropology* 47:91–170. Field Museum of Natural History, Chicago.

Rapoport, Amos

1977 *Human Aspects of Urban Form: Towards a Man-Environment Approach to Urban Form and Design.* Pergamon, New York.

1982 *The Meaning of the Built Environment: A Non-Verbal Communication Approach.* Sage, Beverly Hills, California.

Reed, Nelson A.

1977 Monks and Other Mississippian Mounds. In *Explorations into Cahokia Archaeology,* edited by M. L. Fowler, pp. 31–42. Bulletin 7, Illinois Archaeological Survey, University of Illinois, Urbana.

Reed, Nelson A., John W. Bennett, and James W. Porter

1968 Solid Core Drilling of Monks Mound: Technique and Findings. *American Antiquity* 33:137–48.

Roberts, Wayne

1987 Lithic Artifacts. In *The Toqua Site: A Late Mississippian Dallas Phase Town,* by R. Polhemus, pp. 689–909. Report of Investigations 41, Department of Anthropology, University of Tennessee, Knoxville.

Rolingson, Martha A.

1971 Lakeport: Initial Exploration of a Late Prehistoric Ceremonial Center in Southeastern Arkansas. *Arkansas Archeologist* 12(4):61–80.

1982 Emerging Cultural Patterns at the Toltec Mounds Site. In *Emerging Patterns of Plum Bayou Culture,* edited by M. A. Rolingson, pp. 60–63. Arkansas Archeological Survey Research Series 18, Fayetteville.

1983 *1982 Excavations at the Toltec Mounds State Park.* Arkansas Archeological Society Field Notes 19:3–7.

1984 *Celestial Alignments and Site Planning in the Lower Mississippi Valley.* Paper presented at the forty-first annual meeting of the Southeastern Archaeological Conference, Pensacola, Florida.

1990 The Toltec Mounds Site: A Ceremonial Center in the Arkansas River Lowland. In *The Mississippian Emergence,* edited by B. D. Smith, pp. 27–49, Smithsonian Institution, Washington, D.C.

1992 Excavations of Mound S at the Toltec Mounds Site: Preliminary Report. *Arkansas Archeologist* 31:1–29.

Rolingson, Martha A., and J. Michael Howard

1997 Igneous Lithics of Central Arkansas: Identification, Sources, and Artifact Distribution. *Southeastern Archaeology* 16:33–50.

Romans, Bernard

1962 *A Concise Natural History of East and West Florida.* Facsimile of 1775 edition. University Press of Florida, Gainesville.

Rose, Jerome C., Murray K. Marks, and Larry L. Tieszen

1991 Bioarchaeology and Subsistence in the Central and Lower Portions of the Mississippi Valley. In *What Mean These Bones?,* edited by M. L. Powell, P. S. Bridges, and A. M. W. Mires, pp. 7–21. University of Alabama Press, Tuscaloosa.

Rouse, Irving B.

1939 *Prehistory in Haiti: A Study in Method.* Yale University Publications in Anthropology 21, New Haven, Connecticut.

Rudolph, James L.

1984 Earthlodges and Platform Mounds: Changing Public Architecture in the Southeastern United States. *Southeastern Archaeology* 3:33–45.

Russo, Michael

1994 Why We Don't Believe in Archaic Ceremonial Mounds and Why We Should: The Case from Florida. *Southeastern Archaeology* 13:93–109.

Sahlins, Marshall

1981 *Historical Metaphors and Mythical Realities.* University of Michigan Press, Ann Arbor.

Salo, Lawr V.

1969a Martin Farm (40Mr20). In *Archaeological Investigations in the Tellico Reservoir, Tennessee, 1967–1968: An Interim Report,* edited by L. V. Salo, pp. 87–144. Report of Investigations 7, Department of Anthropology, University of Tennessee, Knoxville.

1969b Mayfield II (40MR27). In *Archaeological Investigations in the Tellico Reservoir, Tennessee, 1967–1968: An Interim Report,* edited by L. V. Salo, pp. 155–65. Report of Investigations 7, Department of Anthropology, University of Tennessee, Knoxville.

Sanders, Donald
1990 Behavioral Conventions and Archaeology: Methods for the Analysis of Ancient Architecture. In *Domestic Architecture and the Use of Space,* edited by S. Kus, pp. 43–72. Cambridge University Press, Cambridge.

Sanders, Therman E.
1981 *Soil Survey of Leon County, Florida.* U.S. Department of Agriculture, Soil Conservation Service, Washington, D.C.

Saucier, Roger T.
1974 *Quaternary Geology of the Lower Mississippi Valley.* Research Series 6, Arkansas Archeological Survey, Fayetteville.

Saunders, Joe W., Thurman Allen, and Roger T. Saucier
1994 Four Archaic? Mound Complexes in Northeast Louisiana. *Southeastern Archaeology* 13:134–53.

Scarry, C. Margaret
1986 *Change in Plant Procurement and Production during the Emergence of the Moundville Chiefdom.* Ph.D. dissertation, Department of Anthropology, University of Michigan, Ann Arbor. University Microfilms, Ann Arbor.
1993 Variability in Mississippian Crop Production Strategies. In *Foraging and Farming in the Eastern Woodlands,* edited by C. M. Scarry, pp. 78–90. University Press of Florida, Gainesville.

Scarry, C. Margaret, and Lee A. Newsom
1992 Archaeobotanical Research in the Calusa Heartland. In *Culture and Environment in the Domain of the Calusa,* edited by W. H. Marquardt with the assistance of C. Payne, pp. 375–402. Monograph 1, Institute of Archaeology and Paleoenvironmental Studies, University of Florida, Gainesville.

Scarry, C. Margaret, and Vincas P. Steponaitis
1997 Between Farmstead and Center. In *People, Plants, and Landscapes: Studies in Paleoethnobotany,* edited by K. J. Gremillion. University of Alabama Press, Tuscaloosa.

Scarry, John F.
1984a *Spatial Organization and Refuse Disposal Patterns at a Late Pre-*

historic Velda Phase Farmstead in the Tallahassee Hills. Paper presented at the forty-first annual meeting of the Southeastern Archaeological Conference, Pensacola.

1984b *Fort Walton Development: Mississippian Chiefdoms in the Lower Southeast.* Ph.D. dissertation, Case Western Reserve University. University Microfilms, Ann Arbor, Michigan.

1985 A Proposed Revision of the Fort Walton Ceramic Typology: A Type-Variety System. *Florida Anthropologist* 38:199–233.

1990 Mississippian Emergence in the Fort Walton Area: The Evolution of the Cayson and Lake Jackson Phases. In *The Mississippian Emergence,* edited by B. D. Smith, pp. 227–50. Smithsonian Institution, Washington, D.C.

1991 *The Apalachee and Mississippian Exchange: Speculations on the Impact of Geographic Location.* Paper presented at the fifty-sixth annual meeting of the Society for American Archaeology, New Orleans.

1992 Political Offices and Political Structure: Ethnohistoric and Archaeological Perspectives on the Native Lords of Apalachee. In *Lords of the Southeast: Social Inequality and the Native Elites of Southeastern North America,* edited by A. W. Barker and T. R. Pauketat, pp. 163–83. Archeological Papers 3, American Anthropological Association, Washington, D.C.

1995 Apalachee Homesteads: The Basal Social and Economic Units of a Mississippian Chiefdom. In *Mississippian Households and Communities,* edited by J. Rogers and B. Smith, pp. 201–23. University of Alabama Press, Tuscaloosa.

Schambach, Frank F.

1993 Some New Interpretations of Spiroan Culture History. In *Archaeology of Eastern North America: Papers in Honor of Stephen Williams,* edited by J. B. Stoltman, pp. 187–230. Archaeological Report 25, Mississippi Department of Archives and History, Jackson.

Schele, Linda, and Mary Ellen Miller

1986 *The Blood of Kings: Dynasty and Ritual in Maya Art.* Kimball Art Museum, Ft. Worth, Texas.

Schnell, Frank T., Vernon J. Knight, Jr., and Gail S. Schnell

1981 *Cemochechobee: Archaeology of a Mississippian Ceremonial Center on the Chattahoochee River.* University Presses of Florida, Gainesville.

Schroedl, Gerald F.

1975 *Archaeological Investigations at the Harrison Branch and Bat Creek Sites in the Tellico Reservoir.* Report of Investigations 10, Department of Anthropology, University of Tennessee, Knoxville.

1977 *Excavations of the Leuty and McDonald Site Mounds in the Watts Bar Nuclear Plant Area.* Report of Investigations 22, Department of Anthropology, University of Tennessee, Knoxville.

1986 Structures. In *Overhill Cherokee Archaeology at Chota-Tanasee,* edited by G. F. Schroedl, pp. 217–72. Report of Investigations 38, Department of Anthropology, University of Tennessee, Knoxville.

1990 *Archaeological Research at 40Re107, 40Re108, and 40Re124.* Report of Investigations 53, Department of Anthropology, University of Tennessee, Knoxville.

1993 Review of *Archaeology of Aboriginal Culture Change in the Interior Southeast,* by M. Smith. *North American Archaeologist* 14:87–92.

Schroedl, Gerald F., and C. Clifford Boyd, Jr.

1991 Late Woodland Period Culture in East Tennessee. In *Stability, Transformation, and Variation: The Late Woodland Southeast,* edited by M. S. Nassaney and C. R. Cobb, pp. 69–90. Plenum, New York.

Schroedl, Gerald F., C. Clifford Boyd, Jr., and R. P. Stephen Davis, Jr.

1990 Explaining Mississippian Origins in East Tennessee. In *The Mississippian Emergence,* edited by B. D. Smith, pp. 175–96. Smithsonian Institution, Washington, D.C.

Schroedl, Gerald F., R. P. Stephen Davis, Jr., and C. Clifford Boyd, Jr.

1985 *Archaeological Contexts and Assemblages at Martin Farm.* Report of Investigations 39, Department of Anthropology, University of Tennessee, Knoxville.

Schroedl, Gerald F., and Richard Polhemus

1977 *A Summary and Preliminary Interpretation of Archaeological Investigations at the Toqua Site (40Mr6).* Report submitted to the National Park Service, Atlanta.

Sellards, E. H.

1910 Some Florida Lakes and Lake Basins. In *Florida Geological Survey Fourth Annual Report,* pp. 1–79. Florida Geological Survey, Tallahassee.

Shapiro, Gary, and Bonnie G. McEwan

1992 Archaeology at San Luis, Part One: The Apalachee Council House. *Florida Archaeology* 6:1–174.

Shea, Andrea B, Jefferson Chapman, and Richard Polhemus
    1987 Paleobotany. In *The Toqua Site: A Late Mississippian Dallas Phase Town,* by R. Polhemus, pp. 1113–1207. Report of Investigations 41, Department of Anthropology, University of Tennessee, Knoxville.

Shelby, Charmion, trans.
    1993 *La Florida,* by Garcilaso de la Vega. In *The De Soto Chronicles: The Expedition of Hernando de Soto to North America in 1539–1543,* vol. 2, edited by L. A. Clayton, V. J. Knight, Jr., and E. C. Moore, pp. 25–559. University of Alabama Press, Tuscaloosa.

Sherrod, P. Clay, and Martha A. Rolingson
    1987 *Surveyors of the Ancient Mississippi Valley: Modules and Alignments in Prehistoric Mound Sites.* Research Series 28, Arkansas Archeological Survey, Fayetteville.

Sherwood, Sarah C.
    1991 *Microartifact Analysis of a Dallas Phase House Floor.* Unpublished master's thesis, Department of Anthropology, University of Tennessee, Knoxville.

Siegel, Sidney
    1956 *Nonparametric Statistics for the Behavioral Sciences.* McGraw-Hill, New York.

Sitte, Camillo
    1965 *City Planning According to Artistic Principles,* translated by George R. Collins and Christiane C. Collins. Columbia University Studies in Art History and Archaeology 2. Phaidon, London.

Smith, Bruce D.
    1978a Variation in Mississippian Settlement Patterns. In *Mississippian Settlement Patterns,* edited by B. D. Smith, pp. 479–503. Academic, New York.
    1978b [Editor] *Mississippian Settlement Patterns.* Academic, New York.
    1990 [Editor] *The Mississippian Emergence.* Smithsonian Institution, Washington, D.C.
    1992 Mississippian Elites and Solar Alignments: A Reflection of Managerial Necessity, or Levers of Social Inequality? In *Lords of the Southeast: Social Inequality and the Native Elites of Southeastern North America,* edited by A. W. Barker and T. R. Pauketat, pp. 11–30. Archeological Papers 3, American Anthropological Association, Washington, D.C.

Smith, Buckingham, trans.

1968 *Narratives of DeSoto in the Conquest of Florida.* Palmetto, Gainesville.

Smith, Hale G.

1973 *Analysis of the Lamar Site (9Bi7) Materials at the Southeastern Archaeological Center.* Submitted to the National Park Service, Contract
CX500031136, 1973. Copies available from the Department of Anthropology, Florida State University, Tallahassee.

Smith, Harriet M.

1969 The Murdock Mound: Cahokia Site. In *Explorations into Cahokia
Archaeology,* edited by M. L. Fowler, pp. 49–88. Bulletin 7, Illinois Archaeological Survey, University of Illinois, Urbana.

Smith, Marvin T.

1987 *Archaeology of Aboriginal Culture Change in the Interior Southeast:
Depopulation during the Early Historic Period.* Ripley P. Bullen Monographs in Anthropology and History 6, Florida State Museum, University Press of Florida, Gainesville.

1988a *An Archaeological Survey of Portions of the Chickamauga Reservoir,
Tennessee 1987–1988.* Report submitted to the Tennessee Valley Authority, Knoxville.

1988b *Mississippian Period Settlement in Eastern Tennessee: The View from
the Chickamauga Reservoir.* Paper presented at the forty-fifth annual
meeting of the Southeastern Archaeological Conference, New Orleans.

Smith, Marvin T., and David J. Hally

1992 Chiefly Behavior: Evidence from Sixteenth Century Spanish Accounts. In *Lords of the Southeast: Social Inequality and the Native Elites
of Southeastern North America,* edited by A. W. Barker and T. R.
Pauketat, pp. 99–109. Archeological Papers 3, American Anthropological Association, Washington, D.C.

Smith, Marvin T., Guy G. Weaver, and Charles H. McNutt

1990 *A Survey of Archaeological Resources in Portions of the Chickamauga
Reservoir, Tennessee, 1987, 1988, and 1989 Field Seasons.* Report submitted to the Tennessee Valley Authority. Garrow & Associates, Atlanta.

Snyder, John Francis

1962 *John Francis Snyder: Selected Writings,* edited by C. C. Walton with
contributions by P. E. Connolly and M. L. Fowler. Illinois State Historical Society, Springfield.

Southerlin, Bobby G.

  1993 *Mississippian Settlement Patterns in the Etowah River Valley near Cartersville, Bartow County, Georgia*. Unpublished master's thesis, Department of Anthropology, University of Georgia, Athens.

Squier, Ephraim G., and Edwin H. Davis

  1848 *Ancient Monuments of the Mississippi Valley*. Smithsonian Contributions 1, Washington, D.C.

Starr, M. E.

  1984 The Parchman Phase in the Northern Yazoo Basin: A Preliminary Analysis. Appendix in *The Wilsford Site (22-CO-516), Cohoma County, Mississippi*, by J. M. Connaway, pp. 163–209. Archaeological Report 14, Mississippi Department of Archives and History, Jackson.

  1991 Powell Bayou: Part I. *Mississippi Archaeology* 26(1):1–38.

Steinen, Karl T.

  1992 Ambushes, Raids, and Palisades: Mississippian Warfare in the Interior Southeast. *Southeastern Archaeology* 11:132–39.

Steponaitis, Vincas P.

  1978 Location Theory and Complex Chiefdoms: A Mississippian Example. In *Mississippian Settlement Patterns*, edited by B. D. Smith, pp. 417–53. Academic, New York.

  1983 *Ceramics, Chronology, and Community Patterns: An Archaeological Study at Moundville*. Academic, New York.

  1986 Prehistoric Archaeology in the Southeastern United States, 1970–1985. *Annual Review of Anthropology* 15:363–404.

  1991 Contrasting Patterns of Mississippian Development. In *Chiefdoms: Power, Economy, and Ideology*, edited by T. Earle, pp. 193–228. Cambridge University Press, New York.

Stoltman, James B.

  1991 Cahokia as Seen from the Peripheries. In *New Perspectives on Cahokia: Views from the Periphery*, edited by J. B. Stoltman, pp. 349–54. Monographs in World Archaeology 2. Prehistory Press, Madison, Wisconsin.

Stout, Charles B.

  1984 Mississippian Sites in Western Kentucky: Variations on a General Mississippian Theme? In *Late Prehistoric Research in Kentucky*, edited by D. Pollack, C. D. Hockensmith, and T. N. Sanders, pp. 167–79. Kentucky Heritage Council, Frankfort.

1989 *The Spatial Patterning of the Adams Site, a Mississippian Town in Western Kentucky.* Unpublished Ph.D. dissertation, University of Illinois at Urbana-Champaign, Urbana.

1991 Adams Meets St. Francis: Lower Mississippi Valley Site Classification Critiqued. In *The Human Landscape in Kentucky's Past: Site Structure and Settlement Patterns,* edited by C. Stout and C. K. Hensley, pp. 128–38. Kentucky Heritage Council, Frankfort.

Stout, Charles, and R. Barry Lewis

1995 Constantine Rafinesque and the Canton Site, a Mississippian Town in Trigg County, Kentucky. *Southeastern Archaeology* 14:87–90.

Stout, Charles, Kathleen Tucker, and Scott Kayse

1995 *Looking below the Surface: Recent Investigations at the Adams Site.* Paper presented at the eleventh annual meeting of the Kentucky Heritage Council, Richmond, Kentucky.

Stout, Charles, Gregory R. Walz, and Jarrod Burks

1996 Investigations at the Canton Site (15Tr1), Trigg County, Kentucky. In *Current Archaeological Research in Kentucky,* vol. 4, edited by S. A. Sanders, T. N. Sanders, and C. Stout, pp. 264–79. Kentucky Heritage Council, Frankfort.

Sullivan, Lynne Peters

1986 *The Late Mississippian Village: Community and Society of the Mouse Creek Phase in Southeastern Tennessee.* Unpublished Ph.D. dissertation, Department of Anthropology, University of Wisconsin-Milwaukee.

1987 The Mouse Creek Phase Household. *Southeastern Archaeology* 6:16–29.

1989a Cultural Change and Continuity in the Late Woodland and Mississippian Occupations of the Mouse Creek Sites. *Tennessee Anthropologist* 14:31–63.

1989b *Household and Community Organization of the Mouse Creek Phase.* Paper presented at the fifty-fourth annual meeting of the Society for American Archaeology, Atlanta.

1989c Household, Community, and Society: An Analysis of Mouse Creek Settlements. In *Households and Communities: Proceedings of the 21st Annual Chacmool Conference,* edited by S. MacEachern, D. Archer, and R. Garvin, pp. 317–27. Calgary, Alberta, Canada.

1995 Mississippian Households and Community Organization in Eastern Tennessee. In *Mississippian Communities and Households,* edited by

J. D. Rogers and B. D. Smith, pp. 99–123. University of Alabama Press, Tuscaloosa.

Swanton, John R.

1911 *Indian Tribes of the Lower Mississippi Valley and Adjacent Coast of the Gulf of Mexico.* Bulletin 43, Bureau of American Ethnology, Smithsonian Institution, Washington, D.C.

1912 The Creek Indians as Mound Builders. *American Anthropologist* 14:320–24.

1922 *Early History of the Creek Indians and Their Neighbors.* Bulletin 73, Bureau of American Ethnology, Smithsonian Institution, Washington, D.C.

1928a *Social Organization and Social Usages of the Indians of the Creek Confederacy.* Forty-second Annual Report of the Bureau of American Ethnology, pp. 23–472, Smithsonian Institution, Washington, D.C.

1928b *Religious Beliefs and Medical Practices of the Creek Indians.* Forty-second Annual Report of the Bureau of American Ethnology, pp. 473–672. Bureau of American Ethnology, Smithsonian Institution, Washington, D.C.

1946 *The Indians of the Southeastern United States.* Bulletin 137, Bureau of American Ethnology, Smithsonian Institution, Washington, D.C.

1952 *The Indian Tribes of North America.* Bulletin 145, Bureau of American Ethnology, Smithsonian Institution, Washington, D.C.

Tacitus, Cornelius

1942 *The Complete Works of Tacitus,* translated by A. J. Church and W. J. Brodribb, edited by M. Hadas. Modern Library, New York.

Tainter, J. A.

1978 Mortuary Practices and the Study of Prehistoric Social Systems. In *Advances in Archaeological Method and Theory 1,* edited by M. B. Schiffer, pp. 105–41. Academic, New York.

Tally, Lucy

1975 Preliminary Demographic Analysis of the King Site Burial Population. *Bulletin of the Southeast Archaeological Conference* 18:74–75.

Teltser, Patrice A.

1992 Settlement Context and Structure at County Line, Missouri. *Southeastern Archaeology* 11:14–30.

Tesar, Louis D.

1980 *The Leon County Bicentennial Survey Report: An Archaeological Survey of Selected Portions of Leon County, Florida*. Miscellaneous Project Report Series 49, Florida Bureau of Historic Sites and Properties, Tallahassee.

Thom, Alexander, and A. S. Thom

1978 *Megalithic Remains in Britain and Brittany*. Oxford University Press, New York.

Thomas, Cyrus

1894 *Report on the Mound Explorations of the Bureau of Ethnology*. Twelfth Annual Report of the Bureau of American Ethnology, Smithsonian Institution, Washington, D.C.

Thornton, Russell, with the assistance of C. W. Snipp and N. Breen

1990 *The Cherokees: A Population History*. University of Nebraska Press, Lincoln.

Tilley, Christopher

1982 Social Formation, Social Structure, and Social Change. In *Symbolic and Structural Archaeology*, edited by I. Hodder, pp. 26–38. Cambridge University Press, Cambridge.

1989 Interpreting Material Culture. In *The Meaning of Things: Material Culture and Symbolic Expression*, edited by I. Hodder, pp. 185–93. Unwin Hyman, London.

1994 *A Phenomenology of Landscape: Places, Paths and Monuments*. Berg, Providence.

Titterington, Paul F.

1938 *The Cahokia Mound Group and Its Village Site Material*. St. Louis, Missouri.

Toth, E. Alan

1974 *Archaeology and Ceramics at the Marksville Site*. Anthropological Papers 56, Museum of Anthropology, University of Michigan, Ann Arbor.

1979 *The Lake St. Agnes Site: A Multi-Component Occupation of Avoyelles Parish, Louisiana*. Mélanges 13, School of Geoscience, Louisiana State University, Baton Rouge.

1988 *Early Marksville Phases in the Lower Mississippi Valley: A Case Study of Culture Contact Dynamics*. Archaeological Report 21, Mississippi Department of Archives and History, Jackson.

Trancik, Roger
   1986 *Finding Lost Space: Theories of Urban Design.* Van Nostrand Reinhold, New York.
Ubelaker, Douglas H.
   1976 The Sources and Methodology for Mooney's Estimates of North American Indian Populations. In *The Native Population of the Americas in 1492,* edited by W. M. Deneven, pp. 243–88. University of Wisconsin Press, Madison.
Vander Leest, Barbara J.
   1980 *The Ramey Field, Cahokia Surface Collection: A Functional Analysis of Spatial Structure.* Unpublished Ph.D. dissertation, Department of Anthropology, University of Wisconsin-Milwaukee.
Varner, John G., and Jeannette J. Varner, trans. and eds.
   1951 *The Florida of the Inca.* University of Texas Press, Austin.
Vatsyayan, Kapila
   1991 *Concepts of Space: Ancient and Modern.* Indira Gandhi National Centre for the Arts, New Delhi.
Vogel, Virgil J.
   1973 *American Indian Medicine.* University of Oklahoma Press, Norman.
Voss, Jerome, and John Blitz
   1988 Archaeological Investigations in the Choctaw Homeland. *American Antiquity* 53:125–45.
Wahls, Richard
   1986 *An Examination of Shared Patterns of Plaza Definition in Mississippian Mound and Plaza Centers.* Unpublished senior honors thesis, Department of Anthropology, University of Illinois, Urbana.
Walker, Karen Jo
   1992 The Zooarchaeology of Charlotte Harbor's Prehistoric Maritime Adaptation: Spatial and Temporal Perspectives. In *Culture and Environment in the Domain of the Calusa,* edited by W. H. Marquardt with the assistance of C. Payne, pp. 265–366. Monograph 1, Institute of Archaeology and Paleoenvironmental Studies, University of Florida, Gainesville.
Ward, H. Trawick
   1965 Correlation of Mississippian Sites and Soil Types. *Southeastern Archaeological Conference Bulletin* 3:42–48.

1985 Social Implications of Storage and Disposal Patterns. In *Structure and Process in Southeastern Archaeology*, edited by R. S. Dickens, Jr., and H. T. Ward, pp. 82–101. University of Alabama Press, Tuscaloosa.

Waring, Antonio J., Jr.

1968 *The Southern Cult and Muskogean Ceremonial*. Papers of the Peabody Museum of American Archaeology and Ethnology 58:2, Harvard University, Cambridge.

Waring, Antonio J., Jr., and Preston Holder

1945 A Prehistoric Ceremonial Complex in the Southeastern United States. *American Anthropologist* 47:1–34.

Webb, Clarence H.

1982 *The Poverty Point Culture*. Geoscience and Man 17 (2d ed., rev.), School of Geoscience, Louisiana State University, Baton Rouge.

Webb, William S.

1938 *An Archaeological Survey of the Norris Basin in Eastern Tennessee*. Bureau of American Ethnology Bulletin 118, Smithsonian Institution, Washington, D.C.

1952 *The Jonathan Creek Village, Site 4, Marshall County, Kentucky*. Reports on Anthropology 8(1), University Press of Kentucky, Lexington.

Webb, William S., and William D. Funkhouser

1931 *The Tolu Site in Crittenden County, Kentucky*. Reports in Archaeology and Anthropology 1(5), University Press of Kentucky, Lexington.

Weinland, Marcia K.

1980 The Rowena Site, Russell County, Kentucky. *Kentucky Archaeological Association Bulletin* 16-17:1–150.

Weinstein, Richard A.

1987 Development and Regional Variation of Plaquemine Culture in South Louisiana. In *The Emergent Mississippian: Proceedings of the Sixth Mid-South Conference, June 6–9, 1985*, edited by R. A. Marshall, pp. 85–106. Occasional Papers 87-01, Cobb Institute of Archaeology, Mississippi State University, Starkville, Mississippi.

Welch, Paul D.

1991 *Moundville's Economy*. University of Alabama Press, Tuscaloosa.

Weltfish, Gene

1965 *The Lost Universe: Pawnee Life and Culture*. University of Nebraska Press, Lincoln.

Wesler, Kit W.

1989 *Archaeological Excavations at Wickliffe Mounds: 15Ba4. Mound D, 1987.* Report 3, Wickliffe Mounds Research Center, Wickliffe, Kentucky.

Wesson, Cameron B.

1996 *Sacred Foundations: Cosmic Order in Public Architecture in the Southeastern United States.* Paper presented at the sixty-first annual meeting of the Society for American Archaeology, New Orleans.

Wheatley, Paul

1971 *The Pivot of the Four Quarters: A Preliminary Enquiry into the Origins and Character of the Ancient Chinese City.* Aldine, Chicago.

White, Nancy M.

1982 *The Curlee Site (8JA7) and Fort Walton Development in the Upper Apalachicola–Lower Chattahoochee Valley.* Unpublished Ph.D. dissertation, Department of Anthropology, Case Western Reserve University, Cleveland.

Whiteford, Andrew H.

1952 A Frame of Reference for the Archeology of Eastern Tennessee. In *Archeology of Eastern United States,* edited by J. B. Griffin, pp. 207–25. University of Chicago Press.

Widmer, Randolph J.

1988 *The Evolution of the Calusa: A Nonagricultural Chiefdom on the Southwest Florida Coast.* University of Alabama Press, Tuscaloosa.

Wied, Maximilian, Prinz von

1982 *People of the First Man: Life among the Plains Indians in Their Final Days of Glory. The Firsthand Account of Prince Maximilian's Expedition up the Missouri River, 1833–34.* Promontory, New York.

Willey, Gordon R.

1940 *Archaeological Site Report of the Lake Jackson Site.* Ms. on file, Florida Museum of Natural History, Gainesville.

1949 *Archeology of the Florida Gulf Coast.* Smithsonian Miscellaneous Collections 113, Government Printing Office, Washington, D.C.

Willey, Gordon R., and Philip Phillips

1958 *Method and Theory in American Archaeology.* University of Chicago Press.

Williams, Mark

1995 Chiefly Compounds. In *Mississippian Communities and Households,* edited by J. D. Rogers and B. D. Smith, pp. 124–34. University of Alabama Press, Tuscaloosa.

Williams, Mark, and Gary Shapiro

1990 *Lamar Archaeology: Mississippian Chiefdoms in the Deep South.* University of Alabama Press, Tuscaloosa.

Williams, Stephen

1967 On the Location of the Historic Taensa Villages. *Conference on Historic Site Archaeology Papers 1965–1966* 1:3–13.

Williams, Stephen, and Jeffrey P. Brain

1983 *Excavations at the Lake George Site, Yazoo County, Mississippi, 1958–1960.* Papers of the Peabody Museum of Archaeology and Ethnology 74, Harvard University, Cambridge, Massachusetts.

Wittry, Warren

1977 The American Woodhenge. In *Explorations into Cahokia Archaeology,* edited by M. L. Fowler, pp. 43–48. Bulletin 7, Illinois Archaeological Survey, University of Illinois, Urbana.

1980 Cahokia Woodhenge Update. *Archaeoastronomy* 3:12–14.

1996 Discovering and Interpreting the Cahokia Woodhenges. *Wisconsin Archaeologist* 77(3-4):26–35.

Woods, William I., and George R. Holley

1989 Current Research at the Cahokia Site (1984–1989). In *The Cahokia Atlas,* edited by M. Fowler, pp. 227–32. Studies in Illinois Archaeology 6, Appendix 5. Illinois Historic Preservation Agency, Springfield.

Young, Jon N.

1962 *Annis Mound: A Late Prehistoric Site on the Green River.* Unpublished master's thesis, Department of Anthropology, University of Kentucky, Lexington.

Zuidema, Reiner Tom

1964 *The Ceque System of Cuzco: The Social Organization of the Capital of the Inca.* E. J. Brill, Leiden.

Contributors

Scott J. Demel received his M.A. in anthropology from the University of Illinois at Chicago and is an advanced graduate student at the University of Wisconsin at Milwaukee. He brings a background as a professional landscape architect to his specialization in community and landscape archaeology. He has done fieldwork in Illinois and Wisconsin and has worked extensively with architectural data from Cahokia.

Robert L. Hall is a professor of anthropology at the University of Illinois at Chicago. He has previously served as curator of anthropology for the Illinois State Museum, director of the Institute of Indian Studies at the University of South Dakota, and assistant curator of anthropology for the Wisconsin State Historical Museum. He received his B.A. and Ph.D. from the University of Wisconsin at Madison. He has conducted field research in Illinois, Wisconsin, Kentucky, South Dakota, North Dakota, and Venezuela.

David J. Hally is an associate professor of anthropology at the University of Georgia in Athens. He received his Ph.D. from Harvard University in 1972. His research interests include the development of Mississippian societies, the analysis of archaeological ceramics, and the anthropology of southeastern food patterns. He has directed excavations at King and many other sites in Georgia.

Hypatia Kelly holds a master's degree in anthropology from the University of Georgia and a master's degree in architecture from the University of Texas at Austin. Currently she has a private design practice in southern California. Her interests include sustainability and the building process, the myth and meaning of spatial forms, and research into the architectural design process of ancient cultures.

Tristram R. Kidder is associate professor of anthropology and director of the Center for Archaeology at Tulane University. He received his M.A. in 1987 and his Ph.D. in 1988 from Harvard University. His research interests include the analysis of prehistoric diets, social change in the evolution of hunter-gatherer and early agricultural communities, the origins and development of ranked societies, and the dynamics of Indian-European contact in eastern North America. He is currently director of the Osceola Project, a long-term multidisciplinary study of prehistoric subsistence and social change in the Tensas Basin of northeast Louisiana.

R. Barry Lewis received his Ph.D. from the University of Illinois at Urbana-Champaign, where he is associate professor of anthropology. Until recently, his research interests and publications focused on the investigation of Mississippian towns in Kentucky and Missouri. He is currently working on a comparative study of late medieval and early modern fortified towns in South India and the Mississippian world.

Jon Muller is a professor of anthropology at Southern Illinois University at Carbondale. He received a Ph.D. in anthropology from Harvard University and is the author of *Archaeology of the Lower Ohio Valley* (Academic Press, 1986) and *Mississippian Political Economy* (Plenum Press, 1997). His research interests include late prehistoric cultures of the Southeast, prehistoric art styles, and political economy.

Claudine Payne is visiting assistant professor of anthropology at the University of Illinois at Urbana-Champaign. She received her Ph.D. in anthropology from the University of Florida. Dr. Payne's research interests include the Mississippi period, political anthropology, and the role of architecture in the acquisition and maintenance of political power.

John F. Scarry is visiting lecturer in the Department of Sociology and Anthropology, North Carolina State University, and research associate professor in the Department of Anthropology at the University of North Carolina-Chapel Hill. He received his doctorate in anthropology from Case Western Reserve University in 1984. His dissertation research focused on the development of Mississippian chiefdoms in northwestern Florida. Since that time, Dr. Scarry's primary research efforts have dealt with the late prehistoric and historic period Apalachee chiefdom and the Spanish missions to the Apalachee. His current research is focused on the articulation of households into larger social formations in the West

Jefferson and Moundville phases of Alabama and how that affected the development of the Moundville chiefdom.

Gerald F. Schroedl is an associate professor at the University of Tennessee, Knoxville. He received his Ph.D. in anthropology from Washington State University. His research interests are focused on Mississippian cultures in the Southeast and on the ethnohistory and archaeology of historic native Americans, especially the Cherokee. He is principal author of *Explaining Mississippian Origins in East Tennessee* (Smithsonian Press, 1990), *Late Woodland Culture in East Tennessee* (Plenum Press, 1991), and *Overhill Cherokee Archaeology at Chota-Tanasee* (University of Tennessee, 1986).

Charles Stout is a partner in the Quantum Muse Company, an international management consulting firm based in Ann Arbor, Michigan, where he develops anthropologically based organizational design and marketing strategies in both profit and not-for-profit sectors. He is an affiliate in the Department of Anthropology at the University of Illinois in Urbana, a member of the teaching faculty in the Graduate School of Business at the University of Michigan in Ann Arbor, and a faculty consultant with the Livonia, Michigan, campus of the University of Phoenix. Since 1983, Dr. Stout's archaeological fieldwork has centered on western Kentucky prehistory, focusing on relationships between site design and community structure. Dr. Stout received his Ph.D. from the University of Illinois at Urbana-Champaign.

Cameron B. Wesson is assistant professor of anthropology at the University of Oklahoma. He holds degrees in anthropology and architecture from Auburn University and received his Ph.D. in anthropology from the University of Illinois. His primary research interests are household archaeology, architecture and culture, dominance and resistance, the development of Mississippian chiefdoms in central Alabama, and the effects of Euroamerican contacts on native groups of the Southeast.

Index